Best-Loved
Passages
of the Bible

Best-loved passages of the Bible

of the

A DEVOTIONAL

CONCORDIA PUBLISHING HOUSE · SAINT LOUIS

As You Begin

Concordia Publishing House asked Christians to tell us about their favorite Bible passages. Through various means, we sought to identify a consensus of the "best loved" portions of the Holy Scripture.

Some jumped immediately to the front—passages often quoted in church, Sunday school, or Bible study: Genesis 1:26; John 3:16; Isaiah 9:6; 1 Corinthians 13; and Psalm 23. Others were offered as best loved because they shed light on God's work in our lives: Joshua 21:45; Isaiah 40:11; 2 Corinthians 1:20; and Titus 3:5–6. For several weeks, the responses poured in.

Then in the best tradition of *Portals of Prayer*, we asked several of our authors, including Roger Sonnenberg and Bobbie Reed, to share their insights into the significance and meaning of these passages for the Christian life. What you now hold in your hands is the outcome of that survey—300 devotions that reflect on those Bible passages we hold most dear.

It is in God's Word that we learn of our sinful condition and God's once-for-all solution to the problem of sin—Jesus Christ. Through the stories of great men and women of the faith, we learn of God's active role in our lives and His continued concern for His people. Through these devotions, you will be reminded again and again of the importance of reading God's Word daily, to hear anew His love in Christ and His will for our lives.

May God send His Holy Spirit to work in your heart and strengthen your faith as you reflect on the words He inspired writers of old to put on paper.

Contributors

Paul J. Albers

David S. Andrus

Debb Andrus

David H. Benke

Luther C. Brunette

Donald L. Deffner

James W. Freese

Henry Gerike

James Heine

Arnold Kuntz

David Lumpp

Ida Mall

Charles S. Mueller

Rudolph F. Norden

Kevin Parviz

Bobbie Reed

Laine Rosin

Donald W. Sandmann

Andrew Simcak Jr.

Roger R. Sonnenberg

Timothy Wesemann

Jim Wiemers

Genesis 1:26

Be a Good Portrait

God said, "Let Us make man in Our image, in Our likeness, and let them rule over the fish of the sea and the birds of the air, over the livestock, over all the earth, and over all the creatures that move along the ground." Genesis 1:26

One of Norman Rockwell's famous paintings is entitled *Self-portrait*. The painting shows Norman Rockwell looking into a mirror and painting a likeness of himself. In fact, many painters do self-portraits. Some self-portraits are very true likenesses; others are virtually unrecognizable as the persons they are supposed to portray.

God created Adam and Eve as three-dimensional and multilevel portraits. God gave human beings the potential for power, authority, and leadership. God designed us humans with the capacity to develop the positive qualities of the Trinity: goodness, gentleness, joy, peace, patience, kindness, forgiveness, faithfulness, faith, self-control, and love. God gave us minds to think, wills to choose, and drives to master. God did all of this so we could become good likenesses of the Divine.

We are all portraits of God. Some of us are excellent likenesses on a human level. Others of us are virtually unrecognizable as likenesses of God. Which type of portrait are you? If you aren't a good portrait, what do you need to do to change your image?

Fortunately, in our case, the portrait is never completed as long as we live. We always have the opportunity to change, to improve, and to become conformed to the image of Jesus Christ. And we have God's promise that through His Word and Sacrament He is even now at work conforming us to the likeness of His Son.

Jesus, give me the courage to make life changes so I can become a good portrait of God to those I meet. Amen.

BOBBIE REED

Genesis 15:6

A Shrink-Proof Faith

Abram believed the LORD, and He credited it to him as righteousness.
Genesis 15:6

A shrink-proof faith. That's what we long for as Christians. And what better example of such faith do we have than that of father Abraham. His faith carries through both Old and New Testaments as persistent, consistent, durable, and expansive, even when he was "as good as dead" (Hebrews 11:12). Childless and uprooted, he is directed to look at the starry sky and count his descendants when he has zero on account. His faith is credited as righteousness by God, and the children of Israel eventually add up to a sky full.

From whence this faith? Consider the source! The source of the promise to Abraham is God. The source, then, of his faith, is outside himself. So it is true for us.

Faith is the gift proceeding from God that enables us to trust ourselves to God. Faith is not belief about something; it is trust in someone. That someone is God made personal in Christ Jesus. The evidence for God's trustworthiness is Christ Jesus.

Our faith, then, as Martin Luther put it, "is a living, daring confidence in God's grace. It is so sure and certain that a man could stake his life on it a thousand times." Abraham put his future completely in God's hands. Can we do any less? Trust the source!

Dear Lord, grant me the faith to cling simply and solely to Christ. Amen.

DAVID H. BENKE

Numbers 6:26

God's Face

The LORD turn His face toward you and give you peace. Numbers 6:26

Do you ever wonder what God's face must look like? While Moses was up on Mt. Sinai, he wanted to see God's face. He asked God to let him see God's glory. God told Moses that He would reveal all of His goodness to Moses, but not His face, for "no one may see Me and live" (Exodus 33:20). And even though Moses saw only God's back, he still came away with a radiant face, and everyone knew that Moses had been in God's presence. Yet, here in Numbers, God tells Moses just how He will bless His people, and part of that blessing is that God will turn His face toward His people. He will let them see Him.

Have you seen the face of God? When Jesus came to earth, He baptized with the Holy Spirit. At our Baptism, the Holy Spirit came to live within us. Our face, the face of a Christian, becomes the face of God. And when people see our face, their face becomes radiant! Doesn't it? Doesn't our face reflect the joy and love that God has for all people? When people see us, don't they smile and eagerly anticipate being in our presence?

Sometimes I suspect not, because unfortunately there is also sin within us. And sometimes that sin shows itself on our face. We do not show God's peace, and we do not bless others with God's peace. But there is good news. By the grace of God in Jesus Christ, He brings us into His presence, and He restores us. Whenever we come to the altar for the Lord's Supper, we see His face. And we come back radiant. And when we need God's peace, He sends us one of His servants, a friend, a relative, another Christian, and we are in the presence of God. They comfort us and give us peace. What an awesome God we have!

Dear God, thank You for showing us Your face. Help us to be radiant and to pass Your peace to others. Amen.

KEVIN PARVIZ

Deuteronomy 6:5–9

Parenthood—A High Calling

These commandments that I give you today are to be upon your hearts. Impress them on your children. Deuteronomy 6:6

These verses from Deuteronomy form a manual for the high calling in the rearing of children to the Lord. Parents are first reminded of the relationship that they are to have with the Lord, which is to love the Lord with all their heart, soul, and strength.

With the commandments rooted deeply in the heart and mind, the same is to be shared with one's children. Any time and any place is the right time and place to talk about God. While talking, sitting, walking, lying down, or getting up, the commandments are to be on your mind and freely expressed.

When our children were in parochial school, the principal stressed these verses. Most likely, it was this emphasis placed on the parents' responsibilities for the Christian upbringing of their children that prompted one saying that I shared with our two children. While they were very young and as they continued to grow, I said, "I will always try to stay out of your business when you are grown except in one area. If you don't go church, it is my business." Even when they married, I continued to share this thought with them.

With God's gift of children, parents are given responsibilities. The highest calling for a parent is to love the Lord with all your heart, soul, and strength and to share that with your children through word and action.

Only the child's faith in Christ will gain him or her eternal salvation, but we can be Christ's examples for our children.

Have you talked with the Lord today? Have you talked with a child about the Lord today?

Dear Father, help us to love You and be an example for our child(ren). Amen.

IDA MALL

Deuteronomy 29:29

I Don't Know Everything, but I Do Know This!

The secret things belong to the LORD our God, but the things revealed belong to us and to our children forever, that we may follow all the words of this law. Deuteronomy 29:29

It has been said in jest that just around the corner inside the pearly gates is an answer booth. All the questions we ask for which we have no answer on earth will be explained when we reach heaven. How can Father, Son, and Holy Spirit be one God? Why did this happen to our family; our mother was so young? How can body really be present in bread, and blood in wine? All these are questions we have asked, but the answers are secret—not so much hidden as beyond our grasp.

But this we do know, for it has been revealed to us and is to be shared: that "God so loved the world that He gave His one and only Son, that whoever believes in Him shall not perish but have eternal life" (John 3:16), and that you shall "love the Lord your God with all your heart and with all your soul and with all your mind" as you "love your neighbor as yourself" (Matthew 22:37, 39). This is the revealed word from God, given to us and shared by us with our children and with all others.

We will never know "how" and "why," though we will persist in asking and wondering. But we will always know that God has loved us with an everlasting love and given us Jesus, and that God has clearly identified a way for His people to live in love.

God, help us to glory in the revealed and leave the hidden to You. Amen.

PAUL J. ALBERS

Deuteronomy 31:6

Overcoming Loneliness

The LORD your God goes with you; He will never leave you nor forsake you. Deuteronomy 31:6

A grandmother was once asked: "Have you ever felt lonely?"

"Who isn't lonely? Who isn't lonely?" she repeated. "From the moment we are born, we are lonely."

Lutheran professor and psychiatrist Paul Morentz says: "Loneliness is still mankind's greatest problem. And it stems from the 'original sin' of man's self-imposed loneliness and isolation from God back in the Garden of Eden."

And this sin of self-imposed isolation from God needs repentance and forgiveness. You and I may be on the run, totally by ourselves. But it is a sin to think we are completely alone and to stay in our loneliness. For our God says: "[I] will never leave you nor forsake you" (Deuteronomy 31:6).

Evangelist-author Elizabeth Elliot, after being widowed twice, offered these practical biblical insights on conquering loneliness:

1. Be still and know that God is God. Study Scripture and pray.
2. Give thanks—for the promise of God's presence.
3. Refuse self-pity—a death that has no resurrection.
4. Accept your loneliness. It can draw you closer to God.
5. Offer up your loneliness to God. Let Him transform it.
6. Live your life for those around you.

(Adapted from "The Ones Who Are Left," *Christianity Today*, February 27, 1976, p. 7.)

Yes, when you are lonely, remember that God says: "I know your depression. I care for you." "[I] will never leave you nor forsake you" (Deuteronomy 31:6).

Lord, remove me from the pit of loneliness. Instead, grant me a well of solitude with You—refreshed by the life-giving waters of my Baptism. Amen.

DONALD L. DEFFNER

Joshua 1:9

Kee-mo-sab-bee

Have I not commanded you? Be strong and courageous. Do not be terrified; do not be discouraged, for the LORD your God will be with you wherever you go. Joshua 1:9

A favorite television program of the fifties was *The Lone Ranger*. The Lone Ranger would always save the day, riding into town at just the right time and riding out immediately afterwards. He was accompanied by an American Indian friend named Tonto, who rode a beautiful spotted pony. Tonto often referred to the Lone Ranger as Kee-mo-sab-bee, a word meaning "faithful friend." No matter what they encountered, the Lone Ranger and Tonto were faithful friends, friends who never left each other's side.

Throughout Scripture, we are reminded that God is such a friend! God reminds Joshua of that truth just before He asks Joshua to lead Israel across the Jordan and into the Promised Land. In essence, God is saying, "I'm your friend. It may seem like an awesome responsibility to lead these thousands of people, but I'll be with you. Be assured of it!"

Remember the challenge placed before the disciples when Jesus commissioned them to "make disciples of all nations" (Matthew 28:19)? The task must have seemed overwhelming for 11 disciples. They were assured and comforted, however, with the promise, "And surely I am with you ..." (Matthew 28:20).

God says the same to us. "I'm with you." He's our Kee-mo-sab-bee, our "faithful friend." Scripture says, "Greater love has no one than this, that he lay down his life for his friends" (John 15:13). That's exactly what Jesus did. He laid down His life for us to pay for our sins and to make us friends with God. Friends for life! Friends for eternity!

Thank You, gracious God, loving friend, for being our Kee-mo-sab-bee, our "faithful friend." Always! Amen.

ROGER R. SONNENBERG

13

Joshua 21:45

Promises to Count On

Not one of all the LORD's good promises to the house of Israel failed; every one was fulfilled. Joshua 21:45

A major irritant in parent-child relationships is broken promises. A father says, "Sure, honey, someday I'll take you to the game." Dad says, "One of these days we will go fishing." A mother declares, "Next month, we will be able to afford those new clothes." And yet, the father never gets around to taking his child to the game. He can't quite find the time to go fishing. And mom never seems to get the cash to buy the new jeans.

God reminds us that all of His promises are true. God is as good as His Word! You may have heard it said: "God said it. I believe it. That settles it." The Bible more accurately proclaims, "God said it. That settles it whether I believe it or not."

God and His promises can be counted on. The proof of the Lord's faithfulness can be seen in Jesus Christ, God's Son. Jesus, the Word made flesh, is the fulfillment of all God's promises to give us life and salvation.

Our faith is secure as we count on Him. He promises to always be there for us and to give us what we need. His promises will never fail us!

Dear Lord, even though my promises can be broken, Yours are always true. Help me always trust in You, through Jesus Christ, Your Son. Amen.

LUTHER C. BRUNETTE

Joshua 24:15

What Are You Here For?

But as for me and my household, we will serve the LORD. Joshua 24:15

It's an old riddle, this business of living. What are we here for? A British poet called life an incurable disease. Disraeli summed it up, "Youth is a blunder, manhood a struggle, and old age a regret." With all these answers in our pocket, we go home after a day at the office and wonder out loud to our spouses whether it's worth the effort and think seriously about quitting our jobs or taking an early retirement.

I'd like to suggest there is a lot more to life than just our failures and our regrets. There's God. Of course, the idea of God, even more, of serving Him, isn't exactly in overwhelming favor today. There are a whole lot of people, the great majority in fact, who earnestly believe the sole end and purpose of life is to be found at the ends of their fingers. To feel it, or taste it, or savor it, that's what life is all about. But our faith gives us a loftier, more satisfying reason to throw back the covers each morning and put our feet on the floor. "We will serve the Lord."

There is no other trip on earth that you would dream to undertake without some knowledge of where you are going and why. It seems to me a good deal of our bewilderment, our feelings of futility, and our anxieties are the result of not knowing what we are here for. It's a matter of getting our bearings, understanding our purpose, and celebrating our commitment to God. Take yourself out of the middle of your life and enthrone your God there, and suddenly life is not just a struggle, a blunder, or a regret. We're not here for ourselves at all. We are here for God, and in His service we find purpose and meaning and satisfaction.

O God, who alone can judge the hearts and deeds of people, help me to glorify Your name, extol Your goodness, and serve You in all blessedness. Amen.

ARNOLD KUNTZ

1 Samuel 7:12

Jesus, Our "Ebenezer"

Then Samuel took a stone and set it up between Mizpah and Shen. He named it Ebenezer, saying, "Thus far has the LORD helped us." 1 Samuel 7:12

Samuel was leading God's people in a sacrifice to the Lord when the Philistines showed up, ready for battle. But God fought the battle for His people, causing the enemy to panic and run away in confusion. In thanks, Samuel set up a stone monument where the people could remember what God had done. He called that stone *Ebenezer*—"stone of help."

The enemies of sin, death, and the devil surround God's people, ready for battle. But God fights this battle also. God the Father sent His only Son, Jesus, to die on the cross to defeat sin. Jesus rose to life on Easter morning to overcome death. The Holy Spirit works faith in Christians to give them strength to overcome the temptations of the devil.

The enemies stand no chance against God. But sometimes God's people forget this and try to fight the battles alone. Then they surrender to sin, death overtakes them, and they give in to the temptations of the devil. But the victory need not be lost, even then. When God's people turn to God in repentance, He washes away their sin, conquers death, and drives away the devil. In panic and confusion, the enemies flee from God's people. In response, God's people worship their Ebenezer, Jesus Christ, the Rock of Ages.

Lord Jesus, we remember the battle You fought for us on the cross and in the grave. We praise You for Your victory! Amen.

DEBB ANDRUS

1 Samuel 30:6

When Nothing Goes Right

David was greatly distressed because the men were talking of stoning him; each one was bitter in spirit because of his sons and daughters. But David found strength in the LORD his God. 1 Samuel 30:6

Have you ever had one of those days where nothing seems to go right? As the verse above attests, David was certainly having one of those days! Shortly after losing an important military alliance, he and his army found the burned remains of the village of Ziklag. The Amalekites had taken captive all the people of the village, including the wives, sons, and daughters of David and his army. David and his men were disheartened, to say the least.

David could have given up, but he didn't. He turned to the Lord for strength. It's not important to know if God delivered David from his physical troubles (He did). What is important is that when David was spiritually distressed, God was there to strengthen him.

God still grants strength to His people. He gives His Word to remind us that there is no problem too big for Him. Through Jesus' death and resurrection, God showed that He is even stronger than sin and death. Our Lord gave us Baptism and His Last Supper to strengthen us. God also works through other believers to encourage us and to remind us of these promises.

You probably won't face stoning in your life, but when you feel overcome by other troubles, remember that you can always turn to the God of strength.

Lord, when we are distressed and bitter, help us to find strength in Your victory over sin, death, and the evils of this world. Amen.

DEBB ANDRUS

2 Samuel 22:3

God, Our Deliverer

My God is my rock, in whom I take refuge, my shield and the horn of my salvation. He is my stronghold, my refuge and my savior—from violent men You save me. 2 Samuel 22:3

God is our rock. Rocks can be big enough to hide behind or small enough to throw at an enemy. Rocks are solid, unbreakable. God's love for us is solid and unbreakable.

God is our shield. God shields us from the arrows of temptation that Satan hurls our way.

God is our horn. Horns are used by animals for protection. Other animals fear being gored. When Jesus died for our sins, He delivered a mortal wound to Satan. The horns of the altar offered sanctuary to anyone who held onto them. Jesus' death and resurrection offer us sanctuary from sin and death. Horns were used by Old Testament priests to hold oil for anointing. We were anointed with water and the Word at our Baptism.

God is our stronghold. When our faith is attacked by doubt, we can find safety in the stronghold of God's Word, which reveals the surety of God's strength over sin, death, and the devil.

God is our refuge. Even when life seems overwhelming, we find refuge in the promises of God, who is always with us.

God is our savior, not just from physical violence, but also from the spiritual violence of eternal damnation.

When we find ourselves battle weary against the trials of life, we can turn to God for deliverance.

Dear God, help us to always remember that You are our rock, our refuge, our shield, our horn, our stronghold, and our savior. Amen.

DEBB ANDRUS

1 Chronicles 4:10

Freedom from Pain

Oh, that You would bless me and enlarge my territory! Let Your hand be with me, and keep me from harm so that I will be free from pain. 1 Chronicles 4:10

She could not walk, for she had no legs. She was often weary, for her elderly body was ravaged by advancing cancer. Confined to bed and wheelchair in the hospice, Mrs. Schmidt was near the end of her days. Yet life and hope were her stock in trade. Coaxing and demanding the nurses to lift her out of bed and wheel her around, she became a fixture on—the children's ward! There, like a mother, she held terminally ill little ones close. She crooned songs of love and faith. She prayed in English and German.

Mrs. Schmidt was the embodiment of this verse. Her territory was small—a wheelchair in the hospital. Yet the Lord enlarged her territory, so to speak, to include the children's ward. Her pain was lessened by the joy of others.

God is the giver of all strength. God is the encourager of the weak. The love for others so manifest in elderly Mrs. Schmidt was the love of God in Christ Jesus. Our God cares for us so much that His only-begotten Son was made weak unto death. In His resurrected life we are relieved from pain not for a season but unto eternity. In Him we will "run and not grow weary." In Him we will "walk and not be faint."

Dear God, thank You for Your promise made true in Christ Jesus to give strength to the weary and to give freedom from the pains of this life. Thank You for Your strong presence in my life each day! Amen.

DAVID H. BENKE

1 Chronicles 29:1–20

What a God Who Makes What a People

Yours, O LORD, is the greatness and the power and the glory and the majesty and the splendor, for everything in heaven and earth is Yours. Yours, O LORD, is the kingdom; You are exalted as head over all. 1 Chronicles 29:11

Read chapter 29 of 1 Chronicles. David wanted to build the temple for God. God, however, said no because David was a warrior whose life had been defined by fighting and shedding the blood of the nations around Israel. David could, however, prepare for the building of the temple by his son Solomon, and this he did. Such preparation started with asking the question: "Who is willing to consecrate himself today to the LORD?" (v. 5). An outpouring of gifts and devotion followed, for "they had given freely and whole-heartedly to the LORD" (v. 9).

Why were these people able to act as they did? Only because of the God they worshiped, the God we worship as well. How can one ever adequately describe God, sufficiently praise God, appropriately give God acclaim other than to repeat as David said, "Yours, O LORD, is the greatness and the power and the glory and the …"

David goes on, and we go on in never-ending praise of the God of all grace and glory. Our praise can even exceed that of David, for we have God's greatest gift, His own Son, Jesus Christ. In this gift we have the completion of our redemption and the fullness of our hope, for we have Jesus, Ruler of all, in the victory of His resurrection.

Help me, Lord, this day and all days to praise You without end. Amen.

PAUL J. ALBERS

2 Chronicles 20:15

The Battle Is Not Yours

He said: "Listen, King Jehoshaphat and all who live in Judah and Jerusalem! This is what the LORD says to you: 'Do not be afraid or discouraged because of this vast army. For the battle is not yours, but God's.'" 2 Chronicles 20:15

The Israelites faced certain defeat at the hands of their enemies. A "great multitude" was about to attack, and King Jehoshaphat and the people of Judah were gravely concerned. But the king knew what to do. He approached the source of the only power that could save God's people; he prayed to the Lord. God's response came through the Levite Jahaziel in the words of our text. God's solution to this dilemma allowed for them to simply stand and watch as He annihilated the enemy troops. Not only did God win a victory for His people, but they also reaped the battle's spoils.

We sometimes find ourselves in seemingly hopeless situations—physically, emotionally, financially, socially, spiritually. We would do well in those times to recognize that our God views our battles as His. He fights with us and for us, and His almighty power cannot fail. Those are minor battles; however, *the* major conflict, the one against the kingdom of the devil, has already been fought and won. The Scriptures boldly declare the battle done and the victory God's in Christ. That victory also belongs to all who are in Christ, who are trusting in Him for everything they need. In Him, they shall have it!

Heavenly King and almighty Father, give us courage as we face each day and its challenges. Continually remind us that our battles are Your battles, that the ultimate war has already been won, and that we, who are in Christ, share in that victory. In the mighty name of Jesus we pray. Amen.

DANIEL SCHLENSKER

2 Chronicles 32:8

Everlasting Arms

With him is only the arm of flesh, but with us is the LORD our God to help us and to fight our battles. 2 Chronicles 32:8

It didn't look good for Hezekiah and the people of Judah. Sennacherib was invading the land, and God's people could see no way to win the battle. That is when Hezekiah spoke the words of our text to uplift their flagging spirits. He reassured the people with the truth that God has His everlasting arms underneath His people.

"Are we weak and heavy laden?" the hymn writer asks. God is never weak, but omnipotent. His strength in our weakness is marvelous. He knows what we need. He acts on our behalf.

He will drive out our enemy. This final enemy, as St. Paul says, is death. God has destroyed death through His Son, Jesus. Because of Christ's victory, we are assured of eternal life in the world to come. Freed from the guilt of sin and its consequences, we are now free to serve.

Hezekiah's assurance is indeed our loving Father's encouragement to us, His redeemed children, as we fight the battles of this life until our eternal victory in heaven. Christ Jesus Himself has fought the fight. He has won the battle.

Gracious God, our shield and deliverer, assure us of Your constant providence and guidance, undergirding and protection. Hold us safely in Your arms until we safely stand in our Promised Land. Amen.

JAMES W. FREESE

Nehemiah 8:10

Rejoice in the Lord

Nehemiah said, "Go and enjoy choice food and sweet drinks, and send some to those who have nothing prepared. This day is sacred to our LORD. Do not grieve, for the joy of the LORD is your strength." Nehemiah 8:10

Tom had more than his share of trouble last year. He was laid off from work because his company lost a large government contract. His mother became ill with what seemed to be Alzheimer's disease. His stepson died unexpectedly of a heart attack at age 29. He was involved in a masters degree program that demanded so much of his time that he was always exhausted. Tom experienced several personal setbacks during this time, and at times felt he might not be able to hang on. Despite all this, Tom seemed calm, peaceful, and able to take whatever came in stride. Friends asked him if he was in denial or unaware of what was going on in his life.

Tom's reply was thoughtful. "My happiness may depend on my circumstances, but deep inside I have the gift of joy from the Lord, and nothing that happens to me can take that joy away. It is mine forever. It gives me strength for each day and each crisis. If I didn't have the Lord, I'd be a basket case!"

We do not always feel happy, but we can always feel joyful. We can have an excited anticipation inside that is confident that God is watching, caring, and intervening in life's circumstances to make all things work together for the good of those who are called according to His purpose (Romans 8:28). That joy from the Lord gives us the strength to endure, the courage to trust, and the determination to keep on doing right without getting weary.

God, thank You for Your joy that You give me. Thank You for empowering me through that joy so that I can bear the burdens in my life. Amen.

BOBBIE REED

Job 5:18

I Shall Not Be Forsaken

For He wounds, but He also binds up; He injures, but His hands also heal.
Job 5:18

Should Christians expect to be free from trials and tribulations in life because of their faith? Some ministers and churches teach a religion of prosperity. They say that God wants us all to be wealthy. They also expect quick and complete healing for their illnesses and injuries.

The question arises, what would these people do if they ever had to face the trials of Job? What would happen to their faith? Surely God wouldn't allow them to suffer!

Martin Luther said, "The book of Job deals with the question, whether misfortune comes from God even to the righteous. Job stands firm and contends that God torments even the righteous without cause other than that this be to God's praise, as Christ also testifies in John 9[:3] of the man who was born blind" (*Luther's Works* 35:251).

Does God wound; does He injure? Today's passage replies, yes. It also adds, however, that He "binds up" and "His hands also heal." "The Lord disciplines those He loves, and He punishes everyone He accepts as a son" (Hebrews 12:6).

We cannot expect a life free from pain and suffering, not when we live in a world full of sin. But with Job we can say, "I know that my Redeemer lives … . And after my skin has been destroyed, yet in my flesh I will see God" (Job 19:25–26). We take comfort in the words expressed by the hymn writer who penned for his sick friend:

> **My God, indeed, In every need**
> **You know well how to shield me;**
> **To You, then, I will yield me. Amen.**
>
> ("What God Ordains Is Always Good," by Samuel Rodigast, paraphrased)

JIM WIEMERS

Job 11:7–9

Trust God's Knowledge

Can you fathom the mysteries of God? Can you probe the limits of the Almighty? They are higher than the heavens—what can you do? They are deeper than the depths of the grave—what can you know? Their measure is longer than the earth and wider than the sea. Job 11:7–9

Dan bought a new computer that came with several powerful and sophisticated software programs. The spread-sheet program could track an incredible array of figures several pages in length. If one figure were changed, the program could recalculate the entire report in micro-seconds. It was amazing. Dan didn't understand how the program worked. That was a mystery to him. But he trusted the accuracy of the program for his business finances.

God's ways are often mysterious to us. We do not always understand why undesirable things happen and why other desirable things do not happen. We may wish that God would act in accordance with our own wishes. We may be confused, disappointed, or upset.

But the correct response to God's direction is to trust God's knowledge. God knows all the possible outcomes of any event. God allows or prevents certain events based on this knowledge. If we truly trust God, we can relax and know that whatever comes our way, God will help us survive. God can even take a negative situation and cause the results to be good.

Lord, I believe in You. Help me to let go of the seeds of unbelief and truly trust You. Amen.

BOBBIE REED

Job 11:16–17

Let Go of the Past

You will surely forget your trouble, recalling it only as waters gone by. Life will be brighter than noonday, and darkness will become like morning. Job 11:16–17

Pat and Harry adopted a baby because they couldn't have one of their own. The adoption process was lengthy and filled with frustrations. During the 20 months of waiting for a baby, Pat and Harry filled out countless forms, answered endless questions, and paid the attorneys large sums of money.

Just when Pat and Harry were told they were approved for a baby, a new requirement was discovered. This happened three times. Often either Pat or Harry considered stopping the process. But each time the other spouse refused to quit. Finally, unbelievably, they had a baby girl. She was truly theirs. The new parents' joy was evident. "She was worth all the pain, all the frustrations, all the trouble!" Harry said as he lovingly held his new daughter.

"What trouble?" Pat asked half jokingly. Pat had already let go of the past. She was beyond the pain and ready for the joy.

We are often tempted by Satan to think that the trouble we experience will last forever. We are told to give up and to quit trusting God. Some trouble seems overwhelming. At times we are not sure we are going to survive.

But our hope is in Christ and through Him we are more than conquerors. We already have the victory. All we have to do is to claim it! And victory brings joy. As Christians, we can have the joy even before the victory comes. Knowing we will be victorious, we can choose to be joyful even in troubled times. And the joy of the Lord gives us the strength to make it through the trouble to the victory.

Lord, thank You for the victories and for the joy. Give me the courage to be joyful each day. Amen.

BOBBIE REED

Job 15:11

Jesus, Our Consolation

Are God's consolations not enough for you, words spoken gently to you? Job 15:11

Sometimes life seems overwhelming. Then we search for a way out of our trials or at least some comfort—some consolation.

Where do you find your consolation? Some people search for consolation among their family. Others seek consolation in their jobs. The lottery and casinos offer gambling as a consolation. Some people turn to music or art for consolation. All these things may offer some relief from our earthly trials, but there is only one consolation that is complete and permanent—God's.

Jesus Christ came to earth and lived as a human being. He knew pain; He knew trials; He knew hunger; He knew poverty; He knew death. But Christ is more than an empathetic figure to imitate or look to as an example. Jesus Christ suffered death so that we might know the consolation of forgiveness. Christ returned alive to this sinful earth to bring us the consolation of eternal life. Then He sent His Holy Spirit to be with us and guide us through trials and temptations and to offer us the consolation of God's Word and Sacrament.

God's Word speaks gently to us. It reminds us of God's consolation of forgiveness and eternal life. The sacraments of Baptism and the Lord's Supper blend the Word with physical elements to offer absolute consolation. Take comfort and live.

Lord Jesus, You are our consolation and comfort. Help us to always turn to You in times of trial and sadness. Amen.

DEBB ANDRUS

Job 16:19–21

Guilty—Not Guilty!

Even now my witness is in heaven; my advocate is on high. My intercessor is my friend as my eyes pour out tears to God; on behalf of a man he pleads with God as a man pleads for his friend. Job 16:19–21

You are on trial for your life—your eternal life. The evidence stacked up against you is damning. You have broken every law in the book in one way or another. How do you plead?

Before the judge can lower his gavel of judgment, your lawyer rises to speak. You cry as he approaches the bench. You know you are guilty; you know you cannot pay for your legal defense. You prepare for a harsh judgment.

But your lawyer pleads with the judge, begging to be sentenced in your place. The judge's gavel falls; he pronounces you free of all guilt. He sentences your lawyer to die in your place. The court clerk erases your name from all the charges and writes in your lawyer's name instead. Your lawyer is led away to die.

The execution takes place on a cross on Calvary. Your lawyer dies an excruciating death. His lifeless body is placed in a grave. After three days, your mourning turns to joy as you hear of his triumph over death. He has returned to life! And now he comes to you, holding something in his hand. Is it a bill for his services? No. It is a gift of everlasting life. You cannot be tried again. Your freedom is guaranteed forever.

Dear Lord Jesus, You pled on my behalf and took my punishment to the cross. Thank You for Your sacrifice. You died for me; now I live for You. Amen.

DEBB ANDRUS

Job 19:26–27

That Amazing Semicircle

And after my skin has been destroyed, yet in my flesh I will see God; I myself will see Him with my own eyes—I, and not another. Job 19:26–27

A little girl, whose baby brother had just died, asked her mother where the baby had gone. Her mother replied, "To be with Jesus."

A few days later, talking to a friend, the mother commented, "I'm so grieved to have lost my baby!"

The little girl heard her and, remembering what her mother had said, looked up to her and asked, "Mommy, is a thing lost when you know where it is?"

"No, of course not," said the mother.

"Then, how can our baby be lost when he is with Jesus?"

Our loved ones who have died in the Lord are not "lost." They are "*with the Lord*"! "Whether we live or die, we belong to the Lord" (Romans 14:8 TEV). And at the resurrection we will see God and them—face to face. Job affirms: "I myself will see Him with my own eyes" (Job 19:27). (See also 1 Corinthians 13:9–10, 12; 2 Samuel 12:23; Matthew 7:14.) Until that blessed day we are one with them in Christ.

In a miraculous way, Holy Communion particularly enacts the mystical fellowship of all the saints on earth and in heaven. Those who have gone before and those who remain are one in Christ's body and blood. In some older church buildings, the Communion rail extends in a half-circle around the altar to symbolize that completeness.

When you commune, you are swept together with these saints into one great host, rejoicing and praising God and saying: "Hosanna in the highest! Blessed is he who comes in the name of the Lord. Hosanna in the highest!" What a comfort! What a foretaste of the feast to come!

Lord, thank You for the blessed assurance of eternal life with You—which I have right now through my Baptism. Amen.

DONALD L. DEFFNER

29

Job 23:10

God's Love in Jesus Is Enough

But He knows the way that I take; when He has tested me, I will come forth as gold. Job 23:10

The story of Job illustrates the sometimes perplexing ways God deals with His children. Sincerely pious conduct or faithfulness are no guarantee that the child of God will not encounter trouble or hardship in life. The Bible tells many stories of how God is able to use the trials of life to achieve the positive purpose of strengthening one's faith and increasing one's trust in Him.

At the same time, the Bible doesn't explicitly say that all of one's difficulties are for the purpose of teaching patience or even to strengthen faith. The Bible doesn't even promise that in this life everything will turn out all right in the end. Sometimes there is no answer to the why questions.

How is it, then, that this Bible verse says that when God has tested us, we will "come forth as gold"? The book of Job in general and this verse in particular remind us that the most important thing—finally, the only important thing—is our relationship with God.

What's more, God brings about and sustains this relationship through His message to us that in Jesus Christ, and through the forgiveness He gives to us, we are His children and heirs of eternal life. God may test us along our way. The tests may be severe and seemingly unbearable.

Still, the definitive expression of God's abiding love for us is that He gave His only Son to bear our sin and death. Our lives and our destiny depend not on what we do or on what happens to us, but on what God has done for us in Jesus Christ. Literally nothing can change that.

God of all comfort, in the midst of the sufferings and trials of life, draw our eyes to the cross and open tomb of Jesus, where we see yet again that You love us and care for us. Amen.

DAVID LUMPP

Job 31:4

Heavenly Medicine

Does He not see my ways and count my every step? Job 31:4

"You should get the results of the biopsy in a few days." "The boss wants to see you." "We need to know your decision now." "I'm going to put you into the hospital." "Storm warnings have been issued!" "The funeral service is about to begin." "I'm tired of arguing!"

Just reading those situations can bring some anxiety into our lives. Many have heard similar words and can easily relate to the feelings that accompany them.

Those realities are often accompanied by sky-rocketing blood pressure, emotions working overtime, nerves that are frayed. What a wonderful time for a dose of medicine—a dose of heavenly medicine that cannot be found in pharmacies.

Reading through God's Word, one finds such "medicine." Zephaniah reminds us of news that is easy to swallow and has life-changing results: "The LORD your God is with you, He is mighty to save. He will take great delight in you, He will quiet you with His love" (Zephaniah 3:17).

The presence, power, and promises of our Lord bring new-found help to the most difficult of situations. In the midst of his troubles Job acknowledges: "Does He not see my ways and count my every step?" Does not everything that happens to me concern Him?

God is present. He is in control. He has saving power. He offers a peace that we can find nowhere else. Confidently, we rest in His arms and recall His loving faithfulness as He miraculously quiets us with His love.

God of peace, when the results of living in a sinful world tempt me to take my focus off of You, bring me to Your Word and quiet me with Your love—a love that counts my every step, a love that sent Jesus to be my Savior. In His name, I pray. Amen.

TIMOTHY WESEMANN

Job 38:2–7

Celestial Architect! Heavenly Chorus!

Oh, the depth of the riches of the wisdom and knowledge of God! How unsearchable His judgments, and His paths beyond tracing out! Romans 11:33

This magnificent passage from Romans is echoed in God's chiding of Job. Sick and devastated, his faith tested to its limits, Job is challenged by God to provide answers to questions that God alone knows.

In this we see God as the celestial architect, fashioning the heavens and the earth while listening to the songs of morning stars—angels! Here we get a picture of our God who sees the end from the beginning, already having angels at hand to minister to mortals whom He had not yet created.

Jeremiah reminds us that our God knows the plans He has for us—plans for our welfare. This is ultimately shown in the person of Jesus Christ, who redeemed us lost and condemned creatures by His innocent suffering and death. "In all things God works for the good of those who love Him," the apostle Paul reminds us.

In days of suffering, darkness, and uncertainty, we are assured of God's perfect care for us, care which will continue until we safely stand in heaven. The following children's song ably sums up this thought: "God who made the earth, The air, the sky, the sea, Who gave the light its birth, Cares now for me."

Dearest Lord, comfort us with the knowledge that You see the end from the beginning and plan everything for our eternal good. Amen.

JAMES W. FREESE

Psalm 1:1–2

Delight in the Lord

Blessed is the man who does not walk in the counsel of the wicked or stand in the way of sinners or sit in the seat of mockers. But his delight is in the law of the LORD, and on His law he meditates day and night. Psalm 1:1–2

The person who is blessed delights in the Law of the Lord, and he meditates on this Law constantly. To delight in the Law of the Lord and to meditate on the Law means more than doing the things the Law demands. The word for "Law" in the Old Testament is Torah, which means more than what we traditionally understand by "law" or commandments. Torah in the Old Testament refers to instruction, or, even better, to "revelation."

The Gospel, in addition to the Law, is a key part of that revelation. The Gospel in the Old Testament relates what God was doing to forgive and save His people under the old covenant. The Gospel in the Old Testament focuses on God's promises and His saving actions like the exodus and the gift of the land of Israel. The commandments are also part of the revelation; they are ways we respond to God's saving acts.

When we avoid the counsel of the wicked and meditate on God's Torah today, we are reminded of all God has done in Jesus Christ to fulfill in a definitive way the promises He made in the Old Testament.

Do we try to obey God's Law? Of course. But above all we focus on the One who came to fulfill all the Law and the Prophets and who bore the consequences of our sin in our place. In Him we find our delight, and we will enjoy His presence for eternity.

Eternal God, You have kept all of Your promises with the coming of Jesus Christ. We await with confidence the fulfillment of His promise to return. Amen.

DAVID LUMPP

Psalm 8:3–5

God of Great and God of Small

When I consider Your heavens, the work of Your fingers, ... what is man that You are mindful of him? Psalm 8:3–4

My generation has seen many notable events in space. *Sputnik*, the fulfillment of President Kennedy's challenge to put a man on the moon, the exploration of Mars, the *Challenger* disaster, the return of Halley's Comet, and the Hubble telescope are but a few of those worthy of mention. All have barely scratched the surface of the vastness of God's heavens. *Mind-boggling* is a word that must be used when trying to comprehend the vastness of outer space. In all this vastness, how can God be mindful of *me?*

The hymn writer begins to grasp the idea of God's perfect knowledge and care for us with the words "But God had seen my wretched state Before the world's foundation, And mindful of His mercies great, He planned for my salvation" ("Dear Christians, One and All," by Martin Luther).

Our God is a God who reveals Himself to us chiefly in showing mercy by sending His one and only Son, Jesus, to bring us back to Himself. This God who formed Adam *by hand* is the same God who watches over you and me, who has counted the very hairs on our head, and who has planned all our days before our life began. We are the crown of His creation, destined to live with Him forever in heaven. Such knowledge brings serenity and joy.

Dear Lord Jesus, guide, strengthen, and enable us to live always for You. Amen.

JAMES W. FREESE

Psalm 9:9–10

God Will Not Forsake Us

The LORD is a refuge ... in times of trouble. Psalm 9:9

I once knew a child whose mother, in the throes of drug addiction, left him on a subway train. He rode alone, abandoned, for 14 hours until delivered up for safekeeping from beneath the earth. Years later, his need for security, protection, and companionship remain extraordinarily high. The human soul does not suffer abandonment with ease.

There must be a place of refuge in time of trouble. There must be a place for healing in a time of brokenness. There must be a shelter when tempests rage in life.

Our rock and hiding place is Jesus. Our place is secure in Him only because He has taken on Himself the ultimate abandonment that we deserve. "My God, My God, why have You forsaken Me?" He cried. In His crucifixion He endured the depth of our emptiness and final loneliness in separation from God. In the gift of His cross and resurrection, we may rest assured that God has not forsaken us.

We are not left to our own devices on a runaway train to nowhere like eternally frightened children. No! When we seek the Lord, we are surrounded by the hosts of heaven. We are covered by the love of God. We are safe!

Lord God, cover me, shield me, protect me, and defend me in every trial, for the sake of Jesus, my rock and hiding place. Amen.

DAVID H. BENKE

Psalm 10:17

He Hears the Needy

You hear, O LORD, the desire of the afflicted; You encourage them, and You listen to their cry. Psalm 10:17

Ours is a day of "felt" needs. Programs are designed, accommodations made, and mission statements developed—all with an eye toward meeting those felt needs.

Ours is also a day of "real" needs. Pleas for help rise from every corner of the world, from all levels of society, from the nooks and crannies of our own life. Hunger, lack of a job, disease, illness, loneliness are very real needs for which we need real ears to hear. From the earliest dealings with His people, God's ears have been opened to our need: "When [the needy] cries out to Me, I will hear, for I am compassionate" (Exodus 22:27).

Our deepest need, though, is forgiveness—forgiveness for the wrong we have done, for the good we have not done, for the guilt that has weighed us down, for the sickness of sin we inherited from our parents Adam and Eve. Our plea echoes that of Solomon: "[O Lord,] hear from heaven, Your dwelling place; and when You hear, forgive" (2 Chronicles 6:21).

Hear God did as He sent His Son, Jesus the Christ, to die in our stead to give us the very forgiveness we need. Hear God did as He sent His Holy Spirit to bring us to faith in Jesus, to apply the forgiveness of sins to us in Baptism, to strengthen us in faith through His Word and Sacrament.

Hear God does with *all* our needs. He sends His answers in His own way. But hear He does, and that is encouragement enough for us in all our needs.

> **When in the hour of deepest need**
> **We know not where to look for aid ... .**
> **[We] cry to You, O faithful God,**
> **For rescue from our sorry lot. Amen.**
>
> ("When in the Hour of Deepest Need," by Paul Eber)

HENRY GERIKE

Psalm 16:8–9

Believing in the Future

I have set the LORD always before me. Because He is at my right hand, I will not be shaken. Therefore my heart is glad and my tongue rejoices; my body also will rest secure. Psalm 16:8–9

Anna lived in a convalescent home. She had lived there for over 20 years and was now celebrating her 100th birthday. Everyone from the home gathered in the main dining room. Streamers hung from the walls. A large birthday cake table with 100 brightly burning candles bedecked the center. Her pastor said some words. A reporter from the local newspaper interviewed her.

"Do you feel 100 years old?" he asked.

"Of course not," she said.

"Do you have any children?"

"Not yet!" she said laughing.

It's good to believe in the future. The psalmist certainly did. "He is at my right hand, I will not be shaken. … my heart is glad and my tongue rejoices; my body also will rest secure." The psalmist knew his future was in God's hands. Even when he couldn't always feel God's presence, he knew he could trust Him.

We also can believe in the future. It's provided for through Jesus Christ. Just before leaving His disciples, Jesus said, "Do not let your hearts be troubled. Trust in God; trust also in Me. In My Father's house are many rooms; if it were not so, I would have told you. I am going there to prepare a place for you" (John 14:1–2). And that's exactly what He did! He prepared it through His own death and resurrection!

Lord God, when our hearts are troubled, remind us that You are always before us. Our future is in Your hands. Thank You. Amen.

ROGER R. SONNENBERG

Psalm 18:28–29

The One Medicine for Despair

You, O LORD, keep my lamp burning; my God turns my darkness into light. With Your help I can advance against a troop; with my God I can scale a wall. Psalm 18:28–29

Another suicide is reported in the paper. Perhaps we read it with greater anguish because it was someone we knew or someone in our own family. Perhaps we may have considered this for ourselves, for the walls of trouble may have surrounded us as it did for that one who felt there was no way out. More than 30,000 people in the United States each year feel they have no way out.

The message of the psalmist comes ever so clearly: there is hope, for there is help; help to turn darkness into light, help to scale any wall or obstacle that seems insurmountable. This message God brings to each one of us that we may have hope today, the helping hand of God taking our hand. We know this because Jesus rose from the dead. That is absolute, and that is light. The darkness of sin or despair is always removed by the glow of the light of the resurrection of Jesus.

God works through us to pass on this gift of hope to others. God strengthens our hand to be the strong hand for another who struggles. A person in our own family, or church, or neighborhood is the one whose darkness can be turned into light as we share the hope Jesus gives.

God, help me in my struggle, and help me to help another in his or her struggle. Amen.

PAUL J. ALBERS

Psalm 19:1

Glory to God!

The heavens declare the glory of God; the skies proclaim the work of
His hands. Psalm 19:1

One of the true pleasures of life is sitting outside on a nice, sunny
day and watching the billowing clouds gently glide across the sky,
observing their interesting shapes, and feeling the warmth of the
sun on our backs.

On a clear summer's night, we might stand quietly and gaze at
the thousands of twinkling stars in the heavens. Perhaps David
was inspired by the Holy Spirit to write some of his psalms while
sitting on a hillside and gazing up into the sky.

The grandeur of the sun, moon, stars, and clouds points to the
Creator, who fills the earth with His presence and controls all the
heavenly bodies.

We have a God who is both all powerful in ruling over all the
elements of the earth and at the same time loving and kind. He
provides for our needs; He comforts, protects, and gives us His joy.

We also have a loving Savior, Jesus Christ, who was also present
at creation. Because He loved us, He willingly set aside His divine
attributes and came to earth as true man and true God to redeem
us by His innocent suffering and death. Along with the heavens
we also declare the glory of God.

**Dear Lord, You alone are worthy of all our praise. Thank You
for the beauty of Your creation and help us to be good stew-
ards of all that You have entrusted to us. Thank You especially for the gift of salvation in Your Son, Jesus. Help us to tell
others what a marvelous God we have in You, our Creator,
Redeemer, and Sanctifier. In Jesus' name we pray. Amen.**

JIM WIEMERS

Psalm 19:14

An Attitude for the Lord

May the words of my mouth and the meditation of my heart be pleasing in Your sight, O LORD, my Rock and my Redeemer. Psalm 19:14

Imagine the condition of the world if all our words and attitudes were pleasing to God. All the problems that beleaguer us day by day would disappear!

The psalmist is talking about a mind-set, an attitude, an outlook that develops when one is united with the Lord by faith. Some people think of Christianity in terms of rules to follow or laws to obey. You can't reduce the Christian religion to a set of rules and regulations. You can't say, "Do thus and so to fulfill the law of Christ," and get by with it. Christianity cannot be reduced to a code of conduct.

Christianity is a relationship between God and people. The relationship was broken by Adam and Eve, who strove to be equal with God. But the New Adam, Jesus, restored that relationship through His death and resurrection. He brings us back into the relationship through faith. What a gift! In thankfulness and praise we want to mimic Christ—to adopt His attitude.

It is this new attitude that prompts us to keep God's commandments. A person can keep the Ten Commandments meticulously, but if he or she is raging all the while with resentment within, that is a long way from Christian living.

More than one who is rather proud or, at least, somewhat satisfied with the way he or she is living up to the rubrics of decency and the guidelines of Christian living, would be less inclined to boast if a little attention were given to motive. When the highway patrol pulls you over to the side of the road, you do what you're told. You obey, or at least conform, but your inward attitude may be that of rebellion and resentment. That kind of obedience is not worthy to be associated with the mind of Christ. His was an attitude of humbleness and obedience that automatically fulfilled the will of God.

Lord Jesus Christ, how different Your ways, how unique Your thoughts. From Your heart come godly words and Christian deeds. Give me such a heart so that from it proceed those things that please You. Amen.

ARNOLD KUNTZ

Psalm 23

A Promise from Our Shepherd-King

The LORD is my shepherd, I shall not be in want. Psalm 23:1

Of all the parts of Holy Scripture, none is better known and loved than the Twenty-third Psalm: "The LORD is my shepherd, I shall not be in want ..." It is so much a part of our culture that TV and movie characters recite its familiar verses. People who have only a passing familiarity with the Christian faith recall its familiar words, the cadence and resonance of its verses: "He makes me lie down in green pastures, He leads me beside quiet waters, He restores my soul."

The Twenty-third Psalm resonated with the people of King David's time as well. In ancient literature, kings were often depicted as shepherds of their people. Wealth and status and family security were counted in flocks of sheep and goats. All the patriarchs were shepherds. Job was a shepherd. And David, as a young man, was in charge of his father's flock. "Your servant has been keeping his father's sheep," David tells King Saul before he redeems Israel by slaying the giant Goliath. "The LORD who delivered me from the paw of the lion and the paw of the bear will deliver me from the hand of this Philistine" (1 Samuel 17:34, 37).

"Even though I walk through the valley of the shadow of death, I will fear no evil, for You are with me; Your rod and Your staff, they comfort me."

We, too, have a Shepherd-King. He is Jesus Christ, God's Son, our Savior: "I am the good shepherd," Jesus told the unbelieving Pharisees. "The good shepherd lays down his life for the sheep. ... I know My sheep and My sheep know Me—just as the Father knows Me and I know the Father" (John 10:11, 14–15).

Jesus is indeed the Good Shepherd. He laid down His life for us on the cross. Now, because of His life, death, and resurrection, we have peace with our heavenly Father, who welcomes us home and no longer counts our transgressions against us.

"Surely goodness and love will follow me all the days of my life, and I will dwell in the house of the LORD forever."

No matter what comes our way, no matter how our adversary, "the old evil Foe," tries to deceive us, our reward is secure, our eternal life guaranteed, "for the Lamb at the center of the throne will be their shepherd; He will lead them to springs of living water. And God will wipe away every tear from their eyes" (Revelation 7:17).

Amen. Alleluia. Come, Lord Jesus!

JAMES HEINE

Psalm 24:7–10

The King of Hearts

Lift up your heads, O you gates ... that the King of glory may come in. Psalm 24:7

This passage, often used during Advent, invites us to prepare for the Lord's coming. "Advent" and "adventure" are related words, not only because they come from the same Latin word (*advenire*, to come to) but also because both point to an exciting event and experience. What an adventure it is for us Christians to prepare ourselves for Jesus Christ, so that at His advent we may open the door of our hearts and let the King of glory come in!

The rule of this King is not political, external, dramatic. Its power lies in the Gospel of the forgiveness of sins. People do not see it here, then there, for Christ's kingdom is within us. He is the King of hearts. He took us over when He redeemed us from sin and death with His own precious blood. Now we are His own blessed.

To "advent" and "adventure" we add a third related word: "venture." We venture forth to the pleasant, delightful task to serve Him who first served us. Our Lord emphasizes that His yoke is easy and His burden light. Gladly and joyfully we assume our tasks as Christ's disciples: to venture forth to tell others the good news of His salvation, to visit the sick, to console the grief-stricken.

The King of grace, who comes to us through His Word and sacraments, also invites us to come to Him. His invitation is most appealing: "Come to Me, all you who are weary and burdened, and I will give you rest" (Matthew 11:28).

Who can refuse this invitation of the King of hearts? Let Him come in!

Dear Lord, continue to come into our hearts and homes and enable us to serve You joyfully. Amen.

RUDOLPH F. NORDEN

Psalm 25:6–7

Sins of Youth

Remember not the sins of my youth and my rebellious ways. Psalm 25:7

"The sins of my youth" is an expression often used when looking back over one's life and recalling blunders made in years long gone. We cringe when past events are brought to mind, wondering why we ever did such things and hoping that no one will remember them. The devil uses these sins of our youth to make us believe that God will neither forgive nor forget them. Were that true, we would be bound for eternal death in hell.

King David himself had much for which to be ashamed in his life. The incident with Bathsheba alone would have been enough to keep David's conscience pointing its finger for the rest of his life. His sin of coveting set off a domino effect of sins culminating in murder. Nathan's accusation and David's confession brought about this sweet sentence from Nathan, "The LORD has taken away your sin."

God is love. This love prompted Him to send His Son, Jesus, to redeem, forgive, and restore us. Day after day we are assured that "as far as the east is from the west, so far has He removed our transgressions from us" (Psalm 103:12). "I will forgive their wickedness and will remember their sins no more" (Jeremiah 31:34). Forgiven and restored, may we also forgive and forget when wronged by others.

Heavenly Father, thanks and praise for Your daily assurance of our complete forgiveness. Help us to forgive others when we are wronged. Amen.

JAMES W. FREESE

Psalm 27:1

Whom Shall I Fear?

The LORD is my light and my salvation—whom shall I fear? The LORD is the stronghold of my life—of whom shall I be afraid? Psalm 27:1

The famous writer Thomas Carlyle built a soundproof chamber in his home to keep all noise out. Particularly bothersome to him was a neighbor's rooster. It was unlike any other rooster he had ever known. Often, the rooster crowed throughout the day. Needless to say, this distracted Carlyle greatly. One day he walked over to his neighbor's house and complained loudly. The owner apologized and promised that he would make sure the rooster crowed no more than three times a day. The owner kept his end of the bargain; however, Carlyle still found it difficult to write. He said, "Now all I do is spend my time waiting for the rooster to crow."

Like Carlyle we are easily distracted. We worry about many things that never happen. We fear the known and the unknown.

The psalmist David also worried. He worried about those who conspired to destroy him. In Psalm 27 he acknowledges, however, that he has no reason to fear because of God's promise to him. David had been promised, "My love will never be taken away from [you]" (2 Samuel 7:15). David, therefore, said "The LORD is my light and my salvation." He knew he had nothing to fear.

We also have nothing to fear. Not even our many sins. Why? Because we have salvation through Jesus Christ. "God made Him who had no sin to be sin for us, so that in Him we might become the righteousness of God" (2 Corinthians 5:21).

Lord God, You are "my light and my salvation—whom shall I fear? [You are] the stronghold of my life—of whom shall I be afraid?" Thank You. Amen.

ROGER R. SONNENBERG

Psalm 27:14

Waiting for the Lord

Wait for the LORD; be strong and take heart and wait for the LORD. Psalm 27:14

Waiting is one of the most frustrating things we know. We wait for the mail to come, the computer to process, the phone to ring, the dinner to cook, the traffic to move, the check to come, the rain to stop, the light to change, the Cubs to win, and on and on. It would be interesting to figure out how much of our lives we spend waiting.

This impatience also spills over into our relationship with God. Waiting for God to make good on His promises is one of life's tremendous challenges. Instead of trusting God to give us what we need when we need it, we would like God to give us what we want when we want it! We pray for loved ones and friends to believe in Christ as their Savior, but if nothing happens, we give up on God and lament, "What's the use, there's nothing I can do!"

Even though we are impatient with God, He is so very patient with us. He forgives us our sins and assures us of life with Him forever. By His grace in Christ Jesus, He invites us to come to Him no matter where we are or what time it is. His love enables us to "be still, and know that [He is] God" (Psalm 46:10).

We never wait for God in vain. God's promises can be trusted! As we wait, sometimes the reasons for our waiting are made clear. Other times, we learn that if the answer had come earlier, we could not have handled it. We can't hurry God, but we can trust Him.

Heavenly Father, give me faith to wait on You! Amen.

LUTHER C. BRUNETTE

Psalm 28:7

Dragged Away or Kept Safe?

The LORD is my strength and my shield; my heart trusts in Him, and I am helped. My heart leaps for joy and I will give thanks to Him in song. Psalm 28:7

In most cities and towns, all law enforcement officers are required to wear bulletproof vests. Though cumbersome and heavy, and very hot in the summer, the officers are happy to wear their vests for the extra protection that could save their life.

In reading Psalm 28, one learns that David was facing many enemies who would drag him away and who harbored malice in their hearts against him. This caused great fear in David, so he pled to God with earnest prayer for mercy and help. We struggle with many of the same enemies as David—sickness, despair, anguish, anger, resentment, hatred.

We share with David the one and only hope: "Praise be to the LORD for He has heard my cry for mercy." We share with David the one and only faith: "The LORD is my strength and my shield, my heart trusts in Him." We share with David the one and only true joy: "I am helped. My heart leaps for joy." We share with David the one and only expression of life joined in Jesus Christ: "I will give thanks to Him in song."

Give me faith, O Lord, that my life may be filled with joy. Amen.

PAUL J. ALBERS

Psalm 30:5

Weeping and Rejoicing

For His anger lasts only a moment, but His favor lasts a lifetime; weeping may remain for a night, but rejoicing comes in the morning. Psalm 30:5

For years wise mothers have counseled, "Get some rest. Things will look better in the morning." It's good advice, and the psalmist feels the same. David would not deny that our weeping and sadness are real, for he experienced them often. But sadness is not to abide for long, for rejoicing comes in the morning.

These words are not merely lovely poetry, though they surely are that. Inherent in them are God's mercy and kindness, His favor directed toward us, which lasts a lifetime, yes, even an eternal lifetime.

But what about those times when our tears are not dried overnight? When the new day dawns, but we still are not rejoicing? Do we doubt David's words of promise? No, we continue to rely on Him who never slumbers or sleeps, with the assurance that He holds us every hour of the day and night in His love.

The life God gives is new life, really an unending life begun at Baptism, when all the love and favor He has for His Son is given to us.

Dear loving Father, please send Your comfort in my hour of sadness. Dry my tears with the sweet assurance that You are with me always. Amen.

LAINE ROSIN

Psalm 31:1–5

Our Times Are in God's Hands

Into Your hands I commit my spirit; redeem me, O LORD, the God of truth. Psalm 31:5

Many of the psalms of David are cries for deliverance, times when he fears for his life at the hands of his enemies. Take another look at verse 5, however. Does it look familiar? Where have you read it before?

Jesus quoted this verse as His final words on the cross (Luke 23:46). His last words before He died were, "Father, into Your hands I commit My spirit." Recognizing that His work of redemption was complete, our Savior released His spirit to the care of His heavenly Father.

The martyr Stephen, as he knelt dying, voiced a similar plea, "Lord Jesus, receive my spirit" (Acts 7:59).

As life ends, what better final words can we utter than committing our souls to our heavenly Father, who loves us and always has the best in store for His children. As David says later in the same psalm, "My times are in Your hands" (v. 15). Again, he uses the metaphor of God taking us into His hands, where we are held safe and secure from all our worries and fears.

In life or death we can find rest in our heavenly Father's hands.

> And last, as life and suff'rings end:
> "O God my Father, I commend
> Into your hands my spirit."
> Be this, dear Lord, my dying prayer;
> O gracious Father, hear it. Amen.

("From Calvary's Cross I Heard Christ Say," by Johann Böschenstain. © 1982 CPH)

JIM WIEMERS

Psalm 31:14–15

Trust in the Lord

But I will trust in You, O LORD; I say, "You are my God." My times are in Your hands. Psalm 31:14–15

One time a small boy stood near the grandfather clock at his house. He loved to count out loud with the chimes marking a new hour. One day, as the noon chimes sounded 12, something happened! Instead of stopping at 12, it kept right on chiming, 13-14-15-16 …

The boy jumped to his feet and ran into the kitchen, shouting, "Mom, Mom! It's later than it has ever been before!"

How true! For each of us, it is later than it has ever been before. We are all getting older, changing by the hour, and heading towards that day when we will meet our Savior face-to-face through our faith in Him.

Yet, before we get depressed, the Lord assures us that our times are in His hands. We can trust in Him! The Lord assures us that when it comes to the times of our lives, He has all the bases covered.

Our past is forgiven through the shed blood of Christ.

Our present is taken care of through His merciful provision.

Our future is secure through the promises of His Word.

Truly our times are in God's hands! We trust in Him!

Eternal Father, as time passes, we praise You that You are outside of time. Order our times around Your will so that we may truly trust in You. In Jesus' name we pray. Amen.

LUTHER C. BRUNETTE

Psalm 32:9–10

God's Love Surrounds Us

Do not be like the horse or the mule, which have no understanding but must be controlled by bit and bridle or they will not come to you. Many are the woes of the wicked, but the LORD's unfailing love surrounds the man who trusts in Him. Psalm 32:9–10

In today's world, the acceptance of an offer that is allegedly free sometimes turns out to have strings attached. Therefore, it may be difficult to identify with the stupidity of resisting a free offer, as the psalmist implies. What offer is it that David wants to make sure people do not turn down? The first part of the psalm contains the answer: David has been describing God's boundless love and forgiveness. That is what the godly ought not to resist or stay away from.

Humankind is not naturally inclined to come to God; in fact, sinful human nature runs in the opposite direction! Natural man needs that bit and bridle; he needs to be jerked around for his own good. But the Holy Spirit has called and enlightened us by the Gospel so that we may come to God for spiritual sustenance, for the forgiveness of sins, and for the assurance of eternal life. That is what trust is all about. At God's invitation and empowered by the Holy Spirit, we place ourselves into the almighty and gracious hands of our loving God. There is no more blessed and secure place in all of creation.

Gracious and loving God, accept our praise and thanks for making it possible, by Your Spirit and through the sacrifice of Your Son on our behalf, for us to approach Your throne. Continue to sustain and strengthen our faith and trust in You that we might experience the abundant life You have promised, through Christ, our Lord. Amen.

DANIEL SCHLENSKER

Psalm 34:10–14

Put God First

Those who seek the Lord lack no good thing. Psalm 34:10

Mark wanted a promotion at work. He knew he was qualified and could do the next level job in the company. He could see himself behind the desk, making decisions and setting policy. He felt he was the best choice for the position.

But the person Mark needed to please was not himself, but the boss. It didn't matter how much Mark felt he deserved the promotion unless the boss also agreed that Mark was the best choice. So, Mark made pleasing the boss with good work a priority. At every opportunity Mark gave an extra effort. He learned not only his assignments, but those of others with whom he worked. He volunteered to fill in wherever he was needed. He was helpful, kind, willing, and dependable. In the process, Mark learned a lot about the company he would not have otherwise known. He actually enjoyed himself. And Mark became more valuable to the company. He got the promotion.

It doesn't matter how good we think we are, or how much we think we have learned, there is always room for improvement. Instead of focusing on what we want for ourselves, we need to spend time and energy becoming the persons God designed us to be. We need to seek to please God. We must study the Word to learn about God and His divine expectations for us. We must allow the Holy Spirit to tune in our hearts to God's heart. In the process, we become more like God wants us to be. We come to want what is right and best in our lives. We find that as we seek the Lord and delight in doing right, the desires of our hearts come into line with right choices. We will lack no good thing!

God, keep me close to You. Help me to know You and what You would have me become. Bring my desires into line with what You want for me. Amen.

BOBBIE REED

Psalm 34:19

The Victory Is Ours

A righteous man may have many troubles, but the LORD delivers him from them all. Psalm 34:19

God's people knew the ups and downs of life. They knew that things did not always go well even for those who sought to be faithful and to do God's will as He had revealed it. They knew that there was no easy correlation between obedience and blessing in this life. Righteous men such as Elijah and Jeremiah and Job had many troubles indeed.

Faith and faithfulness today are likewise no guarantee of a trouble-free existence. What can make matters worse, there is often no discernible reason or explanation for why someone does experience difficulties. And, for the time being, there may be no immediate rescue or way out.

Precisely here the psalmist seems to assert something contrary to experience and reminds his readers that the Lord delivers His people from all of these troubles. The psalmist's point is clear: God keeps His promises, even if He does follow His own schedule.

We are at an advantage today over those who first read the words of this psalm: in Jesus Christ, God has kept His promise. Through the saving work of Jesus, God delivers us from all manner of troubles—from those we bring on ourselves and from those that simply attend life in a sinful world.

God delivers us from our problems by delivering Jesus Christ into death for us. The decisive battle has been won; the final outcome is not in doubt.

Merciful God, keep us mindful of Your promises to be with us, to comfort us, and to deliver us from all that would harm us. Above all, remind us of the victory won by Your Son, Jesus Christ. Amen.

DAVID LUMPP

Psalm 34:22

Trust in the Lord

The LORD redeems His servants; no one will be condemned who takes refuge in Him. Psalm 34:22

The book of Psalms lets us glimpse into David's life. Psalm 34, for instance, is one of 13 psalms linked to one specific incident. As king-elect of God's people, David lost his confidence in God's protection against Saul. In that moment of weakness of faith, David fled to Israel's enemies, the Philistines, and sought refuge with their king. When David realized how foolish he was to trust the Philistines for help, he feigned insanity to escape. Through this experience David learned the truth proclaimed in this psalm: "Blessed is the man who takes refuge in [the Lord]" (v. 8).

By his invitation to "taste and see that the LORD is good" (v. 8), David asks us to learn from his mistake and to trust in the Lord who "redeems His servants." So often we put our trust in our own skill and ingenuity, in our power or the power of the "important" people of life. Even in matters of our salvation we try to trust our good works. When we lean on our abilities, strength, and good works, we collapse under the weight of the guilt of our sin. Nothing we can do will redeem us before God; but He sent His Son—Jesus the Christ—not only to live among us, but to suffer betrayal, to die in our place, and to rise again so that we might have new life.

"Therefore, there is now no condemnation for those who are in Christ Jesus," St. Paul tells us (Romans 8:1). Since "no one will be condemned who takes refuge in Him," we are freed to live our lives for the One in whom we put our trust.

> **In You, Lord, I have put my trust;**
> **Leave me not helpless in the dust,**
> **Let me not be confounded.**
> **Let in Your Word My faith, O Lord,**
> **Be always firmly grounded. Amen.**
>
> ("In You, Lord, I Have Put My Trust," by Adam Reusner)

HENRY GERIKE

Psalm 37:4

Not My Will, but God's

Delight yourself in the LORD and He will give you the desires of your heart. Psalm 37:4

I know I am a child of God, but I can't say I'm always delightful. I know that I belong to Jesus, that He has been killed for my sins, that He rose from the dead, and because of this, I am heaven-bound. Yet, sometimes I put all that aside as I make my own plans.

A few years ago, I was in a ministry in which I felt very comfortable. I was successful, the ministry was bearing fruit, and my family and I were pretty well settled. Then I was called to a different ministry, in a different part of the country, in a city to which I never dreamed I'd go. Well, my plans were to stay put where I was. I was doing the Lord's work there, and I had planned for a long and exciting time there. But guess where I am now? You see, I didn't really find my delight in the *Lord* in that place, but in the *ministry*. Therefore, my plans to stay did not succeed.

To "delight yourself in the LORD" is more than just feeling joyous whenever the name of Jesus is mentioned. It involves committing whatever you do to the Lord. It's saying, "not what I will, God, but what You will." If your desire is to be open to God's plan for you, then the desires of your heart will be met.

Dear Father in heaven, I delight in the plans You have made for me. Help me to be open to Your will and to make plans that will glorify You and succeed in Your kingdom. In Jesus' name I pray. Amen.

KEVIN PARVIZ

Psalm 37:5

Commitment

Commit your way to the LORD; trust in Him and He will do this. Psalm 37:5

The scene is pastoral as an older couple sits on the front porch of their farmhouse, rocking away. Birds are chirping; soft music is playing in the background. Suddenly, with no apparent warning, the scene blurs, the music stops, and the sweet little old lady becomes frightening. Her facial expressions turn hateful as she screams into my living room, "I hate commitments."

This advertisement for a music club with no commitments echoes the sentiments of most of America. We find commitments difficult. Often they are long-term, if not forever, and we find it important to keep our options open.

So, in this spirit, sports heroes hold out to renegotiate their contracts, regardless of the commitment they made to their teams. There is an ever-increasing divorce rate, as people refuse to commit to their spouses, and millions of children go without adequate support, because one or both parents refuse to commit to them. What used to be a society of trust based on a handshake has become one where trust is virtually nonexistent.

It is precisely to us that God speaks when He asks us to commit and trust. The basis upon which our commitment is requested is God's commitment to us. His love is so great that He committed Himself to us when He came to earth as a baby. He committed Himself to us when He walked our paths, experienced our pain, and was killed for our sins. His commitment brings us life, and our trust brings Him joy. Through the power of the Holy Spirit, He has given us the ability to commit and to be blessed in those commitments, to trust and to be trusted. Praise Him!

Father God, through Your Son, Jesus, and the power of the Holy Spirit, give us the strength to commit our way to You and to fulfill our commitments to others. Amen.

BOBBIE REED

Psalm 37:23–26

Lean on God

If the Lord delights in a man's way, He makes his steps firm; though he stumble, he will not fall, for the Lord upholds him with His hand. I was young and now I am old, yet I have never seen the righteous forsaken or their children begging bread. They are always generous and lend freely; their children will be blessed. Psalm 37:23–26

Eighty-year-old Marian was weak and shaky after her long illness and found it difficult to stand or walk on her own. When she needed to get out of bed, she was very grateful for the support of her son Richard's arm around her. Richard cared deeply about his mother. Whatever she needed, Richard tried to provide. He went shopping for groceries, cooked for her, and served her meals on a bed tray.

God cares for us in much the same way. The everlasting arms support us. Our needs are met, often in miraculous ways. God protects us from dangers and problems, some of which we never know are issues.

God cares about the paths we choose in life. The Almighty is ready to guide us in the ways we ought to walk. And when we entrust our Christian walk to God, we please our Lord. God will not only direct our paths, but will also keep us from falling. Anyone may falter at times, even stumble, but God is able to break the fall and draw the person back into fellowship. When the night is long and the way is rough, lean on God.

God, You are the only One on whom I can lean without fear of being let down. Thank You for being there for me. Amen.

BOBBIE REED

Psalm 42:1–2

A Necessity—Water and Word

My soul thirsts for God, for the living God. Psalm 42:2

Hydrated is an often-used word today. Models and actresses attribute their beauty to keeping their body and skin hydrated by drinking large amounts of water. From a medical standpoint, we know that people can exist for an extended period of time by the consumption of water only. When it is extremely hot, we are told to consume liquids, especially water. Cities open fire hydrants so children can be cooled by playing in the water. Water is essential for our well being.

As a child living on a farm, I would stand on the pond bank to watch the various animals, especially the cattle, as they came to drink. With the passing of summer, the water would recede from the bank's edge. This required the cattle to carefully approach the water because their hoofs would sink into the mud. When they finally reached the water, it was easy to see that water satisfied their thirst.

In our Bible passage, the illustration compares the survival needs of the deer and of people. For the deer, water will suffice, but for people, water will quench only the bodily needs, but the soul thirsts for living water.

Our bodies need water, but our souls need to be cleansed with the water of holy Baptism. We also need to be nourished with the spiritual food of God's Word.

Do we thirst to be fed with God's Word, to drink of His water?

Dear Father, help us to understand and thirst for Your life-giving spiritual food—food that lasts forever. Amen.

IDA MALL

Psalm 43:4

Our Joy and Delight

Then will I go to the altar of God, to God, my joy and my delight. I will praise You with the harp, O God, my God. Psalm 43:4

The book of Psalms was the hymnbook of ancient Israel. It was central to their life of worship, for through it they expressed their sorrow and joy, their prayers and praises to God.

Psalm 43 talks about God as His people's "joy and delight." They knew that their identity as God's people came not from their achievement but from what He had done for them to make them His people. God had brought them out of slavery in Egypt and given to them the Promised Land.

Israel often forgot their identity as God's own possession, and they too often forgot that their protection came from Him alone. An important part of the Old Testament's message was to remind them of these fundamental realities.

In their worship, as reflected in this verse from Psalm 43, God's people hear in faith what God has done for them, and they respond with praise. Hearing God's acts of mercy on their behalf, He truly is their "joy and delight."

Christian people today often repeat the story of God's old covenant people in their own lives. Yet God is patient and persistent. He is not about to let His plan be derailed by our unfaithfulness. He keeps coming back to us, even though we don't deserve it.

God is our joy and delight because He has claimed us as His own children, delivers us from slavery to sin and death through the death and resurrection of Jesus Christ, and promises us eternal life with Him. This is *our* occasion for worship, thanksgiving, and praise.

Merciful God, You promise to be present with us in grace in Your Son, Jesus Christ. Continue to remind us of our Baptism, declare to us Your Gospel, and feed us with Your body and blood. Amen.

DAVID LUMPP

Psalm 46:1

A Great Man Lay Dying

God is our refuge and strength, an ever-present help in trouble. Psalm 46:1

A great churchman lay dying. On a tour of world missions, he had contracted a rare disease that left him almost totally paralyzed.

He could not speak, but he could hear. Otherwise, he could barely move his fingers or blink his eyes.

As the days slipped by, the surgeons sought to keep in communication with him. To ascertain his mental clarity, they asked him to tap a finger 50 times. This he did each day, with precision.

Then one day he tapped only 46 times. "Ah," he's slipping, they thought. But the next day it was exactly 46 taps, and the next and the next.

"What's he trying to tell us?" they puzzled.

Then one person realized: "Forty-six, 46, 46! The 46th *psalm!*"

Here lay this great churchman, inert, powerless on his deathbed. But as he lay there facing heavenward, his finger was tapping out the faith-filled message: "God is our refuge and strength, an ever-present help in trouble!" (Psalm 46:1).

Lord, we praise and thank You for being our refuge and strength, the one to whom we can always turn in times of trouble. Amen.

DONALD L. DEFFNER

Psalm 50:15

This Christianity Stuff Really Works!

Call upon Me in the day of trouble; I will deliver you, and you will honor Me. Psalm 50:15

A pastor in Ann Arbor, Michigan, tells of a woman who was well known for her negativity. In fact, she fairly "seethed with hate," he said. She had been a church member, but something had happened that had so changed her that for *20 years* she was literally filled with loathing.

Somehow, the woman happened to visit the church again. She attended services and meetings for about a month. Then one day, the woman walked up to the pastor, and he saw a totally different person. To his amazement the smiling, beaming woman said: "Hey, you know, this Christianity stuff *really* works!"

It's a true story. It really happened. It's no more "dramatic" than that. And yet, it's *quite* "dramatic." "Christianity really works!" The warming fellowship of being with other Christians *really works*. God's means of grace, His Holy Word and sacraments, *really work*. God in His merciful forgiveness, by the power of the Holy Spirit, does that within us which we are unable to do. *Christianity really works*.

What despair or difficulty confronts you? Christ wants you to have His peace and His power to overcome it. He says: "Call upon Me in the day of trouble; I will deliver you, and you will honor Me" (Psalm 50:15).

But God doesn't just operate as a "God of the Zaps" through the thin air. He works through His *means of grace*—His Word and the sacraments. So let us use them faithfully. They are our "hookup" to His power supply. Through them He delivers *us*. And then we honor *Him*.

Lord, keep me ever faithful in searching the Scriptures, affirming my Baptism, and partaking of the Eucharist often—with a joyful heart. Amen.

DONALD L. DEFFNER

Psalm 51:10–12

Forgiven and Made Pure

Create in me a pure heart, O God, and renew a steadfast spirit within me. Do not cast me from Your presence or take Your Holy Spirit from me. Restore to me the joy of Your salvation and grant me a willing spirit, to sustain me. Psalm 51:10–12

When we think of King David, we often think of one of the greatest kings of Israel. David trusted God so much that he faced an armored Philistine giant with nothing more than a sling and a few smooth rocks. God gave David the victory! His love for God was so great that he committed his life to God, and God blessed David. It is from David's seed that the Savior would come, and Jesus is from the house of David. You'd think with that kind of background, David would have some special power to avoid sinning, that his life was about as perfect as you could get.

But David was harassed, persecuted by his own family, and fell into sin. These are the words he prayed after Nathan confronted him with his adultery with Bathsheba. And what a marvelous prayer! Can you imagine how David must have felt? David had experienced all the blessings that God had given him. He had witnessed God's power and mercy, and yet he still rejected God for a pretty face. David is sad; he is lonely; he feels so empty. And in his emptiness, he understands what it feels like to not walk with God. David knows what it is to be in the presence of God. He has experienced the indwelling of the Holy Spirit; he has experienced the joy of salvation. And now, he feels alone. And so, his prayer.

And the beauty of this prayer is that it is answered. In Christ, our sins are forgiven, our heart is made pure, our spirit is renewed, and we have the joy of salvation. Every day, we will be tempted, and we will succumb to the power of sin. And every day, every minute, every time, as we call upon Jesus to forgive us, we are forgiven and made pure. Now that is power.

Pray Psalm 51:10–12.

KEVIN PARVIZ

Psalm 56:3

From Fear to Faith

When I am afraid, I will trust in You. Psalm 56:3

One time, a family gathered around the television for the nightly news. A featured story was the arrival of the Pope as he visited this country. As they watched him step from the plane and symbolically kiss the ground, the 85-year-old aunt turned to her niece and said, "I know how he feels. I'm scared of flying, too!"

Our Lord Jesus Christ knows us better than we know ourselves. He knows that each of us has our own personal fears and worries. He understands that often it is fear that holds us back from being everything that God wants us to be. Fear cuts us off from God so that we turn to our troubles around us and forget about God's sufficient care for our lives.

Like the disciples, Jesus Christ comes to us with those comforting words, "Fear not!" His death on the cross and resurrection assures us that we can trust in Him. Nothing in all the world can separate us from the love of God. The grace of our Savior assures us that our sins are forgiven and that we have a home in heaven prepared for us.

The Holy Spirit works in our hearts to move us from fear to faith—not faith in ourselves and our own abilities to maneuver our way out of our fixes, but faith in the One who willingly suffered and died so that we could experience abundant life. Together we say, "I will trust in You!"

Gracious Lord, move me from my fears to a firm faith in You. Amen.

LUTHER C. BRUNETTE

Psalm 57:1

Overcoming Discouragement

Have mercy on me, O God, have mercy on me, for in You my soul takes refuge. I will take refuge in the shadow of Your wings until the disaster has passed. Psalm 57:1

An old legend tells of an angel sent by God to inform Satan that all the methods he used to defeat Christians would be taken from him. The devil pleaded to be allowed to keep just one: discouragement. Thinking this a modest request, the angel agreed. Later the devil laughed to himself: "In this one tool, discouragement, I have secured all."

Discouragement is an effective tool and weapon of Satan. Our lives are often adversely affected when we allow ourselves to be discouraged.

There is little to be gained by looking to ourselves when discouragement comes on us. We need to look out and up, away from ourselves and our problems. We need to look up to God, placing our problems in His hands. From Him our help comes.

David, hiding in a cave from Saul, says he "was bowed down in distress" (v. 6). He experienced discouragement. And yet he looks up to God, calls upon Him for mercy, and says he will take refuge in the shadow of His wings until the danger passes. He acknowledges that "God sends His love and His faithfulness" (v. 3). He knew that God was with him. "If God is for us, who can be against us?" (Romans 8:31).

God's Word is full of words that encourage: "Cast all your anxiety on Him because He cares for you" (1 Peter 5:7). "Be strong and take heart" (Psalm 31:24). "Do not fear, for I am with you; do not be dismayed, for I am your God (Isaiah 41:10).

By turning as David did to God through faith in our Savior, we can banish discouragement and savor the encouragement that He provides.

Lord, give me more courage, strength, and faith. Amen.

ANDREW SIMCAK JR.

Psalm 59:1–4

Never Outnumbered

Deliver me from my enemies, O God; protect me from those who rise up against me. ... I have done no wrong, yet they are ready to attack me. Arise to help me; look on my plight! Psalm 59:1–4

Do you ever feel that everyone is against you, that you have no one on your side and that you are powerless to overcome the forces arrayed against you? It seems at times we cannot cope because our problems and fears are too numerous and too overwhelming. We feel outnumbered.

No doubt the psalmist David experienced something like that when Saul sent his men to watch David's house and kill him. The prophet Elisha also knew that feeling when the enemies of God surrounded the city of Dothan. He and his allies were completely outnumbered. The servant of Elisha was pushing the panic button when he asked: "Lord, what shall we do?"

We need the reassurance Elisha's words gave to his servant: "Those who are with us are more than those who are with them" (2 Kings 6:16). Though it may appear that there are more who are opposed to us than for us, as Christians we know that God is on our side. That tips the scales in our favor. It gives us a decided advantage. With the psalmist we can pray: "Deliver me from my enemies, O God" and rest assured that He stands with us.

"If God is for us, who can be against us?" (Romans 8:31). With Jesus on our side, we are always in the majority. With Christ we are more than conquerors through Him who loved us (Romans 8:37). Because Jesus died for our sins, we know that God is for us, loves us and numbers us as His sons and daughters, is on our side. No one—nothing—can ever snatch us out of His loving and protecting hands.

Lord, help me never to be afraid, for You have promised to be with me always. Amen.

ANDREW SIMCAK JR.

Psalm 59:16–17

I Will Sing of God's Love

I will sing of Your strength, in the morning I will sing of Your love; for You are my fortress, my refuge in times of trouble. Psalm 59:16

There is an old saying that you can't whistle and be sad at the same time. When you see someone walking down the street whistling, humming, or singing, you are fairly confident that the person is in a good mood.

The beginning verses of today's reading detail a frightening situation where enemy forces lie in wait to destroy the psalmist and the nation of Israel. It is certainly not a time we expect the writer to be "whistlin' Dixie"!

Still, in verse 16 the psalmist says, "I will sing of Your strength." "Your" refers to the Lord God Almighty, our all-powerful, heavenly Father. The psalmist continues, "in the morning I will sing of Your love." Why? "For You are my fortress, my refuge in times of trouble." In the face of eminent danger the writer can be confident of his Father's love and protection.

In times of crisis or on days when we are just feeling "down," turning to the Lord in songs of praise can lift our spirits, too. As we dwell on our Father's love in sending His Son to redeem us, we find refuge and rest in our Savior's care.

> **Oh, that I had a thousand voices**
> **To praise my God with thousand tongues!**
> **My heart, which in the Lord rejoices,**
> **Would then proclaim in grateful songs**
> **To all, wherever I might be,**
> **What great things God has done for me. Amen.**
> ("Oh, that I Had a Thousand Voices," by Johann Menizer)

JIM WIEMERS

Psalm 62:2

The Ultimate Fortress

He alone is my rock and my salvation; He is my fortress, I will never be shaken. Psalm 62:2

Many people have traveled through Europe to see the great castles and fortresses built centuries ago. The purpose of every fortress is the same: protect the inhabitants from the enemies and preserve the kingdom. In one way or another, every such fortress has failed. The enemy has always found a way to gain entrance or to defeat the inhabitants.

King David in this psalm was facing such enemies who would topple his kingdom and destroy his fortress. We might imagine that we can create a fortress in our lives that no one can topple. Such a fortress might be our efforts at financial security, always having enough saved for a rainy day. Or we may try to find security in health and exercise. Look at the health market emphasis on exercise machines and megavitamins that will help to fight off every invasion of weakness as if we can build a fortress of exercise that will preserve life.

Twice in this psalm (verses 2 and 6), David identifies the one fortress in which he will never be shaken. That fortress is God, his rock and salvation. When Jesus says that He will never leave us or forsake us, that He will be with us always to the close of the age, He is building just such a fortress around us that cannot be destroyed. It is His love that surrounds us day by day.

O Lord, let Your fortress of love be my dwelling place forever. Amen.

PAUL J. ALBERS

Psalm 90:1–2

Our God Is Faithful

LORD, You have been our dwelling place throughout all generations. Before the mountains were born or You brought forth the earth and the world, from everlasting to everlasting You are God. Psalm 90:2

Teenagers often talk about their parents, saying things like: "I just can't figure my dad out. One minute he's nice; the next minute he's a bear. One minute he is silent; the next minute he is violent. And Mom is so moody! One minute she is tough on me, and the next minute she is easy on me."

What a comfort to know that even though we are always changing, our God is changeless! Even though we are inconsistent and unfaithful, our eternal God remains the same. God never wakes up grumpy. He is never in a bad mood. He never has a bad day!

Our faithful and consistent God can be counted on to give us everything that we need. He has taken care of our past by forgiving our sins through Jesus Christ, His Son. God gives us His almighty provision for the present to give us all we need.

And our capable God who is from everlasting to everlasting holds our future secure. God who is always the same has all our bases covered! He becomes our dwelling place now and even forevermore.

Eternal God who never changes, thank You for Your provision for my past, my present, and my future. Amen.

LUTHER C. BRUNETTE

Psalm 91:1–2

In the Shelter of the Most High

He who dwells in the shelter of the Most High will rest in the shadow of the Almighty. I will say of the LORD, "He is my refuge and my fortress, my God, in whom I trust." Psalm 91:1-2

Have you ever felt as if your skin was being baked in an oven? While standing in line for an attraction at a nationally famous Florida theme park, the sun coupled with the heat and humidity was almost unbearable. No matter what kind of sunblock we had on our skin, it was still so terribly HOT! What a relief when a big cloud came and rested over us!

The psalmist reminds us where our genuine relief comes from. Those who trust in Jesus Christ as their Savior find refuge from the pressures and heat of this world in Him. A living relationship with Jesus Christ brings comfort and strength to know that in Him we find perfect peace. He who defeated our enemies through His death on the cross and resurrection becomes our refuge and fortress. What a relief to know that He forgives our sins and gives us needed strength in the midst of this hot and bothered world!

We respond to His peace and protection with simple trust. We let go of our own notions of self-sufficiency and rest in the shadow of His almighty love.

Next time you feel as if you are being burned, focus on the shelter of Jesus and His love for you. Find comfort in the shadow of His protection!

Dear Lord, help me dwell in the shelter and shadow of Your protection as I trust completely in You. Amen.

LUTHER C. BRUNETTE

Psalm 96:1

A New Song

Sing to the LORD a new song; sing to the LORD, all the earth. Psalm 96:1

The psalmist encourages us to sing—not any song, mind you, but a new song. A global song. A song sung by "all the earth."

Are you like me? I like the old songs. The tried and true songs. The ones my mother taught me.

Sing to the Lord a new song is, therefore, a word of encouragement that I often need, as do we all. New songs call for new singers, a new choir, fresh composers. And whether we are foghorn monotones or nightingale warblers, all of us are gowned conscripts in the global choir of praise.

In this sense, our lives are a song. The lives of the billions of organisms on this rushing planet are singing the praise of the almighty Creator God. And the best-tuned soulful instruments of all belong to those of us alive in Christ Jesus, for we are being baptismally renewed daily. In the liturgy that is our life a different verse comes forth each day.

I am, therefore, a new song in Christ, my Lord. For I am His new creation. As are you. Our combined paeon of praise will rock the heavens in different holy harmony each day of our lives and for eternity. To the glory of God. Sing on, new songs!

Lord of heaven and earth, let me sing to Your glory in harmony with the love You have placed within me each day. Amen.

DAVID H. BENKE

Psalm 100:2

Your Station in Life

Serve the LORD with gladness. Psalm 100:2 KJV

Who could ever measure how much might be achieved for the kingdom of Jesus Christ if more of the people of that kingdom realized that the position they have been given in it has been given to them by God? High, low, or in between, easy or hard, happy or unhappy, great or insignificant, it's all part of an eternal plan to move this world along toward eternity. It is human nature to grumble and complain. We've been at it since the children of Israel wished out loud that they might go back to the bondage of Egypt, that far back, at least, and farther. But what we are and where and for what is up to God who has made us.

God has divided His gifts among us. Oh, granted, it is not a meticulously equitable division. Over here some have gotten an abundance of the things that make for precociousness; while over there, where most of us hang out, there is nothing spectacular about the abilities people have been dealt. But God isn't so concerned with parity as He is with getting the job done. And in that everyone's part is important. More gifts mean more responsibility. Any gifts at all, even the humblest, are part of the plan.

Life is not an ordeal we have to endure, a routine we have to go through, time to be served, like a convict in a penitentiary. It is an opportunity to cultivate whatever gifts we have been given and whatever time there is left for the glory of God.

God has placed us into what Martin Luther called "[our] station in life." He expects us to be faithful in that station. There is no place for fretting or complaining that we were not given a loftier station or more significant challenges. There is simply place for prayer that through Christ Jesus we be empowered to do faithfully the things God has given us to do wherever He has placed us.

Teach me, Savior to serve You faithfully wherever I am and with whatever I have, and therewith to be content. Amen.

ARNOLD KUNTZ

Psalm 100:5

God's Love Endures Forever

For the LORD is good and His love endures forever; His faithfulness continues through all generations. Psalm 100:5

At the close of each year, TV and magazines remind us of the highlights of the previous 12 months—the top news stories and the people who played prominent roles in politics, sports, arts, and entertainment.

Usually, the top stories of the year concern wars, natural disasters, accidents, and other calamities; and often concerned citizens worry about the direction the world is heading.

At times when we are anxious or prone to look negatively at the future, we do well to read through the book of Psalms, especially verses like today's reading. There we are reminded that God's faithfulness "continues through all generations." Through every century of this world our heavenly Father has watched over and cared for His people. He has no plans to withdraw His protection from us ever.

The psalmist also reminds us that not only is the Lord faithful, but He "is good and His love endures forever." God's plan of redemption, His sending His Son to suffer and die in our place and raising Him on the third day, is effective for all generations—the future as well as the past.

No matter what happens in the world, God is faithful and "His love endures forever."

> **Our God, our help in ages past,**
> **Our hope for years to come,**
> **Still be our guard while troubles last**
> **And our eternal home! Amen.**
> ("Our God, Our Help in Ages Past," by Isaac Watts)

JIM WIEMERS

Psalm 103:12

Forget It!

As far as the east is from the west, so far has He removed our transgressions from us. Psalm 103:12

A young nun once claimed to have had a vision of Jesus. Her bishop decided to test her truthfulness and ordered that the next time she had a vision she should ask Christ what the bishop's primary sin had been before he became a bishop. Some months later the nun returned, and the bishop asked if she had asked Christ the question, to which she affirmed that she had.

"And what did He say?" the bishop asked, apprehensively.

"Christ said ... ," and the nun paused a moment. "He said, '*I don't remember.*' "

We have a God who not only forgives but *forgets!* He tells us: "I am He who blots out your transgressions for My own sake, and I will not remember your sins" (Isaiah 43:25 RSV). Psalm 103:12 affirms: "As far as the east is from the west, so far has He removed our transgressions from us."

Accordingly, we should learn to pray: "O God, forgive me for the sin of coming back to You and asking forgiveness for a sin You forgave—and forgot—*a long time ago*" (O. P. Kretzmann).

So God forgives—and forgets. And then He asks *us* to "forget" our sin. Some people say, "The only thing you can't change is your past." But in one sense that's wrong. God *has* changed your past. Because of Christ's death on the cross for your sin, your past need *not* haunt you with guilt anymore. You can, by the power of the Holy Spirit, "change" your past. You can "forget" it, for God has. You are also called to forgive others as Christ has forgiven you (Mark 11:26).

O Lord, thank You for forgiving and "forgetting" my sin. Now empower me to do the same for others. Amen.

DONALD L. DEFFNER

Psalm 105:3–5

Know That Good Will Come

Glory in His holy name; let the hearts of those who seek the LORD rejoice. Look to the LORD and His strength; seek His face always. Remember the wonders He has done, His miracles, and the judgments He pronounced. Psalm 105:3–5

I sat eagerly waiting for the concert to begin. This was the sixth time I had been to a Neil Diamond concert. I knew it would be good. While I waited, I remembered the last concert. My memory replayed some of the songs. I chuckled as I remembered an unexpectedly funny moment from that evening. As the band took their places on stage and began the musical introduction for Neil, I felt an adrenaline rush. I felt excitement. I knew the concert would be wonderful. It was.

When people (singers, neighbors, or friends) have proven themselves to us in the past, we find it easy to trust them the next time. We even trust people who have let us down once, if they give us believable reasons for their failure. Why don't we give God that same trust?

The Bible is filled with stories of God's faithfulness. Never once has God failed to take care of those who believed. God even listened to and rescued Jonah, who was deliberately disobeying God's orders. God is trustworthy. God has faithfully provided for you and your family. Make a list of the experiences in which God intervened in your life. Think of times when you unexpectedly received a bonus or a gift you very much needed. That was God at work.

Remember God's record. God will not let you down. However bad the circumstances of your life today, God can and will bring good from them. Trust God. Know that good will come.

God, thank You for all the ways You are faithful in my life. Help me to remember Your history and to trust You. Amen.

BOBBIE REED

Psalm 107:2

Speak Up for the Lord

Let the redeemed of the LORD say this—those He redeemed from the hand of the foe. Psalm 107:2

Years ago I saw a poster that read, "If you were arrested for being a Christian, would there be enough evidence to convict you?" That question continues to haunt me.

I wonder if there is evidence in my life that "beyond a reasonable doubt" communicates that I am a believer, that I love the Lord, that I live according to the principles given in Scripture. That's a tall order, but it is no less than what God expects of us.

Is the evidence of faith in your life strong enough to let others know that you are a follower of the Lord? Take stock today.

Check your thoughts. Do you refuse to dwell on inappropriate or immoral things? Do you quickly reject such thoughts and replace them with appropriate ideas? Paul tells us we need to bring every thought under captivity (2 Corinthians 10:5). For as we think in our hearts, we are (Proverbs 23:7).

Check your words. Are the words you choose to speak pleasing to the Lord (Psalm 19:14)? Are there words you need to delete from your vocabulary to give a good witness to the Christian life? What about gossip, spreading rumors, telling tales, breaking confidences, complaining, criticizing, or using sarcasm? Do you need to practice affirming, complimenting, and encouraging skills?

Check your actions. What do people think of Christ when they look at you as a follower of Him? Are you damaging His reputation? Or do your actions point people to the Lord?

Each of us speaks to the world about our relationship with the Lord by our thought patterns, our words, and our actions. Some speak well. Others do not. What about you?

Lord, help me become a good witness for You. Let the words of my mouth and the meditation of my heart be acceptable to You. Let my actions speak well of You. Amen.

BOBBIE REED

Psalm 116:5–9

Alive to Live Again

Be at rest once more, O my soul, for the LORD has been good to you. For You, O LORD, have delivered my soul from death, my eyes from tears, my feet from stumbling, that I may walk before the LORD in the land of the living. Psalm 116:7–9

Don't you wonder what Lazarus was like after Jesus raised him from the dead, or the young man of Nain, or the daughter of Jairus? One cannot imagine that they could live as if nothing had happened.

A pastor and his wife were involved in a chain-reaction collision with several 18-wheelers on a Florida highway. When the state trooper inquired about the passengers in the car, the pastor said, "I was driving and I am fine, as is my wife. The air bags saved us from serious injury and maybe from death." To be sure that pastor drives differently today.

The author of Psalm 116 had a near-death experience and his life was spared. Things were not the same anymore. His life was at rest for he had received from the Lord bountiful blessings. Further, his walk with the Lord was shown clearly to the people around him.

Each of us has a near-death experience every day with temptation and the invitation to sin. Our hope rests only in the deliverance given in Jesus Christ and in His love without end. He dries our tears and keeps us from stumbling that we may walk with Him. Those who don't know the salvation given through Jesus' death and resurrection live as if on a roller-coaster ride of fear and anguish, despair and turmoil.

Hold on to me, dear Lord, hold on to me with strong hands. Amen.

PAUL J. ALBERS

Psalm 117

Praise the Lord!

Praise the Lord, all you nations; extol Him, all you peoples. For great is His love toward us, and the faithfulness of the Lord endures forever. Praise the LORD. Psalm 117

Melissa tore off the gift wrap and opened the box. She pulled out a doll given to her by her aunt Sally. The gift was barely out of the box when Melissa ran to her mother saying, "Look, Mom! Aunt Sally gave me this doll."

Children need to be taught to say thank you; they do no not need to be taught to praise. "Look, Mom! Aunt Sally gave me this doll" is praise. Praise calls to others and focuses on the giver and the gift. This is what we find in this psalm.

The invitation to praise God is issued to all nations and peoples in answer to the Great Commission of our Lord to "go and make disciples of all nations" (Matthew 28:19). In his commentary on Psalm 117, Martin Luther declared that "the whole book of Acts was written because of this psalm," to demonstrate how God's gift of life is for all people.

The psalmist calls to others, and then a reason is given: for—because—God's love is great and His faithfulness lasts forever. God's love is a lavish love, a seeking love that seeks us out in the darkness of our sin. "This is how God showed His love among us: He sent His one and only Son into the world that we might live through Him. This is love: not that we loved God, but that He loved us" (1 John 4:9–10).

If we have our doubts at times as to God's love and purpose for us, we are reminded that "the faithfulness of the Lord endures forever." The promises that God has given us remain intact. They are all based on His love for us in Christ Jesus. We may experience the broken promises of others, but God's "promise gives [us] life" (Psalm 119:50 RSV). His promise and His faithfulness sustain our lives of letting our light shine in the world so that all the world may join us in praising our great God.

From all that dwell below the skies
Let the creator's praise arise: Alleluia, alleluia!
Let the redeemer's name be sung
Through every land by every tongue: Alleluia!
Amen.

("From All That Dwell Below the Skies," by Isaac Watts)

HENRY GERIKE

Psalm 118:14

The Lord Is My Song

The LORD is my strength and my song; He has become my salvation.
Psalm 118:14

Singing on the run is fun. Once while jogging laboriously around a reservoir, I happened upon a group of girls in harmonic choir rehearsal. "Soon and very soon," they clapped and chanted, "we are going to see the King." Just like that my pace picked up, the melody moving my feet. My arms began flapping to keep up with my legs, and off I flew on the wings of that good Gospel beat.

This rhythm of life is what the psalmist describes. We are strengthened on the journey when God is our song. Is God your song? Do you rock to His rhythm and roll to His beat, even if it's your chair that's rocking? This is the joyful declaration of the psalm.

The heart of that God song is salvation. There is no sweeter song than that which sets the soul free. The name of the salvation song is Jesus.

And this song carries us around all the curves, over peaks, and through valleys. Martin Luther believed that music is an "outstanding gift of God." His reason? It "drives away sadness and the devil, and sets us free from great worries." If the song is God in Christ, then the road is straight and narrow, and the run is full of joy.

Lord of the song, fill my heart with the sweet music of salvation and let me sing for joy to You. Amen.

DAVID H. BENKE

Psalm 118:24

Rejoice in This Day

This is the day the LORD has made; let us rejoice and be glad in it. Psalm 118:24

The alarm clock buzzer breaks the stillness of my sleep and shatters the dreams I long to keep. Many of us rue the coming of morning. Alarm clocks are so harsh as they wake us up. A new day brings another opportunity to get frustrated with the kids as they poke along and make us late. Traffic is a nightmare getting to work. There is no possible way we can get everything the boss wants us to accomplish done today. What! You want us to go where tonight? All we want to do is get home, go to bed, and sleep. Tomorrow's another day.

Tomorrow is another day, but this is the day the Lord has made. There is often so little to rejoice about in our day, isn't there? But the alarm clock did wake me up on time; that's something, isn't it? And I'm sure glad the kids are all feeling well and able to go to school. I really enjoy my commute. It gives me a chance to pray and relax with some good music. Boy! I'm really going to earn my salary today ... Lord, give me one opportunity to share about You with someone at work today. It will be nice to get home and spend some time with the family. And yes, sleep is such a blessing!

We do need a reason to rejoice, if only that God has given us a new day! A new day to share the love that we have in Christ, a new day to call on Jesus to get us through. On my desk, I placed a sign to greet me every morning. It says, "Obstacles become opportunities with God." Rejoice, for He has given us new opportunities, and maybe we can also find a kinder, gentler alarm clock.

Gracious Lord, help me to be the witness that You would want me to be. I praise You for Your creation and for a new day. Amen.

KEVIN PARVIZ

Psalm 118:29

Giving Thanks

Give thanks to the LORD, for He is good; His love endures forever. Psalm 118:29

What do you say when someone does something nice for you? What do you do to demonstrate your appreciation concerning an act of compassion and kindness? You do and say what your parents taught you when you were so very small! You say thank you. You appreciate the generosity shown to you.

Throughout the Scriptures, we see how God gives life to His people. His goodness is seen in His creation, making us unique and valuable. His awesome mercy is recognized in God's act of redemption—of purchasing us from our sins through His Son, Jesus Christ. His grace is clearly observed as the Holy Spirit brings us to faith and keeps us close to Himself.

How do we respond to the eternal goodness of God? We give thanks! In our prayer life, we cultivate thanksgiving every day as we enter God's presence and pour out our hearts to Him in gratitude. We recall with God's people of old all that the Lord has done, still does, and promises to do in the future.

How are we responding to God's goodness this day? A thankful heart is a contented heart. Rather than criticizing, condemning, or complaining, let us look up in thanksgiving, for the Lord is good. His love endures forever!

Dear Lord, cultivate in me a thankful heart. Amen.

LUTHER C. BRUNETTE

Psalm 119:105

Jesus, the Word Made Flesh

Your Word is a lamp to my feet and a light for my path. Psalm 119:105

Every time I read this verse, I can't help but hear the song "Thy Word" made popular by Amy Grant. And what I see in my mind's eye is a group of seventh and eighth graders singing that song in the sanctuary of our church. It takes a lot to get seventh and eighth graders excited, but these kids were.

The next time I had them for religion class, I asked them what this psalm meant to them. And they were excited all over again. Singing the song made the psalm alive for them. They were excited about realizing that God's Word is there to guide and protect them in the darkness of our sinful world. God's Word eased their fear.

Have you ever been caught in an unfamiliar room with absolutely no light? Trying to get through a host's home with no light, unaware of the furniture arrangements and doorways, and not knowing even where the light switches are, is an unsettling experience. The first time you bump your shin on a coffee table, you freeze and stand there fearful of moving because you don't know what to expect next. And then your host comes downstairs, switches on the light, and a wave of relief comes over you.

Jesus is God's Word made flesh. Before He came, we were stumbling around in the darkness of our sin, fearful, not knowing what to expect next. But in His light, we see our path. Our path, because of Christ's light shining before us, is to everlasting life in heaven. Sometimes we still stumble and hurt ourselves, but He is there to pick us up and put us back on the path.

Lord Jesus, light of the world, I praise You for Your guidance and strength. Shine on me today as I walk a straight path in Your righteousness. Amen.

KEVIN PARVIZ

Psalm 120:1

No Busy Signal

I call on the LORD in my distress, and He answers me. Psalm 120:1

A few years ago, a lady who was new to town began having an allergic reaction to her medication. Where should she call? Since this happened before today's "911" generation, she decided to phone the local fire station. She dialed the number—busy! She checked the number and tried again—busy! Every time she called, she got a busy signal. The receiver of the phone at the fire station had been accidentally left off the hook. Tragically, she knew of no one else to call.

God reminds us that with Him we never get a busy signal. He is ready and willing to help in any and every situation.

Does God care about the argument we had with our spouse? Of course! Is the Lord interested about our hurt and loneliness? Yes! Does it matter to God that we don't feel well and face an uncertain physical future? For sure!

We can be assured that God knows us and hears us, no matter what the challenge may be. Why? God loves us. The proof of His love is in the person of His only-begotten Son, Jesus Christ. Since we are God's own through Christ, we can be assured that our heavenly Father knows what is best for us. He is always open to hear from us and never gives us the busy signal.

Dear Father in heaven, thank You for knowing me, listening to me, and always being there to answer. In Jesus' name, I pray. Amen.

LUTHER C. BRUNETTE

Psalm 121

Our Journey with Jesus

I lift up my eyes to the hills—where does my help come from? My help comes from the LORD, the Maker of heaven and earth. Psalm 121:1-2

When people walk or march together, they often sing or chant familiar lines. This often helps to set the rhythm or pace of the walk. Sometimes it helps the travelers stay focused on the journey's end, especially when the song or lines speak about what awaits them.

This is the case with Psalm 121. It was spoken by pilgrims as they made their way up to Jerusalem. The holy city sat on top of one of the highest points in the land. The temple, where the worship, praise, and sacrifices took place, was in Jerusalem and was also called Mount Zion. As people journeyed up to the temple, their eyes were drawn to the long climb ahead of them. They used this time to prepare their hearts for God.

Spiritually, we also have a hard, difficult journey. Because of sin, we are weak and unable to walk the wearisome way. God knew, however, that the climb was too much for us, so He came down to us. He then climbed the rough road that went up the hill to the cross. We now journey with Jesus, knowing that our help has come. It came from the hills, the hill of Calvary.

Dear Jesus, thank You for traveling the road of sorrow to take away our sins. Fix our eyes always on that one hill where You died, for we know that from that hill comes our help. Help us to walk today knowing that the Maker of heaven and earth walks with us. Amen.

DAVID S. ANDRUS

Psalm 127:1

The Lord Is Our Master Builder

Unless the LORD builds the house, its builders labor in vain. Psalm 127:1

If you have ever built a new house, you know how important it is to choose the right builder. Nightmare stories abound concerning well-meaning people who trusted in a builder only to later be defrauded and deceived.

In whom are you trusting to build your life? Who is building your family? Who is the master builder of your marriage?

Many people today make the mistake of trusting the world and the things of this world to be the builder of their personal, family, and married lives. But in the end, they become so very disappointed! Can satellite television, a well-balanced stock portfolio, or romantic relationships guarantee a well-built, meaningful life? Of course not!

God reminds us that unless He becomes the master builder, our construction projects will end in failure. In the Sermon on the Mount (Matthew 7:24–27), Jesus tells us that the most sturdy construction takes place when we hear His Word and put it into practice. As our builder, the Lord Jesus forgives our faults, steadies our resolve to follow Him, and promises to one day take us to our heavenly mansion with Him in heaven.

O Lord, be the builder of my life, my family, and my marriage, through Jesus Christ. Amen.

LUTHER C. BRUNETTE

Psalm 130

Wait, Hope

I wait for the LORD, my soul waits, and in His word I put my hope. Psalm 130:5

Do you remember when doctors made house calls? Frequent childhood bouts with strep throat would wake me in the middle of the night in intense pain. I would lie awake all night trying not to swallow, waiting for the first rays of morning light. I knew then that relief was in sight. My doctor would make a house call and bring a cure.

We, too, wait for the good doctor, the Great Physician of our souls, Jesus Christ. The sins of which our conscience accuse us rear up to terrorize us—damnable, never-ending sins upon sins. Were He to withhold His cure, His salvation, from us, we would die in utter despair.

The psalmist captures the essence of our God's love for us: "O Israel, put your hope in the LORD, for with the LORD is unfailing love and with Him is *full* redemption." God heard our cry. While we were yet sinners, Christ died for us. By His all-atoning death and glorious resurrection, Christ has eradicated our sins; He has given us a complete cure! Christ has purchased and won us from all sin, from death, and from the power of the devil.

Now we wait for our final deliverance, deliverance from this life to eternity, knowing we have been cured. Our safe passage is ensured.

O Lord God, slow to anger and abounding in steadfast love, heartfelt thanks for Your deliverance from the sickness of sin through Your Son, Jesus Christ. Amen.

JAMES W. FREESE

Psalm 136:1

Giving Thanks

Give thanks to the LORD, for He is good. His love endures forever. Psalm 136:1

A West German professor surveyed 600 students, asking them, "What would you do if you had only one day to live?"

Twenty percent said they would engage in immoral behavior.

Eighteen percent said they would get drunk or get high on drugs.

Seven percent said they would commit suicide.

Thirty percent said they would spend the time with loved ones.

One girl said she "would find a quiet church and spend the time thanking God for the wonderful life He had given her."

The professor said, "The girl's answer was like a breath of fresh air."

The giving of thanks certainly seems to be less common than grumbling and complaining. Jesus found it to be true when only one returned to give thanks for healing (Luke 17:11–18). The psalmist, however, was assured that God's "love endures forever," and so he could not help but give thanks.

As New Testament people we have every reason to give thanks! Christ suffered, died, was buried, and rose victoriously from the grave. His victory over sin, death, and the power of the devil is our victory. Thanks be to God!

We give thanks to You, O Lord, for You are good. Your love does endure forever. Amen.

ROGER R. SONNENBERG

Psalm 139:1–3

God Knows and Cares

O LORD, You have searched me and You know me. ... You are familiar with all my ways. Psalm 139:1–3

Do you enjoy the fact that people know you? For one entire semester in college, the professor called me by the wrong name. How embarrassing! Even though it bothered me greatly, I didn't have the courage to confront him.

Most of us enjoy being known. It has been said that "to know is to care." Our family and best friends know the most about us here on earth. Yet God assures us that He knows us perfectly. He even knows you better than you know yourself! God knows our mistakes, our shortcomings, and our petty sins that we try to hide. He knows how we stray away from Him and His will for our lives.

Remarkably, even though God knows us perfectly, He still loves us! He covers our sins with His mercy through our Savior, Jesus Christ, and assures us that He provides for all our needs.

As our all-knowing and caring Father, He has our best interests at heart. We can trust Him to know that even when events and circumstances seem contrary to His good plans, God knows and cares! By His grace, we admit our sins, and look to Him for forgiveness and strength.

O Lord, You know and care for me perfectly. Enable me to place my complete confidence in You. In Jesus' name I pray. Amen.

LUTHER C. BRUNETTE

Psalm 143:10

God and You—A Majority

Teach me to do Your will, for You are my God; may Your good Spirit lead me on level ground. Psalm 143:10

It is fascinating, but most disheartening, to observe how the U.S. general public takes for granted that the great issues of life are to be decided by majority vote and the judgment of the people. Once the legislature has crafted a law (more often than not by compromise) or the Supreme Court has affixed its stamp of approval, issues as vital and basic as capital punishment, the right to bear arms, or abortion are settled, and right and wrong with reference to them is established. But right and wrong is not a matter of majority opinion. It is a matter of the will of our God.

That is why making political issues out of moral matters is quite ridiculous. God is the ultimate authority. His Word is the last word for establishing right and wrong. And where He has not spoken, our responsibility is to be as consistent as we know how to be with those concepts on which He has made Himself very clear, indeed. Neither the wisdom of the masses nor the history of humankind's judgments indicates that the combined verdict of the minds of people is impeccable.

So while worldly people work for the majority edge and appeal to the will of the majority, Christians must go back to the clear revelation of God and in prayer and meditation seek what is God's will and God's judgment about those basics in life. With the psalmist, our prayer will be: "Teach [us] to do Your will, for You are [our] God."

Can you picture standing before God and arguing in defense of your daily behavior that the "102nd Congress ruled ..." or "the Supreme Court in its statement of October 8, 1991, declared ..."? St. Peter, who in humankind's imagination has ultimate responsibility over the entry laws and emigration rules of heaven, would chortle in his beard if the upshot weren't so often tragic. God did not listen to the majority of our sin, which was damning us eternally. Instead, He sent Jesus to die on the cross and be raised from the dead so that we might have forgiveness and eternal life.

Your will, not mine, be done. And not this world's either. Open my heart to Your judgments and direct my life along the paths that reflect Your will. Amen.

ARNOLD KUNTZ

Psalm 147:1

Praise God!

Praise the LORD. How good it is to sing praises to our God, how pleasant and fitting to praise Him! Psalm 147:1

Once there was a man, a fine singer, who learned he had cancer of the tongue, and surgery was required. Just before the operation, the man asked the doctor, "Are you sure I will never sing again?" The surgeon found it difficult to answer the man. He simply shook his head no.

The patient then asked if he could sit up for a moment. "I've had many good times singing the praises of God, and now you tell me I can never sing again. I have one song that will be my last."

There in the presence of his doctors, nurses, and most of all, his gracious Lord, he boldly sang the common doxology: "Praise God from whom all blessings flow; Praise Him, all creatures here below; Praise Him above, ye heavenly host; Praise Father, Son, and Holy Ghost. Amen."

In response to all that God has done, is doing, and will do for us into eternity, we joyfully praise Him. To Father, Son, and Holy Ghost, we lift our voices in our songs of adoration and praise, knowing that He hears us and continues to shower His abundant blessings upon us.

O Lord, You are worthy of my praise and thanks. Help me always sing Your praises! Amen.

LUTHER C. BRUNETTE

Proverbs 3:5

Give Him Your *All*

Trust in the LORD with all your heart and lean not on your own understanding. Proverbs 3:5

Are you giving your "all" to God and, through Him, to others?

As a worker and parent, are you more committed to your job than you are to your family? Or do you give your family your total dedication also?

Are you a student? Did you study as hard as you could for that test, or just enough to "get by"?

Do you reach out to other people who really need your help or is "*my* schedule" more important?

Are you giving your "all" in your life for Christ? Are you living for self or for God?

It is only in fully giving our "I" into the hands of God that we can give Him our "all." As Martin Luther said: "The recognition of sin is the beginning of salvation." Charlie Brown would say: "The theological implications of this are staggering." We are "saved by grace through faith alone." And this is not an act we perform to be justified before God, but it is "God at work" in us. (See Ephesians 2:8–9.)

Scripture says our Lord gave us His all. Christ died for our sins and rose again. And everything we are and have comes from God. So whatever we "give" Him belonged to Him in the first place.

Therefore we sing:

> We give You but Your own
> In any gifts we bring;
> All that we have is Yours alone,
> A trust from You, our King.

Lord, move me from partial to total commitment to You. Empower me to give "all my heart" to You as You gave Yourself totally *for me*. Amen.

DONALD L. DEFFNER

Proverbs 3:11–12

God's Heart of Love

My son, do not despise the LORD'S discipline and do not resent His rebuke, because the LORD disciplines those He loves, as a father the son he delights in. Proverbs 3:11–12

All of us would rather enjoy life's blessings than face its trials. Yet both are part of our human experience on this side of heaven. The Lord assures us that He can use our difficulties to strengthen us and bring us closer to His heart of love.

One Christian pastor describes the balance between mercy and discipline: "The Christian life is like the dial of a clock. The hands are God's hands passing over and over again—the short hand of discipline and the long hand of mercy. Slowly and surely, the hand of discipline must pass, and God speaks at each stroke. But over and over passes the hand of mercy, showering many blessings for each stroke of discipline and trial. Both hands are fastened to one secure pivot: the great and unchanging heart of our God of love."

No matter what is happening in our lives, we are assured of God's great and unchanging love. Our eternal future is secure through Christ, knowing that His grace is sufficient for our every need.

Heavenly Father, when times of trial and discipline come, help me to trust in You. In Jesus' name I pray. Amen.

LUTHER C. BRUNETTE

Proverbs 4:23

Real Heart Healthy

Above all else, guard your heart, for it is the wellspring of life. Proverbs 4:23

The writer of this proverb was not a cardiologist, encouraging us to do heart-healthy things. Rather, he urges us to take care of that "heart" from which the key inner things of life flow: things like love and hope and caring. *That* heart is the wellspring of authentic life.

Wellspring? Not a common modern word. Homesteading grandparents of a century ago knew it and used it. The wellspring was the source of the stream that flowed through the farm or the spring that bubbled up sweet water. If the source—the wellspring—was polluted, everything that flowed from it was tainted, too. Ditto hearts. When they are contaminated, the things that flow from them are impure as well.

How can we keep the heart clean? Protect it from outside forces that corrupt. Purify it through prayer, worship, and the Christ life. Best of all ask God for help. Borrow the psalmist's words: "Create in me a pure heart, O God" (Psalm 51:10). He safeguards the wellspring.

Lord, help me guard my heart, keeping it after Your desire. Amen.

CHARLES S. MUELLER

Proverbs 9:10

His Great Sea and Our Small Boat

The fear of the LORD is the beginning of wisdom, and knowledge of the Holy One is understanding. Proverbs 9:10

Power tools are a blessing, but they can do great damage in the blink of an unwary eye. Electric saws nip fingers as easily as they chew through heavy timbers. Can anything make power tools safe? Safer, maybe. Knowledge and understanding can do that. The more we know about the tools, the safer we are. Knowledge helps intelligent users get the most from a lawn mower, a motorcycle, or a power drill—safely.

What's true about power tools is truer about the source of all power: the Lord God Almighty. He cares for all and protects those who follow Him by faith. At the same time He abandons impenitent sinners to their own darkened ignorance and the consequence that follows when we misunderstand great forces.

We see all this in the protection from sin and Satan that we have in Christ's redeeming work, as well as the energy for godly living that comes from Him. With the psalmist we can proclaim: "Great is the LORD and most worthy of praise" (Psalm 145:3).

Lord, help us to fear, love, and trust Your omnipotence and care, especially as You show both in our Savior, Jesus Christ. Amen.

CHARLES S. MUELLER

Proverbs 15:7

Sweet Words

The lips of the wise spread knowledge; not so the hearts of fools.
Proverbs 15:7

What happens when someone doesn't guard their heart as Proverbs 4:23 advises? That heart can become the heart of a fool. There's no way to hide it when that happens. That inside reality spills out over their lips. Their talk tells.

One of God's great commandments tells us that we should not bear false witness against our neighbors. But, of course! At the very least! Who but a fool would lie about his neighbor, not realizing that truth will always finally have its day. Until the public exposure happens, lying makes that neighbor angry and, in turn, the liar's life difficult.

Martin Luther knew there was more to proper speaking than repressing lies. Using the tongue properly includes defending our neighbor, speaking well of her or him, and putting the best construction on everything our neighbor says and does. Not only is that right and proper, but it builds good relationships. Wise people know that. Fools don't. Let your words witness to the world which you are.

Lord, even though I ought and am ready to be a fool for Christ, let not my speech expose me as a fool in things of this world. In Jesus' name I pray. Amen.

CHARLES S. MUELLER

Proverbs 16:2

In the Eyes of the Beholder

All a man's ways seem innocent to him, but motives are weighed by the LORD. Proverbs 16:2

I'm fascinated by how a crafty child deals with wrongdoing. First comes surprise: "What broken dish?" Then feigned innocence: "What makes you think I did it?" Maybe, finally, an admission of distant involvement, with the excuse added: "… but it wasn't my fault." It doesn't change. The difference between crafty children and crafty adults is that adults are better at feigning innocence.

It's a wise parent that doesn't get ensnared in the process of excusing but goes right to the obvious issue. That's the way God does it. Like Jesus, our Father rises above slippery defining of terms, reasoned excuses for things clearly wrong, and explanations of the inexplicable. He ignores muddying questions like that of Satan (Genesis 3:1) and Cain (Genesis 4:9). He goes to the heart and reads it accurately.

And what does He do when He isolates the sorry truth about what's in the heart? He calls us to a confessing that leads to forgiveness, which was earned for us by the Savior and offered by the Spirit.

In the meanwhile, know this: He knows.

Lord, let me see myself as You see me and then, beautiful Savior, see You as You are. Amen.

CHARLES S. MUELLER

Proverbs 16:3

Well Begun

Commit to the LORD whatever you do, and your plans will succeed.
Proverbs 16:3

Well begun is half done. Ever heard that said? It's one of the sayings drummed into my elementary school head decades ago. It's still there on one of my back burners where it has simmered for half a century into a delicious stew of truth and sensibility. Now I try to pass its meaning on to our grandchildren, hoping that they won't take as long comprehending and implementing such an authentic insight as did I.

Proverbs 16:3 abbreviates the approach to all life's better advice into seven basic words: "Commit to the LORD whatever you do." Right. When you start with that, all other good counsel slides into place. For what would you commit to the Lord but what you know is right and proper? And how would you commit it to the Lord in other than the finest manner? And how would you commit to the Lord less than everything needed for success? No wonder plans committed to the Lord succeed.

Our Father, Your plan of creation and Your plan for our redemption were complete in every detail. Bless us that we may plan our work, whatever it may be, as unto You. Amen.

CHARLES S. MUELLER

Proverbs 16:9

A Plan—God Directed

In his heart a man plans his course but the LORD determines his steps.
Proverbs 16:9

Most of us are familiar with the story of the three pigs. Two of the pigs did little to plan for a house that would withstand the elements. One pig carefully planned and built his house.

After the terrible destruction of Hurricane Andrew as well as other storms, the construction codes for houses were increased. Each new house built in certain areas subject to hurricanes is now required to meet special building codes. It is hoped that the loss of property will be reduced.

In our Bible passage, a person seems to be encouraged to plan a course of action—to know where he hopes to go in this life for the Lord. Otherwise, one is subject to every whim. It is similar to the Cheshire Cat's response to Alice when she indicated she wanted to know which road she should take but didn't know where she was going. The cat said, "Then it doesn't much matter which road you take."

Today, both in congregations and as individuals, we are developing mission statements and plans to help focus and give direction to our ministry and service. In doing so we need to remember to pray that the Lord of the church would direct us in our efforts and keep us ever mindful of the work of the Holy Spirit in our midst. For it is God who has the ultimate power and determines the exact steps that we will travel.

Even though we may think that we are in charge of our plans and destiny, ultimately God is bigger and stronger than humankind. He is God. How blessed we are to know that the Lord is in charge of our steps. Are our plans built on solid rock?

Dear Father, thank You that You not only allow us to plan but also give direction to our steps. Amen.

IDA MALL

100

Proverbs 17:14

A Beauty Tip for the Tongue

Starting a quarrel is like breaching a dam; so drop the matter before a dispute breaks out. Proverbs 17:14

We have beauty parlors that give treatments for skin and hair, but unfortunately, there are no beauty parlors for the part of the body we use most often—the tongue! The Bible says, "The tongue is a small part of the body, but it makes great boasts" (James 3:5). The tongue can do many things. It can start a quarrel and break open a dam of poison. It can remain silent and drop a matter before a dispute breaks out. It can make a marriage a paradise or a place of hell. It can kill a church. It can build up another person. It can point the way to heaven.

Isaiah describes Jesus when he says, "He was oppressed and afflicted, yet He did not open His mouth; He was led like a lamb to the slaughter, and as a sheep before her shearers is silent, so He did not open His mouth" (Isaiah 53:7). He didn't open His mouth in His defense for one reason—to win forgiveness for us. To pay for our many sins, including the sin of opening our mouths at times when we shouldn't or of starting quarrels by not dropping a certain matter before a dispute breaks out. He suffered and died for us to make us beautiful! To make us righteous. He did it to help bring our tongues under control. Through His life, death, and resurrection He made even our tongues beautiful.

Lord God, James reminds us: "All kinds of animals, birds, reptiles and creatures of the sea are being tamed and have been tamed by man, but no man can tame the tongue. It is a restless evil, full of deadly poison" (James 3:7–8). So tame our tongues through the power of Your Holy Spirit. Amen.

ROGER R. SONNENBERG

Proverbs 17:22

A Prescription for Health

A cheerful heart is good medicine, but a crushed spirit dries up the bones. Proverbs 17:22

A psychologist at Harvard University discovered that watching uplifting movies helps raise the body's production of antibodies. In contrast, watching films with lots of violence and evil causes the number of antibodies to drop. Since antibodies help fight off infection, it seems important that we focus on what's good, as opposed to what's evil.

In his book of wisdom, Solomon reminds us that "a cheerful heart is good medicine, but a crushed spirit dries up the bones." It's not easy to always be cheerful in a world where sin runs rampant. We see what sin does in our lives and in the lives of others. We ask with St. Paul: "Who will rescue me from this body of death?" But we exclaim with thanksgiving as did Paul, "Thanks be to God— through Jesus Christ our Lord ... the law of the Spirit of life set me free from the law of sin and death" (Romans 7:24–25; 8:2).

What kinds of things do you watch on television or in the movie theater—things that cheer you or that crush you? St. Paul summarizes the truth of Solomon in another way: "Finally, brothers, whatever is true, whatever is noble, whatever is right, whatever is pure, whatever is lovely, whatever is admirable—if anything is excellent or praiseworthy—think about such things. Whatever you have learned or received or heard from me, or seen in me—put it into practice. And the God of peace will be with you" (Philippians 4:8–9).

Lord God, through faith in Jesus Christ, we have every reason for a cheerful heart. Thank You. Amen.

ROGER R. SONNENBERG

Proverbs 18:7

Declare His Praises

A fool's mouth is his undoing, and his lips are a snare to his soul. Proverbs 18:7

There is not much Gospel in this little verse from Proverbs. In fact, it is pure Law—a stiff word of condemnation. The fact that we ruefully acknowledge its accuracy makes it no less threatening.

Indeed, how many times have we said something we wish we could have back the moment after we said it? How many times have we tried to undo something we said that was stupid, thoughtless, or even malicious?

At a superficial level, one response to this verse would be to clean up one's speech and to be more careful about what we say. And, still at a superficial level, that might even work.

But this response to the verse fails to get to the heart of the matter. Rather, God uses verses like this to get us to keep quiet so that we can hear what He says to us. His most important words are not these kinds of condemnations. He says these kinds of things so that He can tell us all about what He has been doing and continues to do for us. God's primary word to us is not "clean up your language" but instead "I forgive you for Jesus' sake. You are My children."

Will we then watch what we say and clean up our language? Sure, but not because we have to or to avoid the consequences of not doing so. We will because we want to, and even more important, because we will have better things to say. We will be saying things that build up instead of destroy. We will be busy declaring the praises of Him who called us out of darkness into His marvelous light (1 Peter 2:9).

Gracious God, help us to speak words that strengthen and console rather than attack and confuse. Above all, keep us focused on the words of forgiveness and life that You speak to us in Jesus Christ. Amen.

DAVID LUMPP

Proverbs 21:30

God Is in Control

There is no wisdom, no insight, no plan that can succeed against the LORD. Proverbs 21:30

In the history of God's old covenant people, there are many instances when they sought to fend for themselves, without God's help and sometimes even in defiance of God's commands—commands that were not arbitrarily given but were intended for Israel's protection and preservation. The prophets constantly reminded the people that their only hope rested within the covenant of promise and care that God had made with them.

Here, in the tradition of Israel's wisdom literature, we are told categorically that God is in control and that any human ambition apart from God's design will come to nothing.

The Gospel message is that God has not left us in doubt as to His design for creation in general or for human beings in particular. God does not leave us to our own wisdom, insight, or plan. God is about the business of rescue, which climaxed in the coming of Jesus Christ into human flesh and blood to assume our sin, suffer our death, and conquer them both at the empty tomb. That is God's plan, fulfilled in Jesus. He makes us participants in this plan by incorporating us in Jesus' death and resurrection in Baptism.

What about now? What do we do between Jesus' first and second coming? We live by His promise. Our own wisdom, insight, and plans will still often fail us. Indeed, God may not give us all that we want or everything for which we ask. All we know is that in Jesus Christ, the very wisdom of God Himself, God has and will keep His promise. Our wisdom, insight, and plans often fail. God's wisdom, insight, and plan always succeeds.

Almighty God, keep us ever focused on the essence of Your saving plan in Jesus Christ, and continue to keep and preserve us in the faith You give us. Amen.

DAVID LUMPP

Proverbs 22:6

The Six-Year-Old Missionary

Train a child in the way he should go, and when he is old he will not turn from it. Proverbs 22:6

Milton L. Rudnick recalls the faith of a six-year-old boy named Billy as he spoke to his friend Celia. "Celia, Jesus was the nicest person who ever lived. He was so good to everyone. If they were sick, He would make them well. If they were hungry, He would feed them. If they were sad, He would cheer them up. He was so nice. But some bad people hated Him, and one day they caught Him and they hurt Him and they killed Him."

"I think I heard about that once," Celia interrupted. "They stuck arrows in Him, didn't they?"

"No, they hung Him on a cross. But He didn't have to let them do that," Billy quickly added. "He wasn't just a man. He was God, too, and He could have stopped them. But He let them do it anyway, and you know why, Celia? He did it for us, so that God would not have to punish us for the bad things that we do."

Celia responded, "Aw, He shouldn't have done that."

"But He didn't stay dead," Billy explained excitedly. "Three days later He came back to life again. He went to see His friends, and were they ever glad to see Him! Then, after a while, He went back to heaven again, but you know what? He's still here anyway. We can't see Him, but He's here all the time. When we're good, it really makes Him happy. When we're bad, it makes Him sad. And someday, Celia, He's going to come back from heaven and we will be able to see Him, and He's going to take us to heaven to be with Him forever. Isn't that wonderful?"

And isn't it wonderful that Billy's parents shared with him the greatest gift of all—Jesus.

Heavenly Father, thank You for the gift of Your Son. Send your Holy Spirit to help me share this Good News with others of every age. Amen.

DONALD L. DEFFNER

Proverbs 23:18–19

True Wisdom

Listen, my son, and be wise, and keep your heart on the right path.
Proverbs 23:19

We all aspire to be wise. People invest time and money to acquire wisdom. They equate wisdom with education and believe it guarantees a full and meaningful life.

A wise person may be educated and an educated person may be wise, but true wisdom is not a matter of schooling. King Solomon reminds us that "the fear of the LORD is the beginning of wisdom" (Proverbs 9:10). To fear God means to "revere Him alone as the highest being, honor Him with our lives, and avoid what displeases Him" (*Martin Luther's Small Catechism with Explanation*).

It needs to be stated that fearing God does not mean to be afraid of God. Christians are not afraid of God. God is our loving, heavenly Father. Through faith in Jesus we are now the sons and daughters of God and are comfortable with Him as children are with loving fathers.

God reminds us: "You have known the holy Scriptures, which are able to make you wise for salvation through faith in Christ Jesus" (2 Timothy 3:15). In God's Word we can learn to know the mind and heart of God and what He has done for us in Christ. This is true wisdom. It enables us to keep on the right path. It motivates and energizes us to live our lives for Him (2 Corinthians 5:15) and in the process to hate evil (Proverbs 8:13).

Father, help me to have and live in true wisdom. Amen.

ANDREW SIMCAK JR.

Proverbs 23:26

Do Not Worry

My son, give me your heart. Proverbs 23:26

God's commandment "Thou shalt not kill" forbids us to worry. Worry can be sin. It causes us to experience physical, mental, and spiritual stress. It is a slow process by which we hurt and harm ourselves.

Worry also causes us to break God's First Commandment: "Thou shalt have no other gods before Me." We keep this commandment when "we fear, love, and trust in God above all things." When we worry, we are not putting our trust in God.

Worry is interest paid on trouble before it is due. It has never ever helped us solve a problem or meet a need. Worry is useless. Worry only produces more worry.

Have you ever stood in a pool and encouraged a child to jump in the water, promising that you would catch him? Maybe he was afraid of the water and didn't trust you to catch him. Then at last he brings himself to trust you. He lets himself go—and you catch him.

Trust is letting ourselves go into the loving hands of our heavenly Father. It is "giving Him our heart," knowing that, whatever circumstance we face, "God works for the good of those who love Him." Because of our Savior's sacrifice for us on the cross, we know God loves us and we can trust Him. Since we are children of the heavenly Father, we can throw all our cares and anxieties upon Him—because He cares for us.

Dear God, You have my heart—I know You are my loving Father. Help me to always fear, love, and trust in You above all things. Amen.

ANDREW SIMCAK JR.

Ecclesiastes 1:2

Life without Christ Is without Meaning

"Meaningless! Meaningless!" says the Teacher. "Utterly meaningless! Everything is meaningless." Ecclesiastes 1:2

Ecclesiastes is one of the most difficult books in the Bible. Some have even wondered whether it belongs in the Bible because it seems there are little or no comforting parts to its message. It seems to be more about skepticism and despair than about certainty or hope.

When we look at this book in the totality of the Christian Bible, however, we begin to appreciate the role that it can play. Ecclesiastes in general and this verse in particular underscore the futility—the meaninglessness—of life lived apart from a relationship with Him who is the Creator and Redeemer.

Ecclesiastes describes life as it is lived outside of the covenant God made with His people. The covenant gave God's people their identity and shaped their whole outlook on life. Apart from it, their lives were bereft of meaning and purpose.

The rest of the Bible makes abundantly clear where meaning and purpose and hope are to be found. These Gospel themes are to be found in and with the God who wouldn't let us go our own aimless way, but who instead went to extraordinary lengths to accomplish our rescue in the life, death, and resurrection of His own Son.

The covenant without which life is meaningless is anchored in God's promise of a new covenant, a promise He kept at the cross and empty tomb and one that He seals in the water of Baptism and in the body and blood of Christ shared in the Lord's Supper.

Such a covenant—a covenant God has kept—gives not only meaning but abundant and eternal life as well.

Almighty God, the meaning and purpose of our lives comes as a gift from You. Keep us in Your care and keep us mindful of the hope that is ours in Jesus Christ. Amen.

DAVID LUMPP

Ecclesiastes 3:1–8

A Time for Everything

There is a time for everything and a season for every activity under heaven. Ecclesiastes 3:1–8

Today, we all seem to want more time. God gifts each one of us with exactly the same number of minutes and hours in a day. For some of us, the minutes and hours seem to disappear faster.

Many years ago we moved from the North to the deep South. On my first excursion to the grocery store, I hurriedly pushed or at least tried to push the cart up and down the aisles. Other patrons were not accustomed to the fast-paced grocery cart. People stopped to greet and talk with one another. They even had the audacity to do this while standing in the middle of the aisles.

During the years of our southern stay, we learned to accept the slower pace and to understand there is a time for everything. We experienced laughter via Wayne, tears at Marilyn's death, empowerment to care for others through a battered women's program, courage to speak out for people of various ethnic groups.

After the passage of 26 years, it was again time to move from the South to the North. The years spent in God's Word during the southern stay helped to make the move easier and helped us know that God truly does have a time for everything. Even when we don't understand and we want to ask why, we are reminded to hang in there because we live in finite time, but God is not bound by time. His timing is perfect even during what we call the "good and bad times."

Dear Father, help us to use the time You give wisely. May we be reminded that there is a time for everything. Amen.

IDA MALL

Ecclesiastes 3:9–15

In His Time

He has made everything beautiful in its time. Ecclesiastes 3:11

The words of verse 11 in our reading were set to music in a popular Christian song "In His Time." This song was used in a wedding of two people who were getting married at an age somewhat older than the national average. Until they met each other, they had been afraid that they might never get married. The words of the song and this reading, "He has made everything beautiful in its time," testified to God's goodness in bringing them together.

As this verse continues, it tells us that God has set eternity in our hearts. While we worry and put stress on ourselves over our day-to-day activities, God's plan for us is far more encompassing. He sees things in terms of eternity. St. Paul reminds us of this when he writes, "I consider that our present sufferings are not worth comparing with the glory that will be revealed in us" (Romans 8:18).

The writer of Ecclesiastes never seems to be shaken by earthly concerns. In verse 15 he says, "Whatever is has already been, and what will be has been before." In a previous chapter he gives us the famous saying, "There is nothing new under the sun" (1:9). The certainty is, "I know that everything God does will endure forever" (Ecclesiastes 3:14).

In the midst of our daily cares and worries God comes to us and says, "Fear not, for I have redeemed you" (Isaiah 43:1). The Father who sent His Son to save us from our sins will preserve us in our times of trouble and make "everything beautiful in its time."

Lord, in those times when earthly concerns weigh me down, please remind me that in terms of eternity You have made all things beautiful. Through Your Son, Jesus Christ, I pray. Amen.

JIM WIEMERS

Ecclesiastes 8:7–8

Our Future

Since no man knows the future, who can tell him what is to come? No man has power over the wind to contain it; so no one has power over the day of his death. Ecclesiastes 8:7–8

Do we really want to know what our future will bring? I don't think so. The knowledge of happy events might easily be overshadowed by that which we would not consider to be good news. No one looks forward to bad news.

God in His wisdom and love does not allow us to foretell or know the future. That's a blessing. He is doing us a favor. He prefers we place our trust in Him with no foreknowledge of events to come. The psalmist assures us: "My times are in Your hands" (Psalm 31:15). An insurance company claims we are in good hands if we buy its insurance. Christians are "good hands people"—our times and lives are in the hands of our living, loving Lord. His hands are very special—they have the marks of the nail in them. Jesus was crucified for us to deliver us from our sins and to give us spiritual life insurance for time and eternity.

While we have no power over the day of our death and little control over the events between now and then, we do not fear the future. Whatever the future brings, we are confident that Jesus Christ is the same yesterday, today, and forever (Hebrews 13:8). He loves us from all eternity, on the cross, yesterday, today, and tomorrow, and for the rest of our lives. That is good news.

Lord, You are for us and with us. Who can be against us? Thank You for this assurance. Amen.

ANDREW SIMCAK JR.

Ecclesiastes 12:1

Christian Education

Remember your Creator in the days of your youth. Ecclesiastes 12:1

Parents generally see the importance of providing Christian instruction to their children, even if they themselves are not faithful in this regard. They may want their children to attend Sunday school, a parochial grade school, or take confirmation instruction. Often the ministers and teachers of these children realize that the only Christian instruction these children are receiving is from them.

Regardless of parental involvement, teaching children about Christ through His Word, the Bible, cannot be emphasized enough. Of primary importance is sharing with them that they are saved by grace through faith in Jesus Christ. Additionally, the more we can teach children about God's plan for their lives found in His Word, the better their chances are for coping with the life ahead of them.

Children usually are not happy about memorizing Bible passages; however, if we can help them to see how these verses will help them in living the abundant life God desires for them, we will have provided them with a valuable tool they can use forever. Words of comfort like Psalm 23 or John 10 can help them through periods of conflict or depression. John 3:16 and Ephesians 2:8–9 explain the plan of salvation. When these verses are committed to memory, they can be retrieved when they are needed for comfort or for witnessing to others.

Remembering our Creator when young will help us when "the days of trouble come."

Lord, thank You for Your Word. Engrave it on my memory and in my heart. Amen.

JIM WIEMERS

Isaiah 1:18

White as Snow

"Come now, let us reason together," says the LORD. "Though your sins are like scarlet, they shall be as white as snow." Isaiah 1:18

The need to be clean is soul deep. "Purge me! Wash me! Cleanse me!" writes the psalmist in anguish on our behalf. For we know what lies within.

I have lost many garments to leaky pens and their ineradicable blue/black/red stains. But my soul—that is not a throwaway item. It is me. It is my essence. And I know that it is unclean. I know that it is stained with sin. And I know that sin to be rebelliously scrub proof. An honest examination reveals that "my sins are ever before me." Confession is good for the soul, but it leaves me exposed. How can my innermost self be cleansed of what St. John Chrysostom called "the one calamity—sin"?

Enter the heart of God. For the heart of God is not to condemn me and leave me stained and sinful. The heart of God is not to expose mercilessly my soul and its "dark blot."

No! The heart of God is to cleanse, to purify, to make my crimson-red sins "as wool." What comfort is this desire from the heart of God on my behalf! And what joy in knowing that God's holy desire for me has come true in the blood of the Lamb, Christ Jesus! The color of pardon is Christ. And I am made clean.

Dear Father, cleanse me in the blood of the Lamb, Your Son, Jesus. Wash me, purify me, claim my heart anew, spotless for You. Amen.

DAVID H. BENKE

Isaiah 7:14

God with Us

Therefore the LORD Himself will give you a sign: The virgin will be with child and will give birth to a son, and will call Him Immanuel. Isaiah 7:14

Have you ever sent a love signal? There is an old song that says, "Knock three times on the ceiling if you love me; twice on the pipes if the answer is no."

When God decided to demonstrate His love for us, He did not knock three times on the ceiling. He became one of us. The true God became true man as He came to us in the person of His Son, Jesus Christ, born of the virgin Mary in the little town of Bethlehem.

Only Immanuel, our "God with us," could be just like us, only without sin. Only the true God-man could take our sins upon Himself and suffer and die for them on the cross to be a sufficient ransom for our disobedience.

Only Jesus Christ, our Immanuel, now promises eternal life through His death and resurrection to all who place their trust in Him.

Jesus, our "God with us," knows our hurts, our frustrations, and our dreams. He sympathizes with our every need and is always there to hear us. Since He is our Immanuel (God with us), may we always respond by being in fellowship with Him.

Lord Jesus, thank You for being Immanuel, my God who is always with me. Help me always to trust in You. Amen.

LUTHER C. BRUNETTE

Isaiah 9:6

The Gift of the Christ Child

For to us a child is born, to us a son is given, and the government will be on His shoulders. And He will be called Wonderful Counselor, Mighty God, Everlasting Father, Prince of Peace. Isaiah 9:6

Isaiah's prophecy of God's gift of the Christ Child, the Messiah, is surely one of the most beautiful promises in Scripture. God's promises are as sure and certain as His Word, so Isaiah knew this prophecy would indeed come to pass.

And come to pass it did years later in Bethlehem, when the virgin brought forth the Child promised to our first parents centuries earlier in a garden. Many times since then the promise was restated to God's faithful people.

It is said that G. F. Handel's favorite oratorio was not the *Messiah*, but it seems to be ours. Handel enhanced the beauty and grandeur of these prophetic words when he graced them with his notes. We read Isaiah's words and many of us hear them set to Handel's music.

The four names of this Child are imposing, and each consists of two elements: Wonderful Counselor; Mighty God; Everlasting Father; Prince of Peace. What a list, even though it is not an exhaustive one. For we also know this Child as Redeemer, as friend, as brother, as life itself.

Foremost we know His name to be Jesus, for He will save His people from their sins. In Him all prophecies are fulfilled. In Him salvation and restoration are complete. All names from beginning to end find their meaning and their essence in Him, who is both Alpha and Omega. Hallelujah!

Dear God, from Your throne You came to earth to live among us and be our Savior. All good gifts are found in You. Amen.

LAINE ROSIN

Isaiah 25:6–9

Banqueting Table

The LORD Almighty will prepare a feast of rich food for all peoples, a banquet of aged wine. Isaiah 25:6

Family holiday dinners are always somewhat bittersweet. The joy of reunions with those from whom we have been separated by time and distance is mingled with the sadness of missing those who have died and are no longer around the table. "Remember when … ?" become the watchwords. My, how times have changed.

By God's power the prophet Isaiah was able to peer all the way to eternity. Filled with overwhelming joy, he saw a banqueting table with *everyone* present. The final shroud, death, had been destroyed. All the faithful had been reunited and sat feasting at the marriage supper of the Lamb in His kingdom. The meal had again become a place where all were reunited. Oh, happy day!

In this life of additions and subtractions, where the pain of separation can be all but unbearable, Isaiah's vision comforts and steels our resolve. Christ Jesus has assured us of this great feast to come by His death and glorious resurrection from the dead. One day soon all God's faithful who have washed their robes and made them white in the blood of the Lamb will eat of the eternal manna and drink of the rivers of His pleasure forevermore. What a day— a never-ending day—of feasting and celebration that will be!

Everlasting Father, keep us strong in faith until the day when we will be the guests at Your eternal banqueting table in heaven. Amen.

JAMES W. FREESE

Isaiah 30:15

Finding Strength for the Inner Life

In repentance and rest is your salvation, in quietness and trust is your strength. Isaiah 30:15

There is a kind of being busy that wounds the spirit. There is a running after things "which have no solid ground" that heads us on a beeline course away from the things that matter within. "Don't look back!" warned timeless baseball pitcher Satchel Paige. "Something might be gaining on you." That "something" lurking just off behind our shoulder, however, needs to be faced.

Isaiah indicates our natural desire opposes internal spiritual examination and growth. "You would have none of it!" says he. Why is that? Why are we so unrepentantly busy?

It is simple—we are by nature unrepentant. Period.

So God calls us to the inner life. The sovereign Lord requires that we look within. And there we will find four key ingredients for daily strength and salvation: repentance, rest, quietness, and trust.

Only His Spirit can initiate that process. Only the power of the living God can turn us within so that we might receive true pardon, rest, and quietness. And only the living God in Christ Jesus can carry us back out to the busy world repaired and refreshed. Be busy then in the things of the soul. Face your "somethings" head on. In Christ your spirit will be restored!

Sovereign Lord, turn me to You. Grant me rest and quietness of the soul. Make me strong within for what lies without. Amen.

DAVID H. BENKE

Isaiah 40:1–2

Comfort

Comfort, comfort My people, says your God. Speak tenderly to Jerusalem, and proclaim to her that her hard service has been completed, that her sin has been paid for, that she has received from the LORD's hand double for all her sins. Isaiah 40:1–2

A pastor friend of mine tells of opening his study door one evening to a mother and her nine-year-old boy. It had been a difficult day for them both. The boy had been expelled from school. As his mother recited a long list of the boy's problems, he sank a notch lower in his chair with each item listed.

My friend asked the boy what he believed was making things go wrong. Thinking for a moment, the boy replied, "I just wish I had a Dad to put his arm around me once in a while, like other kids do." "You mean, like this?" my friend said, placing his arm around the boy's shoulder. Yes, this was exactly what the boy had in mind.

We identify with that nine-year-old. We need the comfort that comes from above and beyond us, whether that be during our anguish at the bedside of a sick loved one or around the warmth of a fire on a cold night. Whether circumstances in our life are all wrong or all right, a longing springs from deep in our souls for some assurance that our lives are not wind-blown leaves but firmly anchored in the mercy and goodness of God.

So God says, "Comfort, comfort My people … . Speak tenderly to Jerusalem, and proclaim to her that her hard service has been completed." From the awful reality of Calvary's hill, Jesus' arms are stretched out on a cross that He might extend His arms around our shoulders and assure us that all, finally, is well.

Lord Jesus, embrace us with Your love and forgiveness now and always. Amen.

DONALD W. SANDMANN

Isaiah 40:8

The Everlasting Word

The grass withers and the flowers fall, but the word of our God stands forever. Isaiah 40:8.

The headlines read: "43 Die in PSA Flight 1771." Within a matter of seconds 43 people had lost their lives. No matter how a person looks at it, life is short. The psalmist reminds us of that truth: "The length of our days is seventy years—or eighty, if we have the strength; yet their span is but trouble and sorrow, for they quickly pass, and we fly away" (Palm 90:10). Isaiah reminds us that everything living dies: "The grass withers and the flowers fall ... ."

What really mattered for those who died in the crash? What really matters for anyone who closes his or her eyelids in death? Certainly not the things they possess! Isaiah reminds us that one thing matters, that which stands forever—the Word of God. When Jesus asked His disciples if they were going to leave Him, impetuous Peter said, "Lord, to whom shall we go? You have the words of eternal life. We believe and know that You are the Holy One of God" (John 6:68–69).

For the 43 who died in PSA Flight 1771, the only thing that mattered was whether they had faith in Jesus Christ. He alone has that which lasts forever. He alone gives eternal life to those who believe. He died so that all people might have their sins paid for. He died so that His people might have life eternal.

Lord God, remind us always, "The grass withers and the flowers fall, ... but [Your] word ... stands forever." Amen.

ROGER R. SONNENBERG

Isaiah 40:11

A Shepherd—the Perfect Shepherd

He tends His flock like a shepherd: He gathers the lambs in His arms.
Isaiah 40:11

Rex, the part German Shepherd dog, had two jobs—keep the children on the quilt and round-up and direct the sheep to shelter.

When my grandmother went to the fields with her three grandchildren, she took a quilt and spread it under the big shade tree. She would instruct us to stay on the quilt and tell Rex to keep us on the quilt and to keep any form of harm away. If we attempted to disobey, Rex would gently "nose" us back, or if necessary his barking would immediately summon our grandmother.

As stated, Rex's other job was to shepherd the sheep. Although the sheep usually spent their days grazing and baaing, there were times especially as winter approached that they had to be herded into pens. In response to my grandfather's voice, Rex would carefully work to gather and direct the sheep to a safe place for the winter.

As grandchildren, we were loved and protected. The sheep were kept warm in the winter. But as God's children, we are blessed to have the perfect Shepherd caring for His sheep. If we are lost, He will look for us until we are found. He carefully nudges us to safety. He carries us close to His heart.

By staying in the care of the Good Shepherd, we will be carried all the days of our lives even for all eternity.

Dear Father, thank You for Your protection from now through eternity. Amen.

IDA MALL

Isaiah 41:1

A Summons to Court

Be silent before Me, you islands! Let the nations renew their strength! Let them come forward and speak; let us meet together at the place of judgment. Isaiah 41:1

In the middle of world upheaval, God calls the nations to court. Cyrus the Persian is on the horizon, defeating all those in his path, including the centuries-old Babylonian Empire. God challenges the nations to renew their strength. But they are as powerless as their immobile gods that they fashion with gold and fasten in place with nails.

The room where God summons us to court may not resemble a courtroom at all. We sit at our desks, check the daily ebb and flow of our stocks through our phone-line umbilical to the markets, and smile that our future is secure. Or we survey the wonders we have built: our business, our home, and our reputation, and settle back into self-satisfied slumber after viewing those poor souls out there on the late news.

Then our loud thoughts are silenced by the gnawing worry that we will never have enough for retirement or that we will never see enough retirement to enjoy what we have. And the false gods of our own building are revealed as the motionless statues they really are.

"Let us meet together at the place of judgment," God says. He takes us to a hill outside Jerusalem where His Son is nailed in place between heaven and earth. He is as immobile, for a moment, as our false gods. But soon He will depart for His Father in heaven so that we might be surrounded by His love. And our silence this time is the silence of reverence and awe before the living God.

Lord God, enable us to be still and know that You are God, through Jesus Christ, our Lord. Amen.

DONALD W. SANDMANN

Isaiah 41:4

Who's in Charge?

Who has done this and carried it through, calling forth the generations from the beginning? I, the LORD—with the first of them and with the last—I am He. Isaiah 41:4

Then it was Babylonians with horses and spears. In our generation it is large artillery and stealth bombers and cruise missiles. The weapons are different, but the effect the same. The maps of the world are shaded with the colors of a new military force conquering first a couple of neighbors, then most of a continent. Our natural question is, "Where's God? Who's in charge?"

The answer, plain and simple, is the Lord! Yet it is not so plain and simple. How could God condone bloodshed and slaughter? Do the armies move at His direction? Is the missile that destroys people guided by His breath? No, a thousand times no. The brilliant mind and heart of humans twisted by sin design terror and conquests. But, plainly and simply put, even the worst that humankind can do has its bounds. God is long-suffering for only so long. Finally, it is the Lord who says "Enough!" and moves the world along according to His good intentions.

But can we be certain that God is indeed watching over us rather than just watching the horror? Yes, for God, the Eternal One, "with the first of them [the generations of humankind] and with the last of them" speaks. He is the One who has lived and proclaimed and saved long before we raised other idols to take His place. He, finally, is "the Alpha and the Omega, the First and the Last, the Beginning and the End" (Revelation 22:13) who loved us enough to take our flesh and suffer with us. This eternal Jesus is coming soon. "Amen. Come, Lord Jesus" (Revelation 22:20).

Lord God, eternal Ruler of the universe and our world, I place my life and the lives of the nations in Your loving, almighty hands. In Jesus' name I pray. Amen.

DONALD W. SANDMANN

Isaiah 41:13

Do Not Fear

For I am the LORD, Your God, who takes hold of your right hand and says to you, "Do not fear; I will help you." Isaiah 41:13

I've always been struck by how some artists portray the appearances of angels to mortals. Picture, for example, the shepherds cowering in fear, hands shielding their eyes from the heavenly light "like thousand snow-clad mountains bright" ("Behold a Host Arrayed in White," by Hans A. Brorson). What is missing is the greeting with which the angels immediately begin their message: *"Do not be afraid!"* So the angel spoke to Zechariah (Luke 1:12–13), to the virgin Mary (Luke 1:30), to the shepherds (Luke 2:10), and to the women at the empty tomb (Matthew 28:5). "Do not be afraid!"

And there are other "Do not fears." An "angel of God" came to Paul and encouraged him (Acts 27:24). We hear "Do not be afraid!" again in Revelation. Here Christ Himself is speaking to us, saying, "I am alive" (Revelation 1:17–18). And that is the beauty of our Lord's approach. Even as He doesn't send angels to frighten us ("Do not be afraid!"), so also His Law and Gospel are declared to draw us back to Him. God's Law and judgment on our sin is declared *in order that* the Good News may be announced that we are forgiven through the precious, shed blood of Jesus Christ.

And as we repent, Luke 15:10 is fulfilled: "There is rejoicing in the presence of the angels of God over one sinner who repents." And then we continue our Christian walk, knowing that our loving God is at our side: *"Do not be afraid, for I am with you"* (Isaiah 43:5). *"Fear not, for I have redeemed you ... you are Mine"* (Isaiah 43:1).

Every day, O Lord, grant me the blessed certainty that You take hold of my right hand and say to me, "Do not fear; I will help you." Amen.

DONALD L. DEFFNER

Isaiah 42:1–8

Gentle Justice

A bruised reed He will not break, and a smoldering wick He will not snuff out. In faithfulness He will bring forth justice; He will not falter or be discouraged till He establishes justice on earth. Isaiah 42:3–4

If a reporter were to stand outside your church after worship next Sunday and ask people, "What did Jesus do?" she would receive fairly consistent answers. "Jesus is the Savior." "Jesus saves us from our sins." These are very good answers, but they have become so common that the words *save* and *Savior* are almost embarrassing clichés, like the "JESUS SAVES" in blinking neon lights above some churches.

Perhaps Isaiah can put other material on the frame of our definition of "savior" or "messiah." The first word people of his day would associate with the Messiah was *justice*. Here the prophet describes the Messiah three times as the one who brings forth or establishes justice. But in contrast to what we associate with justice—"lock up all the criminals"—the picture Isaiah paints is one of gentle justice.

"A bruised reed He will not break, and a smoldering wick He will not snuff out." Too often in history, justice has been a steamroller used by the powerful to crush the poor and the weak. But God's Anointed One doesn't crush others to make Himself look good. He doesn't need to, for He is already holy. He can use His power to fan gently the faltering flame that is our faith. He can love us into being pursuers of justice not for ourselves, but for those who are even weaker than we.

Jesus, justice-bringer and loving friend, fill us with Your Holy Spirit so that we might care for others with Your gentle justice. Amen.

DONALD W. SANDMANN

Isaiah 43:1

You Are Etched on the Palms of His Hands

Fear not, for I have redeemed you; I have summoned you by name; you are Mine. Isaiah 43:1

Having the "cold and clammy claw" of our sinfulness still upon us, even though we are baptized, redeemed, and freed children of God, we can still fall into despair at times. But Christ knows our human weaknesses. "We have one who has been tempted in every way, just as we are—yet was without sin" (Hebrews 4:15).

So remember: "There are always footsteps ahead of you in the Valley of the Shadow, and *they are His*."

What a caring and compassionate God we have! "Behold, I have graven thee upon the palms of My hands" (Isaiah 49:16 KJV).

"Fear not, for I have redeemed you; I have summoned you by name; you are Mine" (Isaiah 43:1).

What a God! He didn't "fail the world" but gave of Himself in His Son's death on the cross. There He made us His own and claimed us for all eternity.

So when you're "down," remember who you are, and whose you are, and where you are going! And if you still despair, remember that He is by your side, step by step, in the Valley of the Shadow.

> Yea, though I walk in death's dark vale,
> Yet will I fear no ill;
> For Thou art with me, and Thy rod
> And staff me comfort still.
>
> ("The Lord's My Shepherd, I'll Not Want," from the Psalms of David in Meeter)

Lord, remind me each day that I am not to despair. For You have redeemed me. You have summoned me by name. You have said, *"You are Mine!"* Amen.

DONALD L. DEFFNER

Isaiah 44:1–8

Offspring?

I will pour out My Spirit on your offspring, and My blessing on your descendants. They will spring up like grass in a meadow, like poplar trees by flowing streams. Isaiah 44:3–4

Each stage of life has its own rewards. While wisdom has not always accompanied the advent of gray hairs on my head, grand-children have, by the blessing of the Lord. Those, however, who first heard these words of Isaiah were trembling at God's judgment: "I will consign Jacob to destruction and Israel to scorn," for "you have burdened Me with your sins and wearied Me with your offenses" (Isaiah 43:28; 43:24). These people couldn't look forward to surviving long enough to have children, let alone grandchildren!

Perhaps it is a disease that ravages our bodies along with our hope of seeing our children mature. Perhaps we despair of shattering the wall that has been slowly, yet surely, built between us and our offspring. Even though we bite our tongues to keep from adding another brick to that wall, the tension in our voice makes our children turn away yet one more time.

As hopeless as it may seem, God promises that our offspring will "spring up like grass in a meadow, like poplar trees by flowing streams." Our hope is never dead if it is founded on the Lord. For He who promises gave His own Offspring to dry thirst on Calvary's hill that He might "pour water on the thirsty land." Our hope is as rich as God is generous, for our trust is not in ourselves but in the Lord.

Giver of hope, speak Your rich promises to us once again. And repeat Your promises often to open our ears stopped by our sin. In Jesus' name we pray. Amen.

DONALD W. SANDMANN

Isaiah 44:21–22

Remember!

Remember these things, O Jacob, for you are My servant, O Israel. ... I will not forget you. I have swept away your offenses like a cloud, your sins like the morning mist. Return to Me, for I have redeemed you. Isaiah 44:21–22

Nothing reminds us of our fallen nature more than the sinful emotion that comes seemingly out of nowhere. Sometime ago I pulled up behind a Mercedes Benz at a toll plaza. My eyes fixed on the license plate: "ONE UP." My usually even temperament immediately boiled over. I wanted to drive that offending message right into the middle of the trunk with the grill of my Chevy! Then I realized my anger wasn't caused by the obviously materialistic message the owner of the Mercedes displayed; it was sparked by my obviously materialistic self that couldn't afford a Mercedes!

Years of training in stewardship principles, years of the habit of writing the check for the Sunday offering first, years of asking whether I really needed that new electronic gizmo had overcome my materialism—so I thought. Yeah, sure! Here I was caught with my hand in the cookie jar, and my real self was revealed. The clouds of doom quickly descended about me. Can I ever hope to receive God's salvation?

No, we can't—if we place our hope in our own abilities, for we are sinfully rotten to the very core of our nature. But remember what God has called us—His servants! He will not forget us! He has swept away our sins like the morning mist by the "Sonshine" of His forgiving love. "Return to Me," He says, "for I *have* redeemed you."

Lord Jesus, You search me and know me. You know my sin, and You have carried it to the cross. Remember me as You sweep away my sin. Help me to live as Your servant. Amen.

DONALD W. SANDMANN

Isaiah 46:4

A Promise Fulfilled

Even to your old age and gray hairs I am He, I am He who will sustain you.
Isaiah 46:4

The elderly, widowed Scandinavian woman lay quietly in her hospital bed. She was a proud woman. She had worked hard for many years. The wrinkles on her face, the gnarled arthritic fingers, and her gray hair indicated the toll of time.

Because she had no children or family in the United States, her church family had assumed responsibility for her care. Members of the church and a few other people visited her. During her later days in the nursing home, she kept asking, "Why doesn't the Lord take me home?" We would share that He wasn't ready for her. He had things for her to do. She was encouraged to pray for specific people and situations.

Now, on this night as I approached her hospital bedside, she again indicated that she wanted to go home—to heaven. During my stay we prayed. The prayer included her desire to go home if it was God's will. We left it in His hands.

The next night I was attending a meeting that was in the vicinity of the hospital. Although it was late and I thought I would see her the next day, the car just seemed to be drawn to the hospital. I went to her hospital room. Immediately, a feeling of peace was there. After checking her, I went to the nurses' station and indicated that they should come.

God had chosen to call her home forever. As He always is, He was faithful to His promise, "Even to your old age and gray hairs I am He, I am He who will sustain you. I have made you and I will carry you; I will sustain you and I will rescue you."

Do we rely on the promises of God?

Dear Father, help us to remain faithful to You until You rescue us for eternity. Amen.

IDA MALL

Isaiah 48:10–11

Not as Silver

See, I have refined you, though not as silver; I have tested you in the furnace of affliction. For My own sake, for My own sake, I do this. How can I let Myself be defamed? I will not yield My glory to another. Isaiah 48:10–11

Circumstances can look bleak when you are in exile far from your homeland. It seemed unrealistic for the Israelites to have confidence in God in view of His apparent inability to protect them from the Babylonians, who boasted of their superior gods.

Circumstances can look bleak when we, far from our heavenly homeland, endure suffering or sickness or betrayal. Is the Lord, after all, able to be victorious for us? He may be allowing these sufferings so that the genuineness of our faith may be shown (1 Peter 1:6–7), but must He turn up the heat until there is no faith left?

Never! "I have refined you, though not as silver." The apparent reason is that if God had turned up the heat on Israel to the point required to release silver, He would have found very little worth saving. But He seeks to reveal His promise, not our unworthiness. To destroy Israel or us would make Him unfaithful to His promises of redemption. But He is faithful and so will reveal our faithfulness. He redeems and desires a full host of the redeemed to be brought home to their heavenly reward. Not by our might, but by His promises will we be sustained.

O God, who suffers with us, increase our love and hope so that we may hold to Your promises of deliverance even in the middle of affliction. Through Jesus Christ, our Lord, we pray. Amen.

DONALD W. SANDMANN

Isaiah 49:1–2

The Best-Kept Secret

Listen to me, you islands; hear this, you distant nations: Before I was born the LORD called me; from my birth He has made mention of my name. He made my mouth like a sharpened sword, in the shadow of His hand He hid me; He made me into a polished arrow and concealed me in His quiver. Isaiah 49:1–2

God's secret is foreshadowed here. He called the Servant, later revealed as Jesus Christ, made Him a "polished arrow" to bear the penetrating will of God to the world, then hid the "arrow" in His quiver until He revealed Jesus in the flesh at the proper time. Here the Servant is pictured as calling to the distant nations and the islands. When He appears, He will not be for Israel only. He will be God's Word for all humankind.

All of us non-Israelites rejoice that the Servant would choose to penetrate our hearts of sin and reveal God's will and salvation to us. But, curiously, we are reluctant to share Him with others. Though we have learned that the wounding of His Word is the prelude to real healing and joy, we fail or refuse to speak of Him in the hearing of those who need similar wounding and healing.

God won't let us rest. When we won't go to distant nations, He moves people from those nations right next door. "Japanese" becomes our neighbor: Yohko, who needs a friend in a strange land. She will find her real friend, Jesus, as God pulls us from His quiver to be His messenger to her.

Think of your neighbor who needs such a friend. Do you feel God's hand reaching into the quiver to find you?

Lord, today make me aware of the lost soul to whom You send me, and help me to stand tall as You reach into Your quiver to find Your messenger arrow. I am reluctant, even afraid. Strengthen me with remembrances of Your great mercy to me. Empower me to speak of Your love in Jesus' name. Amen.

DONALD W. SANDMANN

Isaiah 49:16

Engraved on His Hands

See, I have engraved you on the palms of My hands; your walls are ever before Me. Isaiah 49:16

Remember the time when someone in your history class tried writing notes on his hand to cheat on his test? I've often wondered how that worked and if he ever got caught.

Different than writing important facts on His hand, the Lord tells us that He has our names engraved on His hand. What a comfort to know that God knows us so well! He even knows our name, and He will never forget it.

Maybe you have seen your name in some special places—in the newspaper, on a sports program, on an award or diploma, or on a walnut door. Or maybe you have heard your name from some important people—a coach, a celebrity, a teacher. But to think that our names are written on God's hand ... how wonderful!

Not only does God know our names, but He knows everything about us. Through God's Son, Jesus Christ, God knows and loves us perfectly! He forgives our sins and has our best at heart. The One whose hands were pierced on the cross of Calvary has our names recorded on them. This is why we can always trust in Him.

Dear Savior, Your hands hold me in perfect love. May I always trust in You! Amen.

LUTHER C. BRUNETTE

Isaiah 50:7

Flint-Faced

Because the Sovereign LORD helps me, I will not be disgraced. Therefore have I set my face like flint, and I know I will not be put to shame. Isaiah 50:7

Christians at times appear defenseless, even defeated. In the manner of our Lord who "humbled Himself and became obedient to death—even death on a cross" (Philippians 2:8), we bend our knees in service. As we kneel, we appear to be bowed in shameful powerlessness.

Yet look into our eyes! See compassion in the eyes of a teacher who gets on her knees to assist a student. See mercy in the eyes of a father who kneels to assure his little one a misdeed is forgiven. See determination in the eyes of a sister who is going to tie her brother's shoes—or else! See devotion in the eyes of parent and child as they kneel together in prayer at day's end. Being ashamed is the furthest thing from their minds. The need of another is paramount, and kneeling in humble service is possible because our dignity is given by the Lord who bowed His own head on the cross.

Even when it seemed senseless to His disciples, Jesus could not be sidetracked. He set His face like flint toward Jerusalem, where He would fulfill all that the prophets had foretold. Mission accomplished, His Holy Spirit now sets our determined gaze on the least of Christ's brothers and sisters.

Lord Jesus, kneel with us and fill our eyes with compassion and strength so that we may see Your sisters and brothers through Your love and serve them in Your name. Amen.

DONALD W. SANDMANN

Isaiah 54:17

A Defended, Innocent City

"No weapon forged against you will prevail, and you will refute every tongue that accuses you. This is the heritage of the servants of the LORD, and this is their vindication from Me," declares the LORD. Isaiah 54:17

In Isaiah 53, the Servant's (Christ's) suffering is foretold. The reason for His suffering, and a blessed result of it, is that "He will see His offspring" (Isaiah 53:10). These offspring, the prophet says, are an afflicted city that the Lord will rebuild with precious jewels; it will be a place where "great will be your children's peace" (Isaiah 54:11–13). Moreover, no one can assault the children of the Servant with weapons or false accusations.

What ruins your sleep? Is it the memory of a sin long past for which you have pleaded for God's forgiveness? Is it the injustice of a harsh word hurled against you by someone you thought loved and respected you? Even more revealing are our own accusing words that berate us for failing to live up to God's standards over and over again.

Hush! That's God's word to those sleep-robbing thoughts. For you are, with all God's people, a strong city, "prepared as a bride beautifully dressed for her husband" (Revelation 21:2). No one can accuse you, not even yourself! The Father has passed sentence, declaring His Son guilty. So sleep the peaceful sleep of a child of God, safe within the walls of His strong protection.

Lord, quiet my sleepless nights with remembrances of Your pronouncement of "Not guilty!" In the strong name of Christ let me sleep the sleep of Your innocent child. Amen.

DONALD W. SANDMANN

Isaiah 55:8–9

God's Way

"For My thoughts are not your thoughts, neither are your ways My ways," declares the LORD. "As the heavens are higher than the earth, so are My ways higher than your ways and My thoughts than your thoughts." Isaiah 55:8–9

One of the most haunting questions we face is: Why? Why did this relationship fall apart? Why did that accident have to happen? Why did my loved one have to suffer and then die? Each of us can add our own complaints to the catalog of charges against God.

If we were in charge, life would be quite different. We would make certain that neither we nor our family and friends would have to suffer. In fact, we would do all that we could to make certain that we would enjoy the good life with no troubles at all.

The morning alarm clock, however, awakens us to the realities of life. There are bills for us to pay. We are getting older and more susceptible to illness and disease. Loved ones or we ourselves do suffer from a cancerous invasion or the mysterious ravages of Alzheimer's disease. And the old question still remains: Why?

The life of suffering and disease is not God's way, either. For God designed a life for us that was free from all that. When sin ruined God's perfect creation, God designed a way to recreate the world. That design focused on His Son, Jesus the Christ, who took on our human flesh and bone, fulfilled the Law of God perfectly, and then died and rose again for us. All this was done in God's way because there is no way we could have done it for ourselves. Thank God, His ways are not our ways nor His thoughts our thoughts.

Jesus, still lead on
Till our rest be won;
And although the way be cheerless,
We will follow calm and fearless;
Guide us by your hand
To our fatherland. Amen

("Jesus, Still Lead On," by Nicolaus L. von Zinzendorf)

HENRY GERIKE

Isaiah 64:1–8

Open the Heavens

Since ancient times no one has heard, no ear has perceived, no eye has seen any God besides You, who acts on behalf of those who wait for Him. Isaiah 64:4

At times it isn't enough to know that God has control of our individual fates. When nations march against nations, when natural disasters threaten, we need a cosmic God who has control of the universe! We need God to make sense of all the senseless events around us. The prophet here asks for us all: "Oh, that You would rend the heavens and come down, that the mountains would tremble before You!"

Isaiah won't let this God be a god of our own imagining. This cosmic God is not a figure of our own construction. "For when You did awesome things that we *did not expect*, You came down, and the mountains trembled before You." "You come to the help of those who gladly do right, who remember Your ways."

But where does that leave us? "All of us have become like one who is unclean, and all our righteous acts are like filthy rags." Is it possible to expect that You will tear the heavens open and come down to us who are so unworthy?

Yes, for "at that moment heaven was opened, and [Jesus] saw the Spirit of God descending like a dove and lighting on Him. And a voice from heaven said, 'This is My Son, whom I love; with Him I am well pleased' " (Matthew 3:16b–17). The waters of Christ's Baptism in which we participate by our own washing of the Spirit are mixed with the dust of our sinful humanity, and God molds us to be the work of His hand.

Heavenly Father, as You opened the heavens and came down at the Baptism of Your Son, Christ, our Lord, so convince us of Your power and mold us to be Your vessels of love. Amen.

DONALD W. SANDMANN

Isaiah 65:17–25

Home Again—Now!

Behold, I will create new heavens and a new earth. The former things will not be remembered, nor will they come to mind. ... I will create Jerusalem to be a delight and its people a joy. ... the sound of weeping and of crying will be heard ... no more. Isaiah 65:17–19

The exiles are longing for the rebuilding of Jerusalem so they can have a home in which to live again. Isaiah looks beyond the physical boundaries of that city to a new Jerusalem that God will "create." It won't have a geographic location, for God will "create new heavens and a new earth." Time will no longer be our enemy, for "he who dies at a hundred will be thought a mere youth." No longer will anyone "toil in vain." Hostile animals "will neither harm nor destroy." The people will be home again, and what a home it will be!

Strange, but we find similar language later in the Scriptures, in the last book of the Bible. The Revelation given to the apostle John uses much the same imagery (Revelation 21:1–4). What are we to think? Isaiah shares the word of the Lord. Hundreds of years later John speaks in similar tones. Why didn't God act in those hundreds of years to bring about His new creation? Why hasn't He acted in the hundreds of years since John wrote? Yes, really, our question is "Why doesn't God act *now?*"

He does! "Therefore, if anyone is in Christ, he is a new creation; the old has gone, the new has come!" (2 Corinthians 5:17). We are His new creation, citizens of the heavenly Jerusalem that He will bring when He comes again at the last day. The divisions of time fade. Eternal life is ours now. Even as Christ rose from the dead, we have the spiritual life that knows no boundaries.

Through Christ, we enjoy one special gift of the new Jerusalem right now: "Before they call I will answer; while they are still speaking I will hear." Some years ago my family and I were caught in a snowstorm. The front wheel of the car got into a rut on the edge of the road and would not pull out. A bridge abutment loomed closer and closer. I literally cried, "Lord, Lord, Lord!" The car came back to the center of the road only by God's response and power. In an even more miraculous way Christ said, "When you pray, say, 'Our Father.' " Safe in the Father's heart, we are home!

Heavenly Father, keep us safe in Your arms and bring us finally to the heavenly Jerusalem of which we are already citizens. Through Christ, our Lord, we pray. Amen.

DONALD W. SANDMANN

Isaiah 66:12–13

Mother Love

For this is what the LORD says: "I will extend peace to her like a river, and the wealth of nations like a flooding stream; you will nurse and be carried on her arm and dandled on her knees. As a mother comforts her child, so will I comfort you; and you will be comforted over Jerusalem."
Isaiah 66:12–13

Our first memories are often connected with our mother. It was she in whose presence we felt safe and comforted. Her hug could cure most ills. Her singing voice assured us of her presence and made our lives music. All was well.

"Mother Jerusalem" is the city in whose presence God's people find comfort and safety. We are nursed there and carried by her, and we play on her lap. All is well with us and with the world.

"The LORD says, 'As a mother comforts her child, so will I comfort you.'" The strong, mighty Lord compares Himself to a mother. With tender love He calls us back to Himself when we stray.

But beware lest we ignore His call! "O Jerusalem, Jerusalem, you who kill the prophets and stone those sent to you, how often I have longed to gather your children together, as a hen gathers her chicks under her wings, but you were not willing" (Luke 13:34). We can misunderstand the motherly love of God and believe that it is smothering us and keeping us from being ourselves. But as He opens our ears to answer His call, we know once more that life is full only when it is lived in the comfort of our God.

Lord God, You love us with a mother's love. Restore Your wandering children again, and welcome us into Your heart, through Jesus Christ, our Lord. Amen.

DONALD W. SANDMANN

Jeremiah 10:23–24

Accept Correction

I know, O LORD, that a man's life is not his own; it is not for man to direct his steps. Correct me, LORD, but only with justice—not in Your anger, lest You reduce me to nothing. Jeremiah 10:23–24

Chris could see the freeway she needed to be on but couldn't find the on-ramp. Three times she tried following the road signs, and three times she ended back where she started. Suddenly she had an idea. She would reverse the route. She quickly made a U-turn and expected to see the on-ramp. Instead, she saw the flashing lights of a police car pulling up behind her. Chris was so frustrated she was nearly crying as she told the officer her problem.

"You can't get to the freeway from this road," the officer said gently. "You have to be on that other road." He pointed to a line of cars flowing onto the freeway. The officer wrote Chris a ticket for the U-turn, then told her to follow him, and he would show her the way to the on-ramp.

Sometimes in life we get on the wrong roads. We make wrong turns and get into trouble. We need correction to our routes to get back on track. Sometimes the Holy Spirit corrects us by convicting us in our hearts until we choose to change. Sometimes God corrects us through reproofs and feedback from other people. At other times God corrects us by letting us suffer the consequences of our wrong choices.

But always, God is ready to lead us in the paths of righteousness after we accept correction, repent, and desire to do right.

Holy Spirit, speak to my heart when I am on the wrong path. Help me to listen to Your gentle persuasion and to choose the right paths. Amen.

BOBBIE REED

Jeremiah 29:11–14

Joseph—a Special Person

"For I know the plans I have for you," declares the LORD, "plans to prosper you and not to harm you, plans to give you hope and a future." Jeremiah 29:11

My favorite biblical character has always been Joseph, the son of Jacob and Rachel. When young, I did not realize why Joseph was my hero, my "hope" person. As the years passed, it became apparent that my desire for my family to be restored to the same state as Joseph's in his latter years was not going to happen.

Even though "my dream" did not materialize, God was using Joseph to help me see that he had "plans to prosper [me] and not to harm [me], plans to give [me] hope and a future." Through the years He gave me a Christian husband, Christian children, and opportunities to serve in ways that I had never imagined.

According to some of today's thinking, Joseph would have been justified to retaliate or to get even. He was sold into slavery by his brothers, his youth was spent in a foreign country with people of a different culture and religion, and he was imprisoned on false charges. Joseph's thinking was of God, not man. "You intended to harm me, but God intended it for good to accomplish what is now being done, the saving of many lives" (Genesis 50:20).

Unlike Joseph, who was unfairly placed in captivity, the Israelites' banishment was the judgment of God. Even during their exile, God spoke to them and said, "When seventy years are completed for Babylon, I will come to you and fulfill My gracious promise to bring you back to this place" (Jeremiah 29:10).

These Jeremiah verses, which gave direction and hope for the people of Israel and were exemplified in the life of Joseph, can offer us the push we need when things are tough. We are reminded that God always has the best in mind for us.

Dear Father, thank You for protecting Joseph. Help us to know that You have a plan and a hope for us. Amen.

IDA MALL

Jeremiah 31:3

God's Everlasting Love

The LORD appeared to us in the past, saying: "I have loved you with an everlasting love; I have drawn you with loving-kindness." Jeremiah 31:3

Perhaps one of the hardest things about love and loving is to love unconditionally. If a friend is kind, it's easy to return the favor. If a child is obedient and respectful, it's easy to show love. If a spouse treats us with affection and consideration, it's easy to do likewise.

But God's love is unconditional. Jeremiah says it's also everlasting. It depends on Him and His faithfulness, not on whether we deserve it or respond in kind. For if that were the case, we would have no comfort and no hope.

Even before earth's frame was laid, we were the objects of God's love. He sought us when we didn't even know to look for Him. He draws us to Him with the loving-kindness of the Gospel, the sweet message of salvation in His Son. It is God's loving-kindness, His mercy, that most completely defines His nature. For everything that He is and does is shaped and determined by His love for His creation.

When He disciplines and chastens His children, it is always within the context of that love. His goal is restoration, never destruction or revenge.

God's loving-kindness is gentle and pure, yet it also has great power. It has power to draw us to Him, to keep us in His grace, and to overcome the evil the world would have us follow, until that day when we live forever in His everlasting love.

Loving God, Your mercy is new every morning and lasts forever. Thank You for drawing me to You with Your loving-kindness and keeping me in Your grace. Amen.

LAINE ROSIN

Lamentations 3:22

God's Patient Faithfulness

Because of the LORD's great love we are not consumed, for His compassions never fail. They are new every morning; great is Your faithfulness. Lamentations 3:22

The Chinese have an unusual type of bamboo tree. They plant the tiny seed of this bamboo tree. They water it, weed it, fertilize it, and care for it for five years. During that time, absolutely nothing happens. Then, during the sixth year, a remarkable thing happens. The tiny seed grows one foot each day, until it is 60 feet tall in a mere 60 days.

God's love and patience with us are amazing! He created us. He re-made us in Christ our Savior, and then He watches for the results of a productive Christian life. There are many days when nothing fruitful happens. Yet God's faithfulness never ceases! Despite our faithlessness, He remains faithful. His compassions never fail us.

The faithfulness of our compassionate God is seen most clearly in Jesus Christ, who died and rose for us. God's love and forgiveness in Jesus makes each day new and fresh. Every day becomes a celebration of God's eternal faithfulness.

Dear God, while I am often faithless, You remain faithful. Enable me to enjoy each day as a gift of Your compassion. In Jesus' name. Amen.

LUTHER C. BRUNETTE

Daniel 3:17–18

Know and Serve the Right Master

If we are thrown into the blazing furnace, the God we serve is able to save us from it. Daniel 3:17

Have you ever said, "Oh! I'll do that! You can count on me." At the time the words were said, you really meant it. However, money was tight, bills were due, time was short, and other opportunities appeared. Your "I'll do it!" became "Can you find somebody else?"

For Shadrach, Meshach, and Abednego, "find somebody else" would have seemed appropriate. When Nebuchadnezzar, king of Babylon, summoned the three men and asked them, "Is it true … that you do not serve my gods or worship the image of gold I have set up?" (Daniel 3:14), they knew that a positive response to the inquiry meant placement in the fiery furnace. Even knowing the penalty, they responded, "If we are thrown into the blazing furnace, the God we serve is able to save us from it, and He will rescue us from your hand, O king. But even if He does not, we want you to know, O king, that we will not serve your gods or worship the image of gold you have set up."

These men were faithful to their God. They knew Him well. From past experiences, they knew He was able, if He chose, to deliver them from the blazing furnace. They were committed to following Him even if it meant death.

This story serves as a reminder to us to know and to continue to know our God better on a daily basis so that when we are confronted with "fiery furnaces" we will depend on the one who can deliver us. By knowing and serving the right master, we are insured of deliverance for all eternity.

Dear Father, help us to be faithful to You in our "fiery furnace" times. Amen.

IDA MALL

Daniel 9:9

Not Justice, but Mercy

The LORD our God is merciful and forgiving, even though we have rebelled against Him. Daniel 9:9

The story is told of a woman who had a portrait painted of herself in an expensive studio. When the artist was finished with the portrait, the lady peered onto the canvas in utter dismay. "That painting certainly doesn't do me justice," she uttered. To this the artist quipped back, "Lady, you don't need justice, you need mercy!"

In a way, the same is true for us all. We have all missed the mark of what God expects of us as His creation. We sin against Him in our thoughts, words, and deeds. We not only do the evil God forbids, but we fail to do the good He commands. Justice deserves a guilty verdict! Yet the wonderful news of the Gospel of Jesus Christ is that in Him, God has mercy on us. Instead of giving us what we deserve (eternal damnation) because of the ugliness of our sins, God gives to us what we need most (forgiveness) and what He has earned for us (eternal life).

Through Jesus Christ, we can all personally know and experience God's forgiveness and life. Every day, the newness of God's mercy makes today the best day of our lives. Each day of grace is lived to the glory and honor of Him who suffered the punishment of our sins and won salvation for us.

Dear God, thank You for giving to me not what I deserve, but what I need most—Your love and forgiveness. Amen.

LUTHER C. BRUNETTE

Hosea 6:1

A Mother Crying Piteously

Come, let us return to the LORD. He has torn us to pieces but He will heal us. Hosea 6:1

It was the dead of winter in Montana. A woman and her child were crossing the frozen prairies in a bus. They were the only passengers besides the driver.

It was bitterly cold. But what was worse, the heating system in the bus had failed. And the driver realized that the mother was gradually becoming unconscious from the cold.

So he suddenly did a strange thing. He stopped the bus, grabbed the baby from the mother's arms, and wrapping it warmly, placed it underneath the seat.

Then he seized the mother by the arm, dragged her outside, and drove away, leaving her in the freezing snow.

Stupefied, the mother saw the bus leaving, and ran after it, crying piteously for her baby.

When the bus driver was sure the mother's blood circulation was going again, he allowed her to overtake the bus. He opened the door and restored the child to the mother's outstretched arms.

Only then did she realize that he had saved her life.

Often God permits severe spiritual tests to come to our lives. But then—and sometimes only then—are we restored to faithful, vigorous Christian living.

O Lord, let me not doubt Your ways. Rather grant me Your wisdom to see that "the testing of [my] faith develops perseverance" (James 1:3). In the strong name of Jesus Christ. Amen.

DONALD L. DEFFNER

Joel 2:32

Called Out of Darkness into His Marvelous Light

And everyone who calls on the name of the LORD will be saved. Joel 2:32

Those who call on the name of the Lord will be saved. This is an extraordinary promise God makes through His Old Testament prophet, probably at one of the bleakest times in Judah's history. It was made, in all likelihood, when God's people didn't feel like calling on the name of the Lord and in fact thought that their God had let them down in their struggle against Babylon. What good will calling on this God do? Where had He been?

These questions are not limited to the people of the old covenant, who had experienced national calamity. We ask them, too, in our moments of crisis, and we long for God to deliver us. In those moments, calling on the name of the Lord is very difficult to do.

For precisely that reason, God first calls us. From the very first transgression in Eden, God goes looking for His people and calls to them. Most important of all, He calls us through the Gospel of His Son, Jesus Christ, whose resurrection victory over sin, death, and evil is the definitive expression of God's saving will toward us. He calls us by name in Baptism and makes us His own possession again.

From within this new relationship that He has established, we can now call on His name. We do so not out of despair, discouragement, or hopelessness, but in the assurance that God hears us and that He wants us to call upon Him all the time, in all kinds of situations, with all our needs.

Calling on the name of the Lord is the highest form of worship. Calling on the name of the Lord gives us the chance to tell others how Jesus Christ became our Lord and continues to be the source of our life and salvation.

Merciful God, we give thanks that You not only instruct us to call upon You, but You promise to hear us and be with us as well. Amen.

DAVID LUMPP

Micah 5:2

Though You Are Small

But you, Bethlehem Ephrathah, though you are small among the clans of Judah, out of you will come for Me one who will be ruler over Israel, whose origins are from of old, from ancient times. Micah 5:2

Bethlehem—one of the most recognized places in the Bible. Everyone knows what happened there. No visit to the Holy Land would be complete without a visit to Bethlehem. It's famous!

Yet God did not choose Bethlehem for the birth of His Son because of its greatness; to the contrary, the prophet notes, "though you are small … ." This town was so small it didn't have enough rooms at the inn when census time came. The newborn Messiah had to be laid in an insignificant manger. How could this be!

One of the reasons God chose Bethlehem was because it was small and unpretentious. The Bible is full of instances where God chose things that were foolish, weak, or lowly to shame the wise (1 Corinthians 1:27–31). David (also born in Bethlehem) was only a child when he did the impossible, slaying the great Goliath. When Ruth came to Bethlehem, no one suspected that this Moabite woman, a Gentile, would be chosen by God to be part of His Son's lineage.

Jesus was born in Bethlehem as true God, yet "He humbled Himself and became obedient to death" (Philippians 2:8). "By His wounds we are healed" (Isaiah 53:5). Out of lowly Bethlehem came a humble Savior who overcame sin and death for us and rose victorious.

O holy Child of Bethlehem,
Descend to us, we pray;
Cast out our sin, and enter in,
Be born in us today. Amen.
("O Little Town of Bethlehem," by Phillips Brooks)

JIM WIEMERS

Micah 6:8

Live ... by God's Design

He has showed you, O man, what is good. And what does the LORD require of you? To act justly and to love mercy and to walk humbly with your God. Micah 6:8

While the participants at the 1995 International Women's Missionary League Convention promised to "go into the world, led by the cross of my Lord Jesus Christ," the large, illuminated backdrop cross moved high above them from the front to the middle of the convention setting. It was the finale to four days of living the convention theme, "Live ... by God's Design," based on Micah 6:8.

On the first day of the convention, the theme weaver (program leader) said, "Cars run on gasoline, but Christians run on holy water." By water and Word our God called us to be His. That is His design.

Also at the convention, the people were confronted with a drama of the courtroom case of *God v. Israel*. It didn't take long for everyone to realize that the case was really *God v. Humanity*—then and now. We are all familiar with courtroom trials. Each of us has probably heard of a trial depicted as the "trial of the century."

For the people in Micah's day and for us, we are in a "trial for eternity." God is the prosecutor and our self-righteousness is our only defense. We can be assured that we have lost the case. However, as with Micah, our only hope is in Christ.

In response to our acquittal through Christ, we, like the convention-goers, are given the opportunity to go into the world led by the victorious cross of Jesus Christ "to act justly and to love mercy and to walk humbly with [our] God."

God's Word gives us the pattern to live by His design. Do we wear His specially designed clothing for us each day?

Dear Father, help us to live by Your design. Amen.

IDA MALL

148

Micah 7:8–9

God Keeps His Promises

Do not gloat over me, my enemy! Though I have fallen, I will rise. Though I sit in darkness, the LORD will be my light. Micah 7:8–9

This text is an affirmation of faith in the strength and mercy of God despite all appearances to the contrary. No matter how bad things appear, God will not abandon His people. They are His, and in His own way and at His own time, He will rescue them.

Sometimes the only thing one can count on, the only thing that one has left, is the God who promises never to abandon or leave His children.

How do we know that? Because God has kept the most important promise that He has ever made. To people who have nothing of their own to offer God, to people who all too often flee from God and want nothing to do with Him, God seeks out these very people and gives abundant blessings to them.

God began His search and rescue mission in Eden, and it climaxed on Good Friday and Easter, when God's Son and our Savior demonstrated how far He was willing to go to forgive us and raise us up again.

To be sure, we have fallen and do continue to fall. But in Holy Baptism God raises us from death with Jesus Christ. Left to ourselves, we sit in darkness, with no sign of life getting better or brighter. But Jesus, who is the light of the world, has called us out of the darkness of our sin and brought us into His marvelous light, where there is forgiveness of sins, life, and salvation.

How do we know that God keeps His promises? Because He already has.

Faithful God, we give thanks that You have kept and will keep the promises You make to us, above all Your promise to be with us, protect us, and forgive us through the gift of Your Son for us. Amen.

DAVID LUMPP

Micah 7:18–19

Unstuck by God's Mercy

Who is a God like You, who pardons sin and forgives the transgression of the remnant of His inheritance? You do not stay angry forever but delight to show mercy. You will again have compassion on us; You will tread our sins underfoot and hurl all our iniquities into the depths of the sea. Micah 7:17–18

Sometimes nasty things stick to us. Like a bad nickname—"Stinky," for instance. Or, say, a reputation for being tardy. Or sin. Sin, says Scripture, sticks to us no matter how hard we try to shake it. It's there as if stuck to our shoe, then tangled in our legs, then—whoops!—we're falling, caught up and tossed down as always because we are by nature sinful.

How do we get unstuck? Consider our God! "Who is a God like You?" writes Micah, echoing the meaning of his own Hebrew name. God does not take pleasure in our pratfalls. God does not angrily push us and our sticky situations away and over a cliff.

No! Our God uniquely "delights to show mercy." And in God's mercy we are unstuck. Unstuck from our own unlovely condition. Unstuck by God, who like no other cares enough to "tread our sins underfoot" to release us from their bondage and then hurls the toxic sinful waste "into the depths of the sea."

So often we feel powerless over the sins that beset us. Only God in Christ Jesus can pick the useless baggage of sin off us and throw it away. Trust then and always and only in the compassion of the God who is like no other.

Release me, merciful God, from the sin that has stuck to me. Release me into the arms of Your compassion for the sake of Jesus. Amen.

DAVID H. BENKE

Nahum 1:7

The Refuge of the Lord

The LORD is good, a refuge in times of trouble. He cares for those who trust in Him. Nahum 1:7

One of the most difficult classes of my high school career was freshman biology. Learning all those proper names for plants and animals did not at the time seem like something I wanted to use for my life. Yet I worked harder in that class than for any subject in my life. Why? One day the biology teacher stopped me in the hall and asked how I was doing. He asked about my family. He seemed genuinely interested in me, a 13-year-old, pimple-faced student.

God assures us that He cares for us. He is so interested in you and your well-being that He sent His only Son to be your Savior. The Lord, who knows you perfectly, loves you the way you are. He forgives you through His Son, Jesus Christ, and assures you of His eternal provision.

Since God cares for us and provides everything we need, we know that we can trust Him. He becomes our refuge in times of challenge, change, and conflict. Instead of trying to run our own lives, we place our confidence in Him to guide and direct us, knowing that He is always there for us.

Dear Lord, despite my sins, You care for me. Thank You for being my refuge in times of trouble. Enable me to place my complete trust in You. In Jesus' name. Amen.

LUTHER C. BRUNETTE

Habakkuk 2:4

The Gift of Faith

See, he is puffed up; his desires are not upright—but the righteous will live by his faith. Habakkuk 2:4

This is probably the most famous passage in the book of Habakkuk. It was certainly one of Paul's favorite verses, and he quotes it both in his letter to the Romans and his letter to the Galatians. It is the beginning of God's answer to Habakkuk's complaint that God must not tolerate the evil that is present in the world. It is God's answer to us when we make the same complaint. And God wants Habakkuk to make His answer very plain to us.

"The righteous will live by his faith." Faith is not something everyone can see. It is not tangible—it is not something we can take out and show people to prove that we have it. Sure, we can express our faith, and we do every time we proclaim the creed with the body of Christ or partake of the sacraments.

But, here in this verse, faith is contrasted with things that can be seen. Pride puffs up, and greed betrays itself in its desires. Pride and greed are something that can be seen. And these things not only can be seen but unmistakably point the way to death.

For it is by faith that we live. Our faith in Jesus Christ, given to us by God through the Holy Spirit, makes us righteous and brings us life. This is the message that St. Paul makes so clear to us, too. We are justified by faith alone—not by anything that can be seen nor by anything that we do, but only by our faith and this a gift from God. Praise Him!

Dear Father in heaven, thank You so much for the gift of faith that You have given me. Help me to share my faith so that others might see it and know that Jesus Christ is Lord. Amen.

KEVIN PARVIZ

Zephaniah 3:17

Rest in Confidence

The LORD your God is with you, He is mighty to save. He will take great delight in you, He will quiet you with His love, He will rejoice over you with singing. Zephaniah 3:17

When Michael was a father for the first time, he was captivated by his baby boy. Michael watched the boy every minute they were together and prevented many injuries and falls. Each day Michael cradled his son and sang him to sleep, then lay beside the boy and marveled at the baby.

One of the metaphors used for God in the Bible is that of a parent. God is eager and ready to save us not only from physical dangers but also from the hell of being separated from God for eternity. Through faith in the sacrifice of Jesus Christ on the cross we can know that God's love has saved us for eternal life in heaven. Many of us are aware of this aspect of God's love.

However, our Scripture verse gives a different view of God's love. Zephaniah suggests that God delights in us much like a proud parent does when an offspring does well. Zephaniah says God is ready to comfort us with loving concern. And Zephaniah tells us that God celebrates with us by singing.

How are you doing as God's child? Do you do good, make good decisions, and treat people right so God can take great delight in you? Do you come to God for comfort? Can you point to those spiritual victories in your life that God celebrated with you? Are there different choices you need to make today than you have been making?

Lord, help me to become the kind of child who will delight You, seek You out for comfort, and hear Your singing in my heart. Amen.

BOBBIE REED

Zechariah 4:6

Find Power Within

So He said to me, "This is the word of the LORD to Zerubbabel: 'Not by might nor by power, but by My Spirit,' says the LORD Almighty." Zechariah 4:6

Seven-year-old Spencer opened his birthday present and found a battery-operated toy robot. The box for the toy was illustrated with pictures of all the different things the robot would do. Spencer set the robot on the table and waited. Nothing happened. Spencer reached over and manually tried to force the arm and leg movements depicted on the box. The arms and legs wouldn't move. Spencer tried harder and broke off one of the arms. He was angry and threw the robot on the floor. Spencer didn't realize he had to flip on the off-on switch to tap into the power from the batteries inside the toy.

Many of us are like Spencer. We get an idea of things we want to do, opportunities to minister we want to take advantage of, and ways we want to live. Then we start working in our own strength to reach our goals. Often we find that nothing goes right for us. We do not get to do what we want. We do not find opportunities to use our gifts for singing, writing, speaking, teaching, or administering. We do not reach our goals. We become disillusioned, heartbroken, angry, and bitter.

The problem is that we fail to tap into the power source within us, the Holy Spirit. In our own strength we cannot succeed. If we try to force situations to go our way, we may end up hurt or hurting someone else. If we trust in the guidance of the Holy Spirit, the opportunities for action come at the right times. Then the Holy Spirit empowers us to do the right things. We will succeed.

Lord, help me to recognize the Holy Spirit's power within me and to be empowered for Your will and work. Amen.

BOBBIE REED

Matthew 1:21

How Sweet the Name of Jesus Sounds

Give Him the name Jesus because He will save His people from their sins. Matthew 1:21

> O Jesus, shepherd, guardian, friend,
> My Prophet, Priest, and King,
> My Lord, my life, my way, my end,
> Accept the praise I bring.
> ("How Sweet the Name of Jesus Sounds," by John Newton)

John Newton, formerly captain of a vessel transporting African slaves, wrote that verse. How well Newton knew of whom he wrote! He who had made his living off the sale of human beings into bondage was reclaimed by the name and in the power of Jesus. Newton became a leading voice in the abolition of slavery in the British Empire.

The name Jesus contains the essence of the divine will. The arrival of the Son of God in human flesh was designed to accomplish human salvation from sin and death. Jesus was sent to free us from the profound bondage to sin.

Jesus! The name above all names. The name *Jesus* means "Savior." In the original Hebrew it is pronounced *Yehoshua*, shortened to *Yoshua*, which is translated in the Old Testament as *Joshua*. But the name had to be matched in truth and life by the one carrying it. There have been many boys named Joshua. Only one lived, suffered, died, and was raised for us. It is this Jesus who captures human hearts and frees them for heaven. It is this Jesus whom we praise!

> **Dear name! The rock on which I build,**
> **My shield and hiding place;**
> **My neverfailing treasury filled**
> **With boundless stories of grace. Amen.**
> ("How Sweet the Name of Jesus Sounds," by John Newton)

DAVID H. BENKE

Matthew 5:16

Leave Your Light On

In the same way, let your light shine before men, that they may see your good deeds and praise your Father in heaven. Matthew 5:16

There's nothing more frustrating than driving up and down a dark street, looking for an address, and none of the houses have any lights on, including, apparently, the one you are looking for … the home to which you have been invited. This is an area that you are not very familiar with, and you've had a hard time even finding the right street. Now you are creeping along, peering into the darkness, not even sure you are in the right block, wondering which side of the road you should try. When you finally do find the right house, it sure doesn't seem very inviting.

We invite people to our homes all the time. If our invitation is not very sincere, perhaps a salesman that we couldn't get rid of, we're not very helpful. But if we are excited about our guests' coming, we give them good directions, we describe landmarks, we leave the lights on, and we eagerly greet them. How much more excited, then, could we be than when we invite people into our Father's home?

As we, by the power of the Spirit, witness the love of Jesus Christ to other people, we need to leave our lights on. As people see our lights, the joy that radiates from us, the surety of our salvation, the fruit of the Spirit that dwell within, they will feel invited; they will feel welcome.

Dear Lord Jesus, help us by the power of Your Spirit to shine before all people, and give us Your message of salvation to share. Amen.

KEVIN PARVIZ

Matthew 6:33

Writing the Right Check

But seek first His kingdom and His righteousness, and all these things will be given to you as well. Matthew 6:33

A layman was making a call on a wealthy businessman, asking him to help in the Lord's work. The man wrote a check for $250 and handed it to him. Just then someone in his office brought in a message. The businessman read it with dismay.

"This message tells me I have just suffered a great loss," he said. "It makes a great difference in my affairs. I shall have to write you another check."

"I understand," said the layman and handed back the $250 check.

The businessman's checkbook was still open. He wrote another check and handed it to the layman, who read it with amazement.

"But this check is for $1000," he gasped. "Haven't you made a mistake?"

"No," said the businessman. "That message was really from God. It read, 'Do not store up for yourselves treasures on earth'" (Matthew 6:19).

That man had his priorities in proper order. He had placed the kingdom of God first and his material affairs second.

How often do we put ourselves first and the "things that come from the Spirit of God" (1 Corinthians 2:14) *second?*

God says, "My son, give *Me* your heart and let your eyes keep to My ways" (Proverbs 23:26). Oh, may we always lovingly respond, "With all my heart … I will obey *Your* decrees" (Psalm 119:145).

Summed up, always place Jesus first, Others second, and Yourself third. Then you will truly have J-O-Y.

Lord, give me the J-O-Y that only comes when living for You. In Jesus' name. Amen.

DONALD L. DEFFNER

Matthew 7:7

Set and Achieve Positive Goals

Ask and it will be given to you; seek and you will find; knock and the door will be opened to you. Matthew 7:7

Janet was in debt. She bought things on impulse, never balanced her checkbook, and purchased expensive gifts for friends. Janet often said she wished she were debt free, but she never took steps to change the condition of her personal finances. Eventually Janet died broke and in debt even though she had earned an excellent salary during her 35-year career.

If we are ever to reach our goals, we must take appropriate steps to get on the right track. First, we must ask for what we need. This includes praying to God. It also includes asking for professional advice or feedback from friends about what is needed to make progress in the desired direction.

Next, we must search out the information we need. Research may be involved. We can find information in books, articles, and other published materials that will help us in our quest. The third step is to start taking positive action based on the information discovered in the first two steps.

Ask. Seek. Knock. When Jesus gave this outline, He was speaking of reaching our heavenly goal: Ask God for forgiveness and eternal life. Seek God's Word. Knock on the door of heaven and Jesus will open it to you—He is the key. Jesus' outline works for heavenly goals and earthly goals. Try it today.

Jesus, give us wisdom in asking, discernment in seeking, and courage in knocking on the doors of opportunity. Amen.

BOBBIE REED

Matthew 7:12

How to Love Your Neighbor

So in everything, do to others what you would have them do to you, for this sums up the Law and the Prophets. Matthew 7:12

This is the New Testament version of the Golden Rule, and in the context of the Bible it is usually considered the summary of the second table of the Law, namely, to love our neighbor just as we love ourselves.

It is not always easy to treat others the way we would like to be treated. Some people have a way of aggravating us or of rubbing us the wrong way. It seems to take extra effort to be civil to these kinds of people.

The Gospel is the Good News that God did for us infinitely more than we could ever hope to do for others or for ourselves. God threw away all the scales and all the other ways to measure or calculate fairness. The last thing we need or should want is for God to be fair. If God were fair to us, we would die in our sins, in despair and without hope.

The same Sermon on the Mount that includes today's reading also says that Jesus Himself is the fulfillment of the Law. We do not relate to God on the basis of whether we keep the Law, but on the basis of Jesus Christ and His unconditional promise that our sins are forgiven through His life, death, and resurrection for us.

We are in good stead with God because He has reached down to us in grace and forgiveness. We can now relate to our neighbor, too, not on the basis of who he is or how she might act toward us, but on the basis of the relationship that God has with us in Jesus Christ. The heart of the matter is not what we might get back, but what we have already been given.

Gracious God, constantly remind us that Your Son is our only source of forgiveness and life, with You and with others. Equip us to share that forgiveness with our neighbor. Amen.

DAVID LUMPP

Matthew 7:24–27

The House That Lasts

Therefore everyone who hears these words of Mine and puts them into practice is like a wise man who built his house on the rock. Matthew 7:24

Reading the last words of Jesus' Sermon on the Mount leads us to one conclusion: Everyone is going to face the rains, the floods, and the winds. Jesus makes a comparison between two houses, one built on a rock and one on the sand. Both are besieged with problems.

Our faith is always being blown about and attacked by sin, death, and Satan. Marriage is like this, too; every marriage has its difficulties. Health, also, will not be perfect forever. A business venture, too, may be making a great profit today, but tomorrow? Everyone is besieged with problems.

God has given us a free will; as believers we have the option to pay attention to the words of Jesus or ignore them. That is the choice of rock or sand. We are drawn into the family of God in Baptism through the gift of faith. By the power of the Holy Spirit our ears are opened to the message of Jesus Christ so that we may build our life upon the rock of Jesus. It is only in Him that anyone can ever have hope to face problems, reconcile differences, or overcome obstacles. In this verse, Jesus is speaking of our faith life; but the same tenets can apply to our personal life, marriage, family, friendships, and business ventures. Jesus gives us His Word that our life might be as solid as the rock.

Lord, help my ears always to be opened to Your Word that my life may always be secure in You. Amen.

PAUL J. ALBERS

Matthew 9:38

Harassed and Helpless

Ask the Lord of the harvest, therefore, to send out workers into His harvest field. Matthew 9:38

My uncle's fields were beautiful at harvest time. The corn and oats were in full maturity. Living in northern Wisconsin, he always feared a drought or severe storm, an early frost or freeze. He depended on his sons and older brother to work long, hard hours to safely bring in the crops. Time was of the essence. He always felt a great sense of urgency about harvesting his crops before they were lost.

Our Lord is like-minded. Jesus had compassion on people who were harassed and helpless. For that reason Christ Jesus came into the world, redeeming us, bringing us back to God. "God our Savior … wants all men to be saved and to come to a knowledge of the truth" (1 Timothy 2:3–4). His prayer for workers to go into the harvest is our joyful invitation to go and tell others the great news of salvation. The Spirit will guide and empower us to carry out the command Jesus gave just before He ascended into heaven, "Go into all the world and preach the good news to all creation" (Mark 16:15). Time is short. The night is coming when no man can work. God give us willing hearts to harvest for Him.

Heavenly Father, make us mission minded. Give us a sense of urgency in our witnessing that many may hear the sweet news of salvation through us. Amen.

JAMES W. FREESE

Matthew 10:32

Tell the Story

Whoever acknowledges Me before men, I will also acknowledge him before My Father in heaven. Matthew 10:32

When your first child or grandchild was born, did people have to pry this news from you? Most likely, you sent announcements and told everyone you knew. It has been my experience that grandparents share pictures and tell stories about their wonderful grandchildren even to people who may not be very interested, including store clerks, doctors, and lawyers.

In this Matthew passage, God gives each of us the opportunity to be billboards for Jesus. We have the special privilege of telling the story of Jesus.

We are promised that if we acknowledge Jesus before other people we will be acknowledged by Christ Himself to the Father in heaven. There are many who desire an audience with the pope, an invitation to the White House, or a request to appear before the queen of England. Here is our opportunity to come into the presence of the King of kings. Can there be a more prestigious invitation than the one offered?

If we received an invitation to meet a head of state, it is unlikely that we would keep it a secret. Having an invitation from *the* King, let each one of us accept this special offer to tell our own story about the *King of kings* and *Lord of lords*.

Most of all, let us acknowledge Jesus to our children and to our grandchildren. How are you telling the story?

Dear Father, empower us to tell our story of Your redeeming love. Amen.

IDA MALL

Matthew 11:28–29

An Offer That Sounds Too Good to Be True

Come to Me, all you who are weary and burdened, and I will give you rest. Take My yoke upon you and learn from Me, for I am gentle and humble in heart, and you will find rest for your souls. Matthew 11:28–29

Everyone has heard the statement, "If it sounds too good to be true, it probably is." Many offers and promises sound awfully good until one tears away the packaging or looks at the fine print:

"You're poised to win $10,000,000.00."

"Save an additional 75% off the price"

"No matter how bad your credit, we'll put you in a new Cadillac with no worry about payments for one year."

"Just step up and try the game. Everybody wins."

Who hasn't been stung by some slick salesperson touting his or her goods, some commercial that guarantees riches and happiness, some investment scheme that promises a large monetary lifetime return? They urge us to buy, to invest, to indulge, but after we have, we discover the claims were at best exaggerated. The barker at the circus promises that "everybody wins," but what one wins isn't worth what you've paid to play the game.

In the process of believing and then discovering time and time again that a claim or a promise isn't true, we become cynical and distrustful. We even become skeptical of God's promises, such as the one made by Jesus in Matthew 11:28–29. He invites all who are burdened to come in faith to Him and He'll give them *rest*. It's an offer that seems too fantastic, but it's true. Even in doubt, we need to remember St. Paul's words, "He who did not spare His own Son, but gave Him up for us all—how will He not also, along with Him, graciously give us all things?" (Romans 8:32).

Lord God, we come to You, just as You invite us. Take our burdens, especially these we name. (Silently name your burdens.) As You promise, give us rest. Amen.

ROGER R. SONNENBERG

Matthew 18:19–20

Come Together in My Name

If two of you on earth agree about anything you ask for, it will be done for you by My Father in heaven. For where two or three come together in My name, there am I with them. Matthew 18:19–20

This is the age of the megachurch, congregations with memberships that total in the thousands. Some of these churches have their own orchestras, parking lot attendants, and even restaurants and aerobic classes. They offer families support services that go far beyond what small congregations can offer.

There is one thing, however, that both large churches and small churches must offer, and that is Christ. He is the reason we have church. He must be the center of all we do in our congregation. All our social and entertainment programs, as important and helpful as they are, cannot take the place of "the one thing that is needful."

There are very few places in the gospels where Jesus mentions the function of the church. In the previous verses of Matthew 18 He addresses the issue of church discipline. Now, He mentions that "where two or three come together in My name, there am I with them." Two or three is a pretty small congregation!

It doesn't matter what size our church is or what programs we offer our members. As long as we are meeting in the name of the Savior who suffered, died, and rose again for our salvation, we can be assured of His presence and blessing.

Heavenly Father, help us remember that "Christ is our cornerstone, On Him alone we build." Amen.

JIM WIEMERS

Matthew 19:14

Sowing Seeds for Eternity

Jesus said, "Let the little children come to Me, and do not hinder them, for the kingdom of heaven belongs to such as these." Matthew 19:14

I'm often amazed at my children's memory. "Daddy, do you remember?" often begins a recollection of an incident I'd long since forgotten, told to the most minute detail. They remember and embrace these early memories and tell them back with great joy.

How important a task parents have to tell the stories of our great God to their children at the earliest possible moment. Though not totally understood, these gems of the Gospel become an open door through which the children can run unhindered to their Savior Jesus. The message that Christ died for their sins and the sins of the whole world indeed assures them that their Father's arms are now open in welcome and will remain open until the day when they are safely in His arms in heaven. They will remember and retell these stories throughout their lives as they grow in faith through Word and Sacrament. Grooming them for discipleship, bracing them for their journey through life, assuring them of eternal life in heaven, we have a God-pleasing task. What greater joy could we have than to say, "The kingdom of heaven belongs to such as these"?

Lord Jesus, help us always to trust in You and witness to others with childlike faith. Make us eager to tell the great news of salvation to others. Amen.

JAMES W. FREESE

Matthew 19:16

God's Mercy Is the Key

What ... must I do to get eternal life? Matthew 19:16

Among the various times I can imagine Jesus laughing is when a man asked Him how to get eternal life. Jesus told him to keep the commandments. The man implied that he had—perfectly—since he was a boy.

At this point I can imagine a tremendous hilarity overtaking Jesus, as He mused: "As if you could! Ho! Ho! Ho!"

But Jesus did not laugh at the man. Instead, in the Mark version of the incident, we read that "Jesus looked at him and loved him" (Mark 10:21). Soon the man would turn his back on Jesus and leave. But even in the face of rejection, Jesus had compassion on him.

You and I fail utterly on our own. But throwing ourselves at the feet of Christ, we receive mercy.

Imagine another person has just arrived at the portals of heaven. A voice asks: "What is the password? Speak it and you may enter."

"The password?" the person replies tremulously. "Well, is it: 'Everyone who calls on the name of the Lord will be saved'?"

"No," replies the voice.

"The righteous will live by faith?"

"No."

"For God so loved the world that He gave ...?"

"Those are all true sayings," says the voice, "But they are not the password for which I listen today."

"Well, then, I give up," says the person.

"That's it! Come right on in!"

Lord, I throw myself on Your mercy, calling upon the name of Jesus. Amen.

DONALD L. DEFFNER

Matthew 25:31–46

Who Was That Masked Man?

The King will reply, "I tell you the truth, whatever you did for one of the least of these brothers of Mine, you did for Me." Matthew 25:40

Many adults today enjoyed the Lone Ranger as children. He was always the hero. As he rode away, the person whom he helped always asked the question, "Who was that masked man?"

Two images of that mask come to mind in this parable of Jesus. The persons who helped others, fed them, clothed them, visited them, did not remember or keep track of whom they helped or how often. "When did we see You hungry?" they asked Jesus. It is as if we mask our minds, not keeping track to mount up an account that should be repaid.

Further, the persons who helped did not consider anything about those they helped except their need. Not their skin color, not their personal hygiene, not whether they were handicapped, not their mental ability, only their need. The persons who helped were masked to anything but need.

This happens only when Jesus makes us His brothers and sisters in faith and enables us to make others His brothers and sisters in need. Then what excitement to hear Jesus say, "Come, you who are blessed by My Father; take your inheritance."

Merciful God, help us to be merciful to all as Your children. Amen.

PAUL J. ALBERS

Matthew 28:19

Go!

Therefore go and make disciples of all nations, baptizing them in the name of the Father and of the Son and of the Holy Spirit. Matthew 28:19

The most diversely populated county in the United States by race, ethnicity, and religion is Queens, New York. In several distinct square miles of Queens, more than 120 nationalities speaking 170 languages share a neighborhood. Reaching "all nations" may mean walking around the block!

But even if representatives from every nation on the planet rented rooms in your home, it would make no difference if the two-letter command of Christ were ignored. "Go!" says the risen Lord. Go. Go teach and baptize. Go in the strong name of the Trinity with grace in Word and Sacrament. Go.

So let's take one step. The first step. The most critical step in following the Great Commission. And our first step is to seize as individuals and as the church of God what is given in Holy Baptism. The first step is to walk in union with Father, Son, and Holy Spirit. The life of God is the gift received in Baptism. The Father's love, the Son's grace, the Spirit's fellowship—these are the prerequisites in the Christian spirit empowering the first toddling step. Our spirits are filled to overflowing with the dynamics of our triune, living God. And so we are compelled to go. We go—whether to Queens, New York, or Queensland, Australia—with God!

Oh, blessed, holy Trinity, be strong in me to speak and live Your mission each new day. Amen.

DAVID H. BENKE

Matthew 28:20

With Us Always

... teaching them to obey everything I have commanded you. And surely I am with you always, to the very end of the age. Matthew 28:20

This conclusion to the Great Commission is a great challenge to us. We don't like to be commanded. We are independent, free-thinking, stand-up-on-our-own Americans. While we obey most civil laws, we do so not because they are commands from authority but because we decide that to do so is best for us or because the penalty is severe enough to discourage us. Our attitude towards civil authority and law reflects our inner perversity and sinfulness. We treat God's Law in the same "flip" way, often thinking of the Ten Commandments as the Ten Suggestions.

As a Lutheran school teacher and principal, I have often pondered this verse, because in Christian education, we accept the responsibility of teaching children to obey everything Christ has commanded us. And children are no different from adults as they weigh their options in deciding whether to obey or disobey.

Our challenge here, however, is teaching not just for the acquisition of knowledge or skills so our students can make wise decisions. Our challenge is teaching God's Word so children desire to do no less than obey. Desire of the heart is a little hard to measure, but pastors, teachers, and parents work hard to nurture this.

The beauty of this challenge is the promise given in its conclusion. For we do not accept this responsibility alone. You notice, it does not say that "*if* you do these things, *then* I am with you always." No, the promise is, "Surely I *am* with you always." Jesus Christ through the Holy Spirit is our teacher. He resides within us and is with us always, whether we succeed or whether we fail. And when we do fail, He is there to forgive and restore us. What a great comfort, and what a great teacher.

Precious Lord, teach us and give us the strength to listen as You build the desire in our hearts to follow You. Amen.

KEVIN PARVIZ

Mark 6:31

A Quiet Place

Come with Me by yourselves to a quiet place and get some rest. Mark 6:31

Compassion fatigue. Burnout. Church-worker stress. These are some of the most dreaded maladies today. And they're afflicting the best kinds of people—those who want to help others in Christian love. There's just too much to do and too little time in which to do it! Counseling, teen problems, food pantries, handouts on the street, clothing drives, money for every cause in the book—compassion is stretched until the passion is wrung out of it.

Have your inner fires cooled? Has stress wrenched compassion from your heart? Jesus knows what you are facing. He saw His own followers pressed on all sides, fast-forwarding their prayers for healing, unable to stop and eat. He saw and stated simply, "Come with Me ... to a quiet place and get some rest." Stop, rest, find quiet, get away, refresh. These are the urgings of our Lord Himself. Remember, He regularly withdrew to be alone and pray.

However, remember as you face your fatigue that the mercies of your Lord endure forever. Remember that His compassion fails not. Indeed, the constant compassion of God for fallen humanity includes you. His refreshment for you is in the promise of His constant presence. And when you have been restored to full strength, it will be His hand lifting you up, His arm on your shoulder sending you back out into the world, and His love in your acts of energetic compassion.

Dear Lord, give me the room to rest so I can be restored to serve You more. Amen.

DAVID H. BENKE

Mark 7:32–37

Ephphatha! Be Opened!

He looked up to heaven and with a deep sigh said to him, *"Ephphatha!"* (which means, "Be opened!"). At this, the man's ears were opened, his tongue was loosened and he began to speak plainly. Mark 7:34–35

Mark's astonishing account tells of our ever-caring Lord Jesus healing a man who was deaf and slow of speech. He did so away from the crowd, personally, privately, completely. He touched the man, fixed His eyes on heaven and said, "Be opened!" Note the exclamation point! Mark is the gospel writer who so often used the word *immediately*. He could have done so here, too. The man's tongue was loosened, and he began to speak plainly.

"Ephphatha!" What a fitting watchword for Christians. God's care and concern are so totally focused on us. Touched by the personal healing of Christ in our souls, freed from eternal death, blessed according to our most detailed, intimate, and specific needs, how can our response be anything other than praise, adoration, thanksgiving, and telling forth what great things God has done for us?

Look at the people's response. They were overwhelmed and, glorifying God, they exclaimed, "He has done *everything* well." May the people's response also be ours as our Lord opens us to worship, work, and witness in word and deed, so that others, seeing Christ through our lives, might also exclaim, "He has done *everything* well!"

O Lord, open my lips; and my mouth will declare Your praise. Amen.

JAMES W. FREESE

Mark 8:36

Things Don't Buy Happiness

What good is it for a man to gain the whole world, yet forfeit his soul?
Mark 8:36

Many people are fooled into believing that things buy happiness. Parents promote such thinking by saturating their children with lots of things. It starts in the "nursery of plenty" and goes all the way into college where they're given full tuition and money on the side to buy the term papers they don't have time to write.

P. T. Barnum spent his life proving the statement he coined: "There's a sucker born every minute." Unfortunately, people who truly believe that money will buy happiness are suckers. They have been duped into believing something that isn't true. If it were true, why do so many people who have so much money seem so unhappy? Why do some end their own lives? Why do others jump from one self-help guru to another? The answer is simple: Because happiness is never found in things.

Happiness is found only in relationship—relationship with God and with one another. Such relationships are made possible only through Jesus Christ. Though we had separated ourselves from God because of sin, He reconnected us. He brought us back into relationship through the perfect life He lived for us, through the death He died for us, through the resurrection, which proclaimed victory over sin and death. In being connected back to God through faith in Jesus Christ, we are brought back into relationship not only with God but also with one another.

Lord God, accept our thanks for bringing us into relationship with You and others through Jesus Christ. Keep us from becoming foolish by thinking we can buy happiness. Amen.

ROGER R. SONNENBERG

Mark 11:24

The Answer—Yes

Whatever you ask for in prayer, believe that you have received it, and it will be yours. Mark 11:24

A preschooler was traveling with her family on Interstate 10 over the Atchafalaya basin from Baton Rouge to Houston. It was dark. The darkness was caused both by the time of day and even more by the fog. Because of the fog, one could only see a few feet in front. By the quietness in the car, it was apparent that all were afraid. This fear was heightened when the family met a car going the wrong way on the interstate. At that point, the preschooler inquired if it was all right to ask Jesus to take away the fog.

Trying to make sure that the proper theological answer was provided, the parents carefully explained that God could say yes, but He might say no, or He might say wait a while.

With the conclusion of the answer, the child prayed aloud that Jesus take the fog away. Within five minutes, the fog was completely gone. One could see the stars and, more important, the road very clearly.

Did God take the fog away as requested in the prayer? I don't know. But as the mother of that child, I know that His Word says that He has the power to respond with a resounding yes. The God who created the heavens and earth, who raised the dead to life, and who forgives sins has the power to make and take away fog.

Have you prayed today?

Lord, help us to pray with the faith of a child. Amen.

IDA MALL

Mark 16:15

For Laypeople Only

Go into all the world. Mark 16:15

Although it is important to be a clergyman, in its place, it is important to be a layperson anyplace. For anyplace, as opposed to church, is where important decisions that affect our world are being made. In the layperson's world big things are happening: nuclear power has been discovered, lend-lease, computer chips, and Hula Hoops have been invented. Clergy ponder, dream, hope, pray, and have magnificent visions. Every last one of those is essential. But it is not in church where history's crucial acts are performed or the world's battles are joined. Even the invasion of Satan's kingdom by the army of Christ occurs in the lay world, not in the world of the clergy. Clergy train the troops, map the strategy, and equip the army. But the job is done be laypeople.

Among Christians it's almost a truism to remark that the need of the day is to get people into church. There is a need, too, to get Christian people out of the church. It is part of God's strategy that His people go into all the world, invade it, and take possession of it in His name.

In the final analysis it's not a matter of getting Christians out of the church, exactly. It's a matter of getting the church out of its sanctuary, out of its preoccupation with its own machinery and interests, and into the battlefield. Interestingly the Bible does not say, "Whether you worship or pray or whatever churchly thing you do, do it all for the glory of God." It says, "Whether you eat or drink or whatever (day to day, homely thing) you do, do it all for the glory of God" (1 Corinthians 10:31).

I would not be of the world, Lord and King, but in it to do Your will on earth as it is done in heaven. Amen.

ARNOLD KUNTZ

Luke 1:37

Pray Believingly

For nothing is impossible with God. Luke 1:37

What an awesome God we serve!
God formed the world by a word.
God parted the Red Sea.
God provided manna for the Israelites.
God brought down the walls of Jericho.
Jesus turned water into wine.
Jesus healed the blind, the lame, and the sick.
Jesus walked on the water.
The Holy Spirit empowered Peter and the disciples to speak up
  for God.
The Holy Spirit brings comfort to those in pain.
The Holy Spirit convicts the world of sin.
God is involved in all areas of our lives. Knowing this gives us the courage to come boldly to the throne of grace and to make our requests known. No matter how dark the night or how impossible the situation seems, we can have hope. Nothing is impossible with God!

Therefore, if God chooses to intervene in our lives, nothing will stop that intervention. So when you are faced with a difficult choice, pray for guidance. When you are hurt, pray for comfort. When you need wisdom, pray for it. When all odds are against you, pray.

We have limitations. God does not. Pray believingly.

Lord, don't let my fears limit my faith. Remind me of Your power and Your sovereignty. Amen.

BOBBIE REED

Luke 2:9–12

Do Not Be Afraid

An angel of the Lord appeared to them, and the glory of the Lord shone around them, and they were terrified. But the angel said to them, "Do not be afraid. I bring you good news of great joy that will be for all the people. Today in the town of David a Savior has been born to you; He is Christ the Lord. This will be a sign to you: You will find a baby wrapped in cloths and lying in a manger." Luke 2:9–12

As parents we were so excited about Jacob's first birthday party. We wanted it to be special, but then Jacob came down with a virus. The seriousness of his illness became apparent when the doctor insisted he be hospitalized.

A stern-faced, bulbous nurse sarcastically said to us, "Your son will never get better unless you make him stay under the oxygen tent."

"But how can I when he cries all the time?" Mom's plea drifted on dead, and unsympathetic, ears.

My wife knew she had to try to follow orders and so she came up with an ingenious plan. She placed Jacob gently into the oxygen tent, and, as awkward as it was, she climbed into the small crib with Jacob. The walls of the oxygen tent slapped against her face as she tried to make herself comfortable.

In an even more sublime way, God did the same thing for us at Christmas. God left heaven, came to earth, and climbed in with us. Our spiritual sickness made it necessary. There was no other way to bring healing to the world. "The Word became flesh and made His dwelling among us" (John 1:14). Literally, He "pitched a tent" alongside ours. What love! Is it any wonder that the angel said to the frightened shepherds, "Do not be afraid"?

Lord God, for coming to earth, for becoming flesh, for us, we give You our thanks. Amen.

ROGER R. SONNENBERG

Luke 2:49

The Focused Life

"Why were you searching for Me?" He asked. "Didn't you know I had to be in My Father's house?" Luke 2:49

If you want to succeed—really succeed—you need to focus on your task. So say athletes, business professionals, farmers. And Jesus, in Luke 9:57–62. He not only taught His followers to be focused, but He lived a focused life, even as a lost twelve-year-old.

Accidentally left behind, He found His way into His Father's house. Maybe He had never left it. It was the logical place to be for one focused on His Father's will and plan. While in the Father's house He went about His Father's work for the young: listening, asking questions, and answering as asked.

Later in life He continued identifying with His Father's will when He "resolutely set out for Jerusalem" (Luke 9:51), even though He knew that road led to the cross. But He knew more. It would lead to crowns: His and ours. Such focused intentionality!

Within the limitations of our humanity, redeemed children of today need lives just as focused.

Lord, give us clear vision, needed courage, and appropriate endurance to live focused lives until, by Your Spirit's work, we can claim the crown You earned for us on the cross. Amen.

CHARLES S. MUELLER

Luke 6:38

A Divine Formula That Never Fails

Give and it will be given to you ... with the measure you use, it will be measured to you. Luke 6:38

This verse scares some Christians. They'd rather that Jesus had said something like, "Charity begins at home" or "Take care of your own responsibilities—first—and if some is left over help others, too." Truth to tell that's exactly what He said. But He said it this way: "Want to get? Give. The getting always comes, whether it's a matter of money or love. But *after* the giving."

For almost 40 years I've asked tithers, "Did you get when you gave?" They always say yes. Sideline interpreters of my question hasten to insert, "But you mean satisfaction, pleasure, and joy—right?" To which the tithers chorus, "That, too. But we have received money, too. And more. We learned how life works."

With that they tell of how forgiving brought them forgiveness; giving love returned as more love; understanding toward others blossomed as understanding toward them; encouragement generated encouragement. And on and on and on.

God's way is that first you give and then you get—in kind. I can't find any givers who disagree.

Lord, thank You for giving first that we might through Your grace get what we need. Now help us to give from that bounty, whatever it is. Amen.

CHARLES S. MUELLER

Luke 11:13

Father Knows Best

If you then, though you are evil, know how to give good gifts to your children, how much more will your Father in heaven give the Holy Spirit to those who ask Him! Luke 11:13

Well? What do you think? Do most parents know how to care for their children? They must, for about the most common reluctant commendations of even evil people is, "He/she was a caring father/mother." The police have captured some wanted men in the past by keeping watch of their children, confident that the criminal father would contact his child.

Jesus makes His point: If it's true that bad folks can do good things for their sons and daughters, just imagine the great good that the author of good, the heavenly Father, will do for His! No evil comes from Him. No harm hides within His active care. Even the worst things that befall us, Paul testifies, are worked by our loving Lord into something very good (see Romans 8:28).

Do you want proof that that is true? Look at Calvary, on a Friday that only children of the Father could call good. What a great thing He did there for us!

Father, teach us to live confident that all things are in Your loving hands. Amen.

CHARLES S. MUELLER

Luke 11:28

The Basics: Hear and Do

Blessed rather are those who hear the word of God and obey it. Luke 11:28

Jesus was not about to be distracted in His ministry even if the distraction was someone who said something nice about His mother. After hearing Him speak, a woman in the crowd said, "Blessed is the mother who gave You birth and nursed You." Jesus responded with our text. In essence He said, "There are a lot of nice things in life, but when it comes down to it, nothing is nicer than the hearing, and then doing, of what God wants."

That's the sequence. First comes hearing. Then, hopefully, the doing. Doing never precedes hearing. Godly hearing gathers the data on which godly doing is based. Hearing God is essential to the Christian life.

That means that the hearing that takes place in Bible study, in worship, and in Christian conversation is important—fundamental. It is the point of beginning, but it's not the end of it. The end of each listening session is on the other side of doing.

Jesus, You heard Your Father's will and obediently acted. As a result we have been saved. We praise You for Your hearing and Your doing. Amen.

CHARLES S. MUELLER

Luke 12:7

Talk about Attention to Detail!

Indeed, the very hairs of your head are all numbered. Don't be afraid; you are worth more than many sparrows. Luke 12:7

Jesus had just pointed out the birds in their commonness, their number, the way God cares for them. He stressed to His listeners that the Father knows the birds, *each and every one of them!*

And then He pushes the illustration either to absurdity or awe by adding that the Father even keeps track of the hair count of every human head!

But neither the birds or human hair are the point of His conversation. The point is us. The same God who has all that detailed, technical curiosity about birds and hair has an even more intense, watchful concern for every one of us. So says Jesus.

And proof? Then and now the proof is in the redemptive work of Christ so clearly spelled out in Scripture. He not only died to save all His children but sent His Spirit that we might believe in what He has done. Some God!

And if all that's so, what's to worry? About anything?

Lamb of God, who takes away the sins of the world, send the Spirit that we may have faith in You and all that You do for us. Amen.

CHARLES S. MUELLER

Luke 12:15

It's Not What You Own but What Owns You

Then He said to them, "Watch out! Be on your guard against all kinds of greed; a man's life does not consist in the abundance of his possessions." Luke 12:15

We know there are no trailer hitches on hearses. But judging by how much we all own, maybe there ought to be. What a commentary those storage sheds are on America! After we've loaded suitcases, houses, and cars, we still need more room for all our stuff. We really *are* materialistic, almost without conscious effort! That's why these words of the Lord are so important. He's telling us to watch out! There's more to life than what you own!

All our "stuff" will be destroyed when our Lord returns. Only people will survive. Check out Matthew 24 and 25 for some of the details. Meanwhile, what do we do with the stuff we have?

Use it, of course. That's why He gave it to us. Use it for things He would approve of and in ways that He would appreciate. Don't store it. Use it responsibly. Now.

Lord, I thank You for everything You have given me. Help me steward it as You want. Amen.

CHARLES S. MUELLER

Luke 12:27–28, 31

Keeping Perspective

Consider how the lilies grow. They do not labor or spin. Yet I tell you, not even Solomon in all his splendor was dressed like one of these. If that is how God clothes the grass of the field, which is here today, and tomorrow is thrown into the fire, how much more will He clothe you, O you of little faith! ... But seek His kingdom, and these things will be given to you as well. Luke 12:27–28, 31

Because of dental surgery, a tuba player in a large philharmonic orchestra was unable to play for several weeks. He saw this as an opportunity to actually sit down and listen to the famous orchestra. He reserved the best seat in the auditorium. He was thrilled as he heard the orchestra play. Afterwards, he ran backstage and shouted, "You were wonderful. Do you know that for the first time I realized the symphony doesn't go 'oompah, oompah, oompah' all the time?" The tuba player had gotten a new perspective.

Sometimes we can lose perspective. We get caught up in our indispensability, thinking we're in control of our destinies. Thus, we worry. The truth of the matter is we would have reason to worry if our destinies depended on us.

Jesus makes it clear that we shouldn't worry. We should instead "seek His kingdom, and these things will be given to [us]." He reminds us that we should at times stand back and see the world from a broader, fuller perspective. See that God has not abandoned His people. Be reminded that He loved His people enough to rescue them from death, sin, and the power of the devil. When He arose, He made it clear, "I'll never leave you." The one who loved us so much says, "Consider how the lilies grow ... If that is how God clothes the grass of the field, which is here today, and tomorrow is thrown into the fire, how much more will He clothe you."

Gracious Father, keep us from losing perspective by thinking we're in control of our destinies. May we "seek [Your] kingdom," assured that all we need will be given to us. Amen.

ROGER R. SONNENBERG

Luke 12:32

Do Not Be Anxious

Do not be afraid, little flock, for your Father has been pleased to give you the kingdom. Luke 12:32

Anxiety is a big issue in life for many people. It is fostered by concern over our health, our family, our job, and our financial security. Anxiety can drive us into thinking that we are responsible for getting ourselves out of whatever mess we're in. As we attempt to get out of the quagmire of our anxiety, we only seem to succeed in plunging ourselves deeper.

Anxiety is really a matter of misplaced trust—trusting ourselves instead of God. We find it difficult to take God at His Word, trusting that He knows what we need. How could a God who seems so remote know the ordeals that we have to suffer on the human scene? In answer to our doubts about God's care for us, we build up our own self-sufficient kingdoms—kingdoms in which we are the masters of our destiny. We try to be the creators of our own lifestyles and providers for all our desires and needs. We slave away at getting the things that make for the good life.

Slaving away is probably the best description because it aptly describes our condition before God. We are enslaved to sin, to our evil desires, to our self-centeredness. We try to earn what we deserve—and we succeed because we have earned death.

Our trust has been misplaced. And our anxiety grows. But God in His lavish love gives us the gift of His kingdom. It is to be His kingdom, not ours; His righteousness, not our pride or efforts. God, "who did not spare His own Son, but gave Him up for us all" (Romans 8:32), gives us the kingdom of His grace, mercy, and forgiveness. His Son, Jesus, took a cross, the load of our sin, and cruel death to free us from anxiety, to relieve us of the burden of trying to play king of our own kingdoms. Through Christ's death and resurrection we have been made children of God, inheritors of the kingdom of God. We can trust our Lord to provide for us. Thus we follow in the footsteps of His lavish love.

With You, Lord, I have cast my lot;
O faithful God, forsake me not,
To you my soul commending.
Lord, be my stay
And lead the way
Now and when life is ending. Amen.

("In You, I Have Put My Trust," by Adam Reusner)

HENRY GERIKE

Luke 12:35

The Duty Roster

Be dressed ready for service and keep your lamps burning. Luke 12:35

The preponderance of Christians are in the receiving line. After all, Christianity isn't something we do, not at its heart, but what God does, for us, in Christ Jesus. A disciple, nonetheless, is someone who has moved to the serving end of the table. Disciples are Christians who have gone to work, and sometimes at considerable cost and no small effort.

In discipleship we do not enter upon a broad and comfortable way. As often as not the road is narrow and full of demanding potholes, and sometimes it calls for painful privations. Discipleship doesn't simplify life or make it easier. In fact, if you are the kind who is inordinately concerned about a dichondra lawn, an arbored patio, or just a roof over your head, discipleship may not be your cup of tea. Disciples are guaranteed no minimum wage and offered no fringe benefits. I'm not just making this up. Jesus said it; He said it again and again, knowing, I suppose, we wouldn't really believe it at first: "Foxes have holes [so if the safety of that appeals to you, be a fox] and birds of the air have nests [be a bird, if protection is that high on your list of priorities], but the Son of Man has no place to lay His head" (Matthew 8:20). Follow Jesus, be His disciple, and you can pretty well count on some sleepless nights.

We like to think of our Christian faith in terms of its comfort and peace and all the things it freely gives us. All that is true. But so is this: There is what someone has called "the stormy north side of Christ." To follow Christ, where He leads, to be His disciple, entails some sacrifice on your part, too.

Holy Spirit, who has made my heart Your dwelling place, raise up out of me the fruits of my faith and make me Your faithful servant. Amen.

ARNOLD KUNTZ

Luke 15:4

Lost and Found

Suppose one of you has a hundred sheep and loses one of them. Does he not leave the ninety-nine in the open country and go after the lost sheep until he finds it? Luke 15:4

Lost. Lost and in trouble. In the gloom of the subterranean parking garage, I got lost 14 floors beneath New York's World Trade Center. My heartbeat began to quicken, my mind went to jelly, my voice quavered as I sought out assistance, my steps faltered as one door after another on one wall after another denied external access. Finally, the lights of an incoming motorist lit my exit path. But the sensation of being lost and in trouble is in my bones now. I don't want to be there again.

Lost. Lost and in trouble. As Martin Luther stated in his explanation to the Second Article, each of us is, by nature, a "lost and condemned person" before God. The parable of the lost sheep does not apply first of all to someone "out there." It applies to each of us.

Found. Found and safe. My Good Shepherd has hunted me down, time and time again, out there on my own. My Good Shepherd has reached for me when I was caught in the brambles over the edge of the cliff and picked me up safe. My Good Shepherd has cared for me when the wounds and worries of life have bruised and battered my soul. My Good Shepherd has claimed me. Kept me. Brought me back.

This lost sheep is found.

Loving Jesus, thank You for finding this lost sheep. Amen.

DAVID H. BENKE

Luke 15:10

The Angels' Party

There is rejoicing in the presence of the angels of God over one sinner who repents. Luke 15:10

It is Sunday morning. In the early service, identical twins, John and Thomas, are baptized. At the late service, five adults, Marilyn, Carlos, Shauntel, Martin, and Lois, are received into membership by adult Baptism and reaffirmation of faith. As God's people, are we ecstatic and happy? Are we concerned about the length of the service? Are the angels rejoicing?

Although I don't have a complete understanding or clear picture of what is meant by "rejoicing in the presence of the angels," this verse is sandwiched among the parables of the lost sheep, lost coin, and lost son. In each of the parables there is great concern or sorrow over the loss and great joy and excitement over finding the lost item or person.

It would seem that the greatest party on earth would be appropriate when a person who was lost is found just like the party the father had for the prodigal (lost) but found son. For us, does that happen when a person is called into a saving relationship with Christ by the Word or through Baptism? As God's people, do we rejoice when the lost are found? There are parties for school graduations and weddings. It is most fitting that we have parties for Baptisms and confirmations.

Let us join in the biggest and best party with the angels as each and every person is added to the Book of Life.

Dear Father, thank You for adding our names to Your book. Help us to reach out to others. Amen.

IDA MALL

Luke 15:20

Reconcile Quickly

So he got up and went to his father. But while he was still a long way off, his father saw him and was filled with compassion for him; he ran to his son, threw his arms around him and kissed him. Luke 15:20

Joan and Sally argued, said hurtful words, and broke off a three-year friendship. Although they each missed the other, neither would pick up the telephone to apologize. The breach lasted six long months.

One day Joan heard from a mutual friend that Sally's daughter was seriously ill and near death. Without a minute's hesitation, Joan grabbed her car keys and drove to the hospital. Sally looked up as Joan entered the little girl's room and saw that Joan's eyes were filled with love and concern. Sally reached out to Joan and the two women hugged. "I'm sorry," Joan whispered.

"Me, too," Sally responded, regretting the lost six months of her friend's companionship and support.

How often do we let petty issues create a rift in precious friendships? Our pride may keep us from apologizing or forgiving or both. So few of the issues we argue or disagree about are of eternal significance. Jesus said that we ought to reconcile with one another. He said that before we worship God we need to ensure that all is right between us and others. And often, when we do reach out or give in a little, we find that the other person is ready to resume the relationship. If you have a relationship that needs repair, begin the effort of reconciliation right away.

There was a rift between us and God; but Jesus reconciled the relationship through His death on the cross. We have His forgiveness to strengthen us as we forgive others.

God, help me to keep the eternal values in perspective and to be willing to reconcile the relationships in my life. Amen.

BOBBIE REED

Luke 16:13

A Priceless Treasure

No servant can serve two masters. Either he will hate the one and love the other, or he will be devoted to one and despise the other. You cannot serve both God and Money. Luke 16:13

One evening on our college choir tour, four of us in the choir stayed at the home of an extremely wealthy couple. They had the best of everything. After supper the husband said, "Boys, how do you like this place? I want you to know something: Everything I have here is a gift from God. He's the most important part of our lives." How refreshing! What a humble yet powerful witness this man gave! He liked the gifts; he *loved* the giver.

In his explanation of the First Article of the Apostles' Creed, Martin Luther gives a lengthy list of blessings from the hand of our gracious Father. The greatest gift He has given us is the gift of redemption through faith in Christ Jesus, our priceless treasure. With our eyes focused on Him, all other blessings fall into their proper place. Money, or material blessings, will be left behind when we close our eyes in death. Our higher good, Christ Jesus, offers life eternal in heaven for free to those who believe in Him. "No eye has seen, no ear has heard, no mind has conceived what God has prepared for those who love Him" (1 Corinthians 2:9). Yes, we should love and trust in God above all things, loving Him who first loved us.

Lord, our God, help us to love and trust in You above all things, always holding You as our eternal, priceless treasure. Amen.

JAMES W. FREESE

Luke 23:43

The Blink of Death

Jesus answered him, "I tell you the truth, today you will be with Me in paradise." Luke 23:43

Blink your eyes. That went quickly, didn't it. Did the darkness during the blink bother you? I doubt it. "What darkness?" you might ask.

As children of God, His very own, redeemed by Christ Jesus, we are never away from Him. He is always with us. In Him there is no darkness at all. We can be in one of two places: earth or heaven. There is no "in between" with God. There is no waiting period at death to enter heaven. The transfer is immediate.

Jesus' assuring words to the thief on the cross are His words to every Christian staring death in the face: *truth, today, paradise*. The psalmist writes, "When I awake I am still with You" (139:18). So it will be with us.

When Jesus ascended into heaven He said, "Surely I am with you always, to the very end of the age" (Matthew 28:20). Each day He assures us, "Today I am with you," until finally one day He will tell us, "Today you are with Me in paradise." As Christians, we live a blink away from eternity. May He make us ever ready for that great day when we are translated from here to eternity.

Abide among us always,
O Lord, our faithful friend,
And take us to Your mansions
When time and world shall end. Amen.

("Abide with Us, Our Savior," by Josua Stegmann)

JAMES W. FREESE

Luke 24:32

Let Us See Jesus

They asked each other, "Were not our hearts burning within us while He talked with us on the road and opened the Scriptures to us?" Luke 24:32

The men on the road to Emmaus were in a quandary. They thought that Jesus of Nazareth was a great prophet who was going to redeem Israel; however, their Jewish rulers handed Him over to the Romans to be crucified. Now, they were hearing stories that Jesus was no longer in the grave, that He was alive. They weren't certain what to believe.

Then the stranger walking with them (who was actually Jesus Himself) opened the Scriptures to them and explained how the Old Testament prophets had foretold the very events that had just taken place. Later, when Jesus shared a meal with them, their eyes were opened and they recognized Him. After finally comprehending the truth, they marveled, "Were not our hearts burning within us?"

Salvation comes to us as the Holy Spirit works faith in us through the Word and through the gift of Baptism. We may not necessarily feel a "burning in our hearts," but we may be assured that we are saved by faith, not by feeling.

Just as Jesus appeared and spoke to the men at a time when they were seeking the truth, so also will He "appear" to us as we seek Him through His Holy Word.

O Holy Spirit, open our eyes to see Jesus as we seek His guidance and assurance of our salvation through Your Holy Word, the Bible. In His name we pray. Amen.

JIM WIEMERS

John 1:1–4

The Light of Men

In the beginning was the Word, and the Word was with God, and the Word was God. He was with God in the beginning. Through Him all things were made; without Him nothing was made that has been made. In Him was life, and that life was the light of men. John 1:1–4

Why do we decorate our businesses, homes, and churches with so many lights at Christmas? How do we explain our penchant for feasting and merrymaking at that time of year? Some might say it is because we are foolishly trying to keep the darkness of evil and sin away from our doors.

But our lights and merrymaking are more than that. The reasons we light them are deeper than that. Down deep within us, we might say primordially deep within us, is a remembrance that says darkness wasn't what God intended. Somewhere deep within our psyches is the recollection that God intended that we should have a close, loving relationship with Him. Our celebrations and feasts are responses to the way it once was and the way we wish it could be.

The only way God's original intent for His world can be restored is to begin all over again! So the evangelist John tells us that is just what God did. He gave new life, spiritual life, to us by the birth of His Son, Jesus Christ.

In the darkness of the night around Bethlehem, the heavens opened and the angels sang of God's bright Word and the glory of the Lord shone around the shepherds. Later darkness closed in again for three hours over Calvary. But in the bright light of Easter morning, sin and death are overcome and God's new creation is complete!

Creating God, shine Your new life within me and renew the joy of Your salvation, through Jesus Christ. Amen.

DONALD W. SANDMANN

John 1:12–14

He Pitched His Tent among Us

Yet to all who received Him, to those who believed in His name, He gave the right to become children of God—children born not of natural descent, nor of human decision or a husband's will, but born of God. The Word became flesh and made His dwelling among us. We have seen His glory, the glory of the One and Only, who came from the Father, full of grace and truth. John 1:12–14

Children of God—that's what God calls us. He "gave [us] the right to become children of God" as He brought us to faith in Christ. We who have been "born of God" live as God's children.

Really? This pastor hasn't always lived as a child of God. In fact, it was at the time of the celebration of Christ's birth that he acted very unchildlike toward the young children God had placed in his home. There was always so much to do on Christmas Eve that the normal tendency of children to dawdle and to take one last look at the Christmas tree became very annoying. He told his children so in unkind terms. Thank God, he also had a wife who called him to task by her tears.

But even tears would not have been enough to change this pastor for very long. After all, there's always the Lord's business to do! But God made it His business to come and sit down among us. "The Word became flesh and made His dwelling [pitched His tent] among us." He came to bring restoration and renewal to our relationship with the Father. He also brings restoration and renewal wherever we have tortured and twisted our relationships with other human beings.

Eternal Son of God, live among us that we may live in You. Heal our broken relationships and bring us all at last to the home You have prepared for us. Amen.

DONALD W. SANDMANN

John 1:29

Look, the Lamb of God

The next day John saw Jesus coming toward him and said, "Look, the Lamb of God, who takes away the sin of the world!" John 1:29

Certain phrases in Scripture stand out like a beacon, tying an event or an individual into the entire history of God's dealing with creation and His people. One of these is John the Baptist's acclamation about Jesus: "Look, the Lamb of God!"

An unblemished lamb was sacrificed every year at Passover in remembrance of God's delivering His people from Egypt centuries before. As St. John unfolds the events of Holy Week we see the significance of this "Lamb of God" title as Christ is led to His slaughter on Golgotha at the precise hour when the lambs for the Passover celebration are being sacrificed in the temple. Jesus was indeed the final Lamb to be sacrificed, this time on the altar of the cross. We are eternally grateful to God for that sacrifice. In fact, we commemorate that sacrifice every time we come to the Lord's Table to receive the body and blood of Christ.

But two questions remain to be asked. Can we picture John the Baptist pointing to Christ and saying, "Look"? More important, do we point others to Him? The church of God is not a comfortable capsule in which we are transported to the throne of the Lamb in heaven. It is the freedom train through whose windows we wave and beckon to people to "Get on board, little children, for there's room for many a more!" To whom will you beckon today?

Lamb of God, You take away the sins of the world. Hear our prayer for mercy, and help us to sound the call for others to hear. Amen.

DONALD W. SANDMANN

John 3:16

The Gospel in a Nutshell

For God so loved the world that He gave His one and only Son, that whoever believes in Him shall not perish but have eternal life. John 3:16

Occasionally, we see someone in the bleachers at a baseball or football game holding up a sign bearing the Bible reference John 3:16. What is the significance of this verse? Why do we remember it and proclaim it to the world?

It is one of the best remembered and loved verses in the Bible, frequently referred to as the Gospel in a nutshell, because in it we learn of God's entire plan for salvation: "For God so loved the world that He gave His one and only Son, ..." We were helpless to save ourselves and doomed to perish in eternal damnation. But out of God's great love for us, He sent "His one and only Son" to suffer our punishment on the cruel cross. Now, "whoever believes in Him shall *not* perish but have eternal life."

Redemption was completed at Calvary. By God's grace we are saved, through faith (Ephesians 2:8). In Baptism we are received into fellowship with God.

John 3:16 sums up God's plan for our salvation, and we in turn can use it to witness to a dying world.

> **Be of good cheer, for God's own Son**
> **Forgives all sins which you have done;**
> **You're justified by Jesus' blood;**
> **Baptized, you have the highest good. Amen.**
>
> ("God Loved the World So that He Gave," by L. Bollhagen)

JIM WIEMERS

John 5:24

Tell Me Quickly—I'm Dying!

I tell you the truth, whoever hears My word and believes Him who sent Me has eternal life and will not be condemned; he has crossed over from death to life. John 5:24

Billy Graham tells a powerful story of something that happened as he addressed a large college assembly in California. Throughout the first part of his speech there were catcalls and derogatory remarks from some of the students; however, there was silence when he started to tell the story of a college student who had been in a car accident.

The girl's mother was informed that the injuries were such that the girl would more than likely die within a few days. The mother rushed to her daughter's bedside. As she held her daughter's hand, the young woman said, "Mother, you taught me how to hold a cocktail glass. You taught me how to have safe sex, but you never taught me how to die. Teach me quickly because I'm dying."

The ultimate question is, "What happens to me when I die?" The answer is found only in God's Word: "I tell you the truth, whoever hears My word and believes Him who sent Me has eternal life and will not be condemned." The moment one is brought to faith through the Spirit of God, he or she "has crossed over from death to life"—eternal life.

Lord God, for the truth, that "whoever hears My word and believes Him who sent Me has eternal life," our thanks. Amen.

ROGER R. SONNENBERG

John 5:39–40

Another How-to Book?

You diligently study the Scriptures because you think that by them you possess eternal life. These are the Scriptures that testify about Me, yet you refuse to come to Me to have life. John 5:39–40

Perhaps you have read books about the Christian life that tout the seven steps toward an effective prayer life or the five attributes of a Christian giver. To be fair, Scriptures often do address practical issues of the Christian life. But such how-to books can give the impression that our walk with God is a series of stepping stones that finally bring us home to the Father. In reality, our walk with God begins with the Father's sending Jesus Christ to us, thereby bringing us home. Out of the living faith He gives us, we respond by searching the ways in which Christ's love and forgiveness apply to our lives.

Jesus addresses just this issue here in John 5. We can diligently study the Scriptures without ever discovering their focal point. To learn "how to" without learning of Jesus and His saving work provides us with a manual for right living without giving us Christ's righteousness. So we are left destitute of the one and only thing that counts: the eternal life He wishes to shower on us.

But the Scriptures testify about Him as they grab us and make us see the futility of our own efforts at godly living. At the moment when we realize all is hopeless, they give us new hope because He suffered and died and rose again for us. So search the Scriptures, for in them is found His eternal life.

Lord, create in us the desire to search the Scriptures diligently that we may discover again and again Your great love for us through Jesus Christ. Amen.

DONALD W. SANDMANN

John 6:35

Bread of Life

Then Jesus declared, "I am the bread of life. He who comes to Me will never go hungry, and he who believes in Me will never be thirsty." John 6:35

Jesus has just fed 5,000 men and probably many others who were with them in the area of Tiberias. When He departs for Capernaum, the crowd follows. After all, this is some bargain! We can sense the pounding of their hearts as they feel the beginning of a new time when their meager existence would be enriched with daily bread provided by their new king!

Most of us aren't asking for the world and don't expect to win the *Reader's Digest* sweepstakes. But our life experience is confined to limits imposed by life and death. So we are wary of throwing our lot in with someone who claims to be "the bread of life." We can taste the food on our table, even if it is only peanut butter. How can we let go and trust Jesus to provide for all our needs, spiritual and material?

Jesus tells us that if we will let go of our lunch pail we will have a much greater banquet in store. Still, we take along our sandwiches in case the great wedding feast fizzles. Finally He meets us at the door with the wedding garment of salvation, and we know that we have to drop everything to put it on. And, miraculously, we do! And we discover the Bread of Life is more than adequate to all our needs.

Bread of Life, fill our hungry souls with Your salvation and welcome us to Your heavenly banquet. Amen.

DONALD W. SANDMANN

John 8:12

Jesus, the Light of the World

When Jesus spoke again to the people, He said, "I am the light of the world. Whoever follows Me will never walk in darkness, but will have the light of life." John 8:12

No matter how long you may have lived in your house or how often you have walked back and forth from room to room each day, whenever the electricity goes off at night, your house becomes foreign territory. In the darkness you bump into chairs and trip over things on the floor. Chaos reigns until you find a flashlight or candle.

As you turn on the flashlight, suddenly you can see where to walk. There is still darkness all around you, but the light provides a way for you to avoid the obstacles that had previously caused you to trip.

Jesus compared Himself to light. He is the flashlight that reveals our pathway through the obstacles of sin and darkness in this world and leads us to our goal—eternal life. In that dark Good Friday Christ gave up His life to redeem us. His cross of suffering is our access to light and life. His light also shines through us to guide others to the source of all light and life—Jesus Christ.

> Hold Thou Thy cross before my closing eyes,
> Shine through the gloom, and point me to the
>   skies;
> Heav'n's morning breaks, and earth's vain shadows
>   flee;
> In life, in death, O Lord, abide with me. Amen.

("Abide with Me," by Henry F. Lyte)

JIM WIEMERS

John 8:31–32

The Truth

To the Jews who had believed Him, Jesus said, "If you hold to My teaching, you are really My disciples. Then you will know the truth, and the truth will set you free." John 8:31–32

We often ask, as did Pilate, "What is truth?" In the context of this passage and of other passages, *truth* is another word for *reality*. The real state of affairs in this world is that we are connected to God through the work of His Son. God welcomes us as His fully forgiven people because of the cross. If we live by that promise, we know truth, we know reality, and we are freed from trying to storm heaven. That's God's plan for us, and it's a grand one!

Too grand, we decide. The world isn't like that. There's no free lunch. When the auto salesman offers an option package as a free bonus, we are wary. Somehow we know we will pay for it before the deal is closed. And we believe it is the same way with our relationship to God. Our church-going begins as a free response to the Gospel but becomes a bargaining chip when the chips of life are down. So our lives are tainted by the *unreality* that we have to earn our way after all.

But the truth is that God has given us new life by splashing us with the waters of Baptism. The truth is that our good works are the result of His daily living in us, strengthening us with the Gospel, and refreshing us at His Table. This preserves us from having to preserve our own "rights" by trampling on our neighbors. Yes, we are truly free!

Lord Jesus Christ, speak the truth into our hearts that we may truly live in the freedom of the Gospel. Amen.

DONALD W. SANDMANN

John 8:36

Freedom

So if the Son sets you free, you will be free indeed. John 8:36

Born Free is the title of a book and movie that describes the plight of lions and their captivity at the hands of human beings. As the title suggests, these lions were born to be free as the rulers of the jungle.

Many people today, expressing their desire for individual rights, claim that they have been born free. Citizens of the United States claim "inalienable rights" as defined in the Declaration of Independence.

Yet, in reality, we are not free. Sin binds us in its chains, making us confess with the apostle Paul, "For what I do is not the good I want to do; no, the evil I do not want to do—this I keep on doing" (Romans 7:19).

All of us have times in our lives when we feel the binding frustration of sin hold us back from being all that God wants us to be. Where may we turn? Ultimately, it is God's Son, Jesus Christ, who alone sets us free. His death and resurrection assures us that we cannot be bound by our sins. He carries our sins to the cross so that we are forgiven.

God assures us that through our faith in Jesus Christ we are reborn to be free: free to live with Him today and forever; free to love as He has loved us; free to give our lives away in service to Him and others.

Gracious Lord, thank You for making me free in Your Son. Amen.

LUTHER C. BRUNETTE

John 9:3

What Goes around Comes Around

This happened so that the work of God might be displayed. John 9:3

Cause and effect, also referred to as the "law of the Medes and Persians" (what goes around comes around) is and has been through the centuries one of the tried and true counsels of wisdom passed on from the old to the young. "Don't do it. It'll come back to haunt you." And there is human truth in this counsel. Divine truth, however, runs deeper.

Conventional "wisdom" dictates that blindness, birth defects, or any human tragedy reveals in its malfunction the reality that "what's going around is coming around." To this Jesus says emphatically *no!*

Every human situation is redeemable in Christ. Every tragedy, every difficulty, every hard edge can and does bring us to a place where the "work of God might be displayed." That place, for you and for me, is at the foot of the cross. There God was reconciling the world in Christ. There God delivered healing and salvation in His Son. There what goes around and what comes around are stripped of their power to destroy. And what remains is life eternal in Christ Jesus.

If you have been laid low by some terrifying agony, take it to the cross. There the work of God will be displayed in your life.

Dear God, when the changes and chances of life threaten to do me in, reveal to me Your eternal work in my life and heart. Amen.

DAVID H. BENKE

John 10:9

Jesus, the Gate to Salvation

I am the gate; whoever enters through Me will be saved. He will come in and go out, and find pasture. John 10:9

A Jewish survivor of the Dachau concentration camp related this story. He was a university professor in Berlin during the early years of the Nazi regime. He had always considered himself a German first and had served proudly in the military during World War I. He had never dreamed that the Nazis would come for him.

On the night when he was arrested, a friend of his who was still an officer in the military sent him warning that his family was going to be arrested that night. He hurriedly packed his family up and sought refuge at the American Embassy in Berlin. But when he got there, the gate was locked, and he was arrested on the road out front while diplomats looked on from behind the gate. He never saw his family again after that night.

Many years later he tracked down a friend of his who had worked with him at the university. He was surprised to find out that his friend was now a Christian. His friend, also being hunted by the Nazis, had managed to make it to the gates of a church, which he found open. The church, through the underground, helped his friend to safety. And this church proclaimed the truth of Jesus to him. In this church, his friend found life, both on earth and forever.

Jesus is the gate, and the gate is never locked. We are often chased by the minions of the devil. Sin, temptation, greed, and lust seek to consume us. But in Jesus, we know that we have safety from these soldiers and that through the gate is salvation. Praise Him!

Our Savior, through the power of Your Holy Spirit, put someone on my heart who needs to be lead to the gate, and give me the words to lead this person to You. Amen.

KEVIN PARVIZ

John 10:11

What a Shepherd!

I am the good shepherd. The good shepherd lays down His life for the sheep. John 10:11

The Associated Press reported that in Pine Bluff, Arkansas, a youth shaved his head as a sign of love and support for his mother. His mother always had beautiful hair but had lost it because of cancer treatments. However, when the young man went to school, some of the students beat him up thinking he was trying to be a skinhead. Support for his mother ended up giving him a black eye!

Young and old alike support others in a variety of ways. They shave their heads. They walk or jog in a rally. They protest. They sit by a bedside holding a friend's hand.

Few, however, give their life for another. It is the greatest act of love someone can show. Yet that's exactly what God did. He who created us perfect was saddened to see us flagrantly disobey Him; nevertheless, He did not give up on us. He continued to love us even though we continued to turn our backs on Him. He loved us enough to lay down His life for us on the cross. He died in our place, rescuing us from the consequences of our sin—death. He did it so that we might "have life, and have it to the full" (John 10:10). It is what a good shepherd does for his sheep!

Loving Shepherd, thank You. Thank You for life and life to the fullest through Your sacrificial death and triumphant resurrection. Amen.

ROGER R. SONNENBERG

John 10:14–15

The Good Shepherd

I am the good shepherd; I know My sheep and My sheep know Me—just as the Father knows Me and I know the Father—and I lay down My life for the sheep. John 10:14–15

My Shepherd knows me. This is the first great realization of the heart. That I, of all people, am Jesus' little lamb! I belong to Him. I am not some insignificant nameless number at the bottom of the corporate barrel. My Shepherd knows me even as I know Him. Our relationship is mutual.

Second, my Shepherd knows me in the same way He knows His Father. And They are one! This means that the life of God— Father, Son/Shepherd, and Comforter—is life in me. The heart of God is in my heart. The Holy Trinity has chosen, as my Shepherd said, to come and make a home in … me!

Finally, my Shepherd laid down His life for me. He knows me as I am. He knows that I love to wander. He knows that I am by nature sinful and unclean. He knows that I am frail unto death. He knows all this! And as a result, He laid down His life—for me— that I may be His own. There is no greater love than the love of my Good Shepherd for me. And for you. There is no greater love than the love of our God for all the lost and wandering sheep of the world, including me.

My dear and kind Shepherd, feed me, lead me, guide me, and keep me always in Your tender care. Amen.

DAVID H. BENKE

John 10:27–28

The Shepherd's Hands

My sheep listen to My voice; I know them, and they follow Me. I give them eternal life, and they shall never perish; no one can snatch them out of My hand. John 10:27–28

Of all the people you have met, who has the strongest hands? Pastors shake and hold numerous kinds of hands, and many of the clergy would agree that farmers have some of the largest and most powerful hands of anyone around. Evidently, their daily work builds incredible strength in their hands.

The Lord reminds us that as His sheep nothing and no one can snatch us out of the almighty and loving hands of our Good Shepherd. He is the one who gave His life for us, the sheep, when He died on the cross of Calvary. He is the one who rose from the dead and defeated Satan, sin, and death. His conquering and caring hands assure us of a life with meaning and purpose that is for today, but goes on for eternity.

Jesus Christ has us in His powerful grip. We can know and trust in the one who holds us and strengthens us as we listen to His voice and follow Him. His Word becomes His loving and guiding voice as we listen to it, study it, meditate on it, and memorize it. What a comfort to know that with Jesus as our Good Shepherd, nothing can snatch us out of His mighty hands.

Your hands, O Lord, surround me with comfort and strength. Help me to listen to You and follow You. Amen.

LUTHER C. BRUNETTE

John 11:10

The Light of the World

It is when he walks by night that he stumbles, for he has no light. John 11:10

How illuminating it is for our lives that Jesus is the light of the world! Without light there is only darkness. And as Jesus teaches in the passage above, those who walk in darkness stumble. Were it not for Jesus shining His light upon us through His death and rising again we would still be walking in that darkness of sin. By God's undeserved love, however, we can assert with Isaiah: "The people walking in darkness have seen a great light" (Isaiah 9:2).

Even as the sun gives light to the moon and the moon reflects that light, so Jesus gives light to us who are His children and we reflect that light. We are the light of the world. We reflect His light to those with whom we live.

What a contrast! "You were once darkness, but now you are light in the Lord. Live as children of light" (Ephesians 5:8). Our source of power as lights in this world comes from the light of the world, Jesus Christ. Even as the moon cannot shine unless it receives light from the sun and reflects that, so we cannot give light to others unless we receive and reflect from the Son of God the light which He gives to dispel the darkness of sin and to guide people on their journey in life.

With the psalmist we affirm: "The LORD is my light and my salvation—whom shall I fear?" (Psalm 27:1).

Light of the world, shine into my heart and let me reflect Your light to all the world. Amen.

ANDREW SIMCAK JR.

John 11:25–26

Do You Believe This?

Jesus said to her, "I am the resurrection and the life. He who believes in Me will live, even though he dies; and whoever lives and believes in Me will never die. Do you believe this?" John 11:25–26

Bethany is a town very near Jerusalem. When Jesus arrived there not long before Holy Week and His triumphal entry into Jerusalem, He found friends mourning the death of Lazarus, brother of Mary and Martha and also a dear friend of Jesus. Lazarus had been in the grave four days. The two sisters both insisted that had Jesus arrived earlier their brother wouldn't have died. They knew Jesus, the Great Physician, had power to restore health.

But power to restore *life?* That belonged to the glory and power of God, and it was for this very reason—that Jesus would be glorified and seen as God's Son—that Jesus delayed His Bethany arrival until after Lazarus' death.

Jesus' words to Martha in our verses above are loved for their comfort and assurance, especially when we face death, both our own and that of loved ones.

"Do you believe this?" Jesus asked Martha. It is an important question that He also asks us. Through the power of the Holy Spirit, we answer confidently along with Martha, "Yes!" The words that sound like a riddle are as clear as can be. Because of Jesus, we will live and never die. His resurrection secures our own.

Dear heavenly Father, thank You for the gift of Your Son, who is the resurrection and the life and the source of eternal life. In His name we pray. Amen.

LAINE ROSIN

John 11:43–44

Nike!

Jesus called in a loud voice, "Lazarus, come out!" The dead man came out, his hands and feet wrapped with strips of linen, and a cloth around his face. Jesus said to them, "Take off the grave clothes and let him go." John 11:43–44

Children acquire likes and dislikes very early in life. Already at the age of three, our son Jacob had some very definite opinions on clothes and shoes. On Easter morning, Robin thought it was a good idea for Jacob to wear his new oxford shoes.

"Today, Jacob, we're going to really dress up because we're going to celebrate Jesus' resurrection," Robin said. Jacob ran off to get the shoes he intended on wearing, his Nike tennis shoes. "No, Jacob, you're going to wear the special shoes your Ama and Papa bought you. You're going to wear your new oxfords."

Jacob insisted he would not. His mother insisted he would. Robin won! The oxfords bedecked Jacob's feet for the special resurrection service.

Perhaps, however, Jacob did not have such a bad idea after all. He wanted to wear his Nike tennis shoes. *Nike* is a Greek word that means "victory." In ancient times, after a victory had been won, the announcement would be made throughout the cities, "Nike! Nike!" It meant a victory had been achieved.

Easter should be a time when the shout of victory is proclaimed with voice, and yes, even with the shoes we wear. Already in the raising of Lazarus, Jesus had given a prelude of what would happen because of His life, death, and resurrection; " 'Lazarus, come out!' The dead man came out" (John 11:43–44). So through His victory we celebrate our victory from death, from sin, and from the power of the devil.

Nike! Nike!

Lord Jesus, thank You for the shout of victory we can make because of Your death and resurrection. Amen.

ROGER R. SONNENBERG

John 12:24

Death to Life

I tell you the truth, unless a kernel of wheat falls to the ground and dies, it remains only a single seed. But if it dies, it produces many seeds. John 12:24

Anyone who likes to garden or comes from an agricultural background understands this image. It is always amazing to think that something so lifeless as a seed—dried up, hard, dead—can, with God's help, grow into a vibrant, green, living plant.

Jesus here is describing what must happen to Him for life to blossom. He was to become dead. Alive, during His ministry on earth, He had many followers. They flocked to Him, witnessed miracles, and listened to His teaching. Yet while still alive, He was abandoned by all but a few of His followers, and He died nearly alone.

But in that death, and the glorious resurrection that followed, the seeds of His ministry, by all appearances dead, were brought to life in faith and grew to a vibrant, living church.

I often start my garden in the basement in pots under a grow light. This gives me a good opportunity to watch the change in the lifeless seeds. And they give me a good lesson in faith. Some never grow. But some, and often the hardiest of the bunch, grow and come out of the soil with the husk of the seed attached to a leaf or a stem. They grow well and are alive and vibrant, but there is a reminder of their death that grows with them.

We, too, grow with a reminder of our death. We have died, but we have been reborn. In our Baptism, and with the seeds of faith that Christ has planted in us, we live and grow in Him. Yet we remember our death. Not only our death in Christ, which He accomplished for us, but our death to sin. And in that death, there is life—everlasting life in Christ.

Jesus, in Your death You give us life. Thank You for the seed of faith that grows in me, and may I help to plant seeds in others. Amen.

KEVIN PARVIZ

John 14:1–3

Glorious Preparations

Do not let your hearts be troubled. Trust in God; trust also in Me. In My Father's house are many rooms; if it were not so, I would have told you. I am going there to prepare a place for you. And if I go and prepare a place for you, I will come back and take you to be with Me that you also may be where I am. John 14:1–3

Clean the house. Shop for groceries. Cook a lovely dinner. Set out the good china. Light the candles. The company will arrive soon. Preparations have been underway for some time, and we are ready to welcome our guests. Out of love, we prepare for their coming.

In a far more majestic way, Christ is preparing a place for us and for all who believe in Him. It is His Father's house, a mansion grander by far than we deserve. His preparations are also done out of love, but it, too, is a love more majestic than the love we show for our earthly guests.

Christ has attended to every detail, and He assures us that everything will be ready when He takes us safely there. This preparation began long ago and culminated in His perfect life, death, and resurrection.

In this farewell discourse, Jesus had just predicted Judas' betrayal and Peter's denial. Yet in these words He seeks to comfort those He loves and bring peace to their troubled hearts. In His dark hours, Jesus was characteristically thinking of others.

Jesus promised to return for His disciples, and that promise includes us. He desires that we be with Him eternally—what perfect love. Do not let your heart be troubled. He is waiting to welcome you home.

Dear heavenly Father, Your Son is preparing a place for those who believe in Him. There we will live forever with You. Amen.

LAINE ROSIN

John 14:6

Christ Is the Only Way

I am the way and the truth and the life. No one comes to the Father except through Me. John 14:6

"Many roads go up the mountain, but they all get to the top."
"All religions are essentially the same."
"One religion is as good as another."

Weird statements, right? The funny thing is, often the same people who make these statements select their *one* doctor very carefully!

These commonly heard views summarize what is known as "universalism," the myth that ultimately all people will be saved regardless of what they believe or what religion they follow.

But the "Gospel in a nutshell" says, "For God so loved the world that He gave His one and only Son, that whoever believes in Him shall not perish but have eternal life" (John 3:16).

There is the universal salvation. God offers salvation to *all* people but only *through* belief in Jesus Christ. And that atonement, grasped by our Spirit-empowered faith, effects our justification: We are declared righteous, forgiven, by God. We are saved, that is, rescued from our sins, and made God's children and heirs of eternal life through the death and resurrection of His Son.

This is why it's so important to get the Good News about Christ out to everyone in the world as quickly as possible. And we must not forget to be faithful witnesses to Him in our own backyards.

We thank God daily for the salvation He offers to all believers. We pray that all humanity may come to know and believe in Jesus Christ, the only way to the Father and eternal life.

Thank You, heavenly Father, for showing me the road back to God—the only way, the truth, and the life: Jesus Christ. Amen.

DONALD L. DEFFNER

John 14:18–19

Snatched from the Orphanage of Sin

I will not leave you as orphans; I will come to you. John 14:18

The great global tragedies always involve children. War and pestilence leave them vulnerable, exposed, and unable to make it on their own. In the televised starving faces of overcrowded hospital wards and orphanages, we understand how truly dependent children are.

Through Baptism we are claimed as members of God's family. We will forever remain children of God. We are forever dependent on God's love, God's nurture, God's care for our very lives. An understanding of our utter dependence on God for everything in life is where baptismal life begins.

As Jesus' words promise, we are swept into the arms of God's love and care. We will not be abandoned. We will not be children without families, sad eyes searching some vast compound for a familiar face. We will not be left alone. "I will not," says our brother Jesus, "leave you as orphans; I will come to you."

The heart of God is for His children, of whom I am one. Jesus has come for me. The Comforter teaches me all things concerning Him. And now God—Father, Son, and Holy Spirit—makes His home in me. I live because the full life of Christ in God is in me—and in all who believe in Jesus as their Savior.

Dear Jesus, thank You for coming to me and for claiming me as a member of Your family. Amen.

DAVID H. BENKE

John 14:27

Be at Peace

Peace I leave with you; My peace I give you. I do not give to you as the world gives. Do not let your hearts be troubled and do not be afraid. John 14:27

Marilyn sighed as the office telephone rang for the 20th time in as many minutes. She was on her way to a meeting, but as she left her office she encountered four people who "had to see her." Each had an "emergency" situation only Marilyn could solve. When she got to the meeting, it seemed that every discussion turned into an argument. Marilyn had a major headache by noon.

Marilyn returned to her office, closed the door, and told her secretary to hold her calls. "I need a few minutes of peace," Marilyn confided.

The peace the world offers is an absence of demands, conflict, competition, unreasonable expectations, and excessive noise. A quiet stream in a large meadow conjures up a sense of peace. The moments alone at dawn before the children arise can be very peaceful. But finding this type of peace is not always easy because we live in a hurry-scurry world where there are many demands and lots of conflicts.

The peace that Jesus offers is different. It is an internal peace—a quiet confidence that no matter what the consequences, no matter what the circumstances, God is in control and will take care of us. With the peace that Jesus offers, we can sleep soundly during the storms of life, free of worry. We can maintain our calm when others are fighting around us. We can control our tempers and refuse to get angry. We may not know what tomorrow will bring, but we know who is in control of all our tomorrows, and we believe in that God.

Jesus, I want Your peace in my heart. I need help with living peacefully in this troubled world. Thank You for the gift of peace. Amen.

BOBBIE REED

John 15:1

Heavenly Nourishment; Heavenly Caretaker

I am the true vine, and My Father is the gardener. John 15:1

A friend of ours is an avid gardener. She is always out fussing in her garden, tilling, pulling weeds, fertilizing, watering, and pruning. You can imagine the results! Her garden is a showpiece. She loves to have others admire it just as much as she does herself.

Our heavenly Father has a similar interest in us. The crown of His creation, we receive His utmost care and attention. At our Baptism we are grafted to Jesus, our Savior and Lord, receiving from Him nourishment for our souls. Jesus poignantly explains this in John 15:5 when He says, "Apart from Me you can do *nothing*." Our lives are totally dependent on Him.

What an intimate, personal relationship this is. Nourished, forgiven, and groomed with perfect, never-ending care, we become an object of beauty to our God and a beautiful witness for others to see. The fruit of the Spirit—love, joy, peace, patience, kindness, goodness, faithfulness, gentleness, and self-control—can only be produced if we stay connected to the true vine, Jesus Christ. Thanks be to God for His perfect nourishment and care.

O almighty God, keep us firmly rooted in Your Word and nourished in body and spirit, that all we are and do may be pleasing in Your sight. Amen.

JAMES W. FREESE

John 15:5

I Can't Do It on My Own

I am the vine; you are the branches. If a man remains in Me and I in him, he will bear much fruit; apart from Me you can do nothing. John 15:5

"Pastor, I'm working on being a better Christian; one by one, I'm looking at the virtues in Christ's life and trying to be like Him."

Any problem with that statement? *Absolutely!* It's a completely false view of what it means to be a Christian, and a misunderstanding of Christ's words, "Follow Me" (Matthew 4:19).

Jesus Christ is no mere model to emulate. To think so is to fall prey to the sin of "moralism." Moralism holds up certain values to follow to attain salvation, rather than seeing those values as *consequences* of the Gospel. We don't "work on" traits of Christian character. Christ is not just our example. He is, rather, a prototype. He is the firstfruits of those who believe in Him. Therefore we do not focus on His humility as a precept to follow, but on His humiliation—His sacrifice—*for us!*

Also we do not "work on" "giving our all"—total commitment—but see His total commitment—*for us!* For we fail totally. But through His death and resurrection we are forgiven and then called to the fruit of faith, empowered totally by the Holy Spirit. It is "Christ in you" (Colossians 1:27). "Apart from Me you can do nothing" (John 15:5). (Also see Philippians 2:13.)

That is the Gospel—what Christ has done *for us*. That is what Christian living is all about.

Lord, lead me to focus not on what I think I can do for You but on what *You are* doing in *me*. To You alone be the glory. Amen.

DONALD L. DEFFNER

John 15:12

Love As Jesus Loved

My command is this: Love each other as I have loved you. John 15:12

Jesus told the disciples to love one another as He had loved them. By application He gave the same commandment to each of us. So how did Jesus show love?

Jesus loved first (1 John 4:19). We often wait for someone to reach out to us in friendship before we respond. We must learn to risk making the first move.

Jesus sacrificed for us before we were friends (Romans 5:8). We often do nice things for friends, but when was the last time you gave sacrificially to a stranger or a casual acquaintance?

Jesus spoke the truth (Luke 22:31–34). Jesus told Peter that he would deny his Lord and turn away. But Jesus also said He prayed for Peter and knew he would turn back again to the Lord. There are times when we must confront others, but when we do, we must speak the truth in love.

Jesus affirmed people (John 1:47). When Philip brought Nathanael to Jesus, He said, "Here is a true Israelite, in whom there is nothing false." We need to be ready to affirm the good qualities and achievements of others.

Jesus prayed for people (John 17:6–26). Jesus spent a lot of time in prayer. Sometimes it was intercessory prayer for others. An important way for us to show love is to pray for one another.

Jesus encouraged people to take risks of faith (Matthew 14:28–31). When Peter wanted to walk on the water, he was encouraged to do so by the Lord. When our friends feel the Lord's call, we need to encourage them to follow and to take appropriate risks.

Jesus spent time with friends. He ate meals with them, talked with them, prayed with them, and healed family members.

These are only a few of the ways Jesus showed love. The greatest example of Jesus' love was when He stretched out His arms on the cross and died so that we might have forgiveness of sins. This is the most important love that we can share with others.

Jesus, teach me to love others as You love me. Amen.

BOBBIE REED

John 15:16–17

Bear Much Fruit

You did not choose Me, but I chose you and appointed you to go and bear fruit—fruit that will last. Then the Father will give you whatever you ask in My name. This is My command: Love each other. John 15:16–17

Five years ago Ed went to a nursery and walked through the rows of avocado saplings for sale. After extensive questioning of the salesperson and careful consideration of all the trees, Ed finally picked the tree he wanted in his front yard. He chose the tree he believed would bear the most fruit. Ed loved avocados.

Ed planted the tree and tended it with care. He kept the roots moist and fed with an avocado-tree fertilizer. He sprayed for bugs. Whatever Ed believed the tree needed, he did for it. Then Ed waited for the tree to give him avocados. This year the tree produced an abundance of fruit. Ed was pleased.

Jesus said that each of us was chosen by God to be a member of the heavenly family. God lovingly provides for our needs: physical, social, emotional, and spiritual. But there is an expectation that as Christians we will bring forth fruit for God. The fruit of the Spirit is love, joy, peace, patience, kindness, goodness, faithfulness, gentleness, and self-control. These are important and need to be present in our lives as we mature in the faith. But the most important of these is love. Jesus said that love for one another would be a sign to the world of a genuine believer. The commandment was given more than once that we are to love one another.

Are you a loving friend? a loving family member? a loving church member? a loving employee? a loving Christian?

Jesus, it isn't always easy to be loving. Sometimes people do things that hurt, anger, or frustrate me. Give me strength to remain loving. Amen.

BOBBIE REED

John 16:33

The Peace of Christ

I have told you these things, so that in Me you may have peace. In this world you will have trouble. But take heart! I have overcome the world. John 16:33

As the plane took off, a man pulled out his pocket New Testament and began to read. Eventually the man sitting next to him remarked, "I don't go much for religion."

"Oh?" said the other. "Well, I surely feel you're missing something."

"Well," replied the second man in a rather nettled tone, "I don't see much reason in believing in a Christ that's been dead 2,000 years."

"What's that?" replied the other. "Christ—dead? Why, that can't be! I was just talking to Him a few minutes ago."

What's bugging you today? For many of us it's anxiety—worry about something confronting us.

Well, whatever it is, let me ask you a question: Is Christ *alive* to you? Do you feel in your heart that peace that Christ is *within* you?

If not, I affirm that the clue to being free of any kind of emotional conflict, any kind of defeat or difficulty, any hardship or sorrow, is to have the peace that man did. Christ was so alive in him that he could talk with Him at any place, at any time.

Jesus conquered the world so that you might have the peace of forgiveness. Jesus conquered death so that you might have life eternally.

That's the "secret." No. Better yet, it's God's sure *promise!*

Thank You, Lord, for overcoming the world so I might be filled with Your peace and life. Amen.

DONALD L. DEFFNER

John 17:1–12

The Answer to a Prayer

Now this is eternal life: that they may know You, the only true God, and Jesus Christ, whom You have sent. John 17:3

Jesus was praying to the Father: Glorify Your Son. You granted Him authority over all people that He might give eternal life. Eternal life is knowing the only true God and His Son, Jesus Christ.

You have seen the bumper sticker with the saying, "Jesus is the answer." Sometimes in ridicule people have asked, "If Jesus is the answer, what's the question?" Christians might respond, "If Jesus is the answer, the question is, 'Who gives life?' "

What happens to those who believe that only Jesus gives life is a sure confidence about *all* of living. There is confidence when facing struggles and when experiencing joys. This life begins in faith and continues in love without end. For each one of us Jesus has died; and for each one of us Jesus lives again to draw us to Himself. Without Him we would desire only to participate in the ridicule, in searching for other direction and attempting other securities. With Him, however, we are joined in the Father's love and gathered into the Father's inheritance of hope. This is living, real living.

Father, glorify Your Son through our faith, and magnify Your Son through our witness. Amen.

PAUL J. ALBERS

John 20:29

Faith to Sight and Prayer to Praise

Blessed are those who have not seen and yet have believed. John 20:29

Thomas is often looked on in a bad light. Shamefaced along with all the other disciples who forsook Jesus as He went to the cross for the sins of all humankind, he suffers the misfortune of being absent during Jesus' first two post-resurrection appearances to His disciples. Stubbornly Thomas clings to his skepticism, only to have it melt at the sound of his Master's voice, "Stop doubting and believe."

"Blessed are those who have not seen and yet have believed." *We* are those people. St. Peter wrote, "Though you have not seen Him, you love Him; and even though you do not see Him now, you believe in Him and are filled with an inexpressible and glorious joy" (1 Peter 1:8). To be sure, we have our "Thomas" moments when our faith wavers and we stubbornly cling to our unbelief. It is then when our Savior, who has called us by our name, assures us of His guiding presence. Redeemed by our precious Savior, whom yet unseen we love, we are assured of eternity in heaven, where we will see God face to face. Then our faith will be changed to sight and our prayer to praise. "I do believe; help me overcome my unbelief!" (Mark 9:24).

Loving Father, strengthen us when we doubt Your promises. Keep us strong in faith until the day when our faith is changed to sight and prayer to praise. Amen.

JAMES W. FREESE

222

Acts 1:8

Washed in Power

You will receive power when the Holy Spirit comes on you; and you will be My witnesses in Jerusalem, and in all Judea and Samaria, and to the ends of the earth. Acts 1:8

My eighth-grade English students were asked to choose a moment in Bible history about which they could write an eyewitness account. One student immediately chose Pentecost, claiming she would love to have heard the rushing wind, seen the tongues of fire, and heard Peter boom his first sermon. Great choice! What a sight that must have been! What a transformation for this three-time denier!

We ourselves have already witnessed and experienced this transformation. This scene is repeated time after time at the baptismal font. At our Baptism our sins are washed away, we become God's beloved children redeemed by Christ, and we receive the promised Holy Spirit. This *same* Spirit who guided the disciples' powerful witness is ours throughout our lives, helping, strengthening, guiding, and empowering us to be God's faithful witnesses whatever our earthly station. The tongues of fire may be gone, the instant foreign language capabilities are missing, we may never see 3,000 people converted after one message from our lips, yet we are given the same promise heard by the disciples, "You will be My witnesses," and the assurance, "I am with you always" (Matthew 28:20).

Yes, we *have* received power. God gives us an abundance of opportunities to go into all the world and preach the Good News to all creation.

Lord, our God, make us strong witnesses for You that many may come to the knowledge of the truth by our words and actions. Amen.

JAMES W. FREESE

Acts 2:25–26

You Can See It on Their Faces

David said about Him: "I saw the Lord always before me. Because He is at my right hand, I will not be shaken. Therefore my heart is glad and my tongue rejoices; my body also will live in hope." Acts 2:25–26

When a bride comes down the aisle, people often comment, "Isn't she radiant?" The eyes of a child light up with a special joy as a gift is opened. You can tell from the look on his face that something very special is happening.

Sadness is also evident. Eyes are dull from crying; lips turn down at the corners from sorrow. You can tell from the look on their faces when people are suffering. But when the downcast look is turned into a smile, when the frown is replaced by laughter, then you know something dramatic has happened.

In the Psalms David frequently shares such experiences. For instance, in one psalm David speaks of his gratitude to God for delivering him from King Saul: "I sought the LORD, and He answered me; He delivered me from all my fears. Those who look to Him are radiant" (Psalm 34:4–5). All around David knew that God had rescued him from what was troubling him, for you could see it on David's face. It was radiant. David knew that God was "at his right hand"—always with him; He could be trusted to hear David's prayers and deliver him. Because of this assurance, David's heart was glad and his tongue rejoiced.

God will hear our prayers, too. He has invited us to pray, has promised to hear our prayers, and has assured us that our prayers are answered according to His grace and mercy. With Jesus' love, sorrow can be turned into joy and despair to hope. For this He died and to complete this He rose again on the third day, that we may have the look of radiance on our faces.

Merciful Father, let radiance shine from my face through Your help. Amen.

PAUL J. ALBERS

Acts 4:12

One Way

Salvation is found in no one else, for there is no other name under heaven given to men by which we must be saved. Acts 4:12

Many people believe in universal salvation for all people. They say it makes little difference what one believes as long as one really believes it. They say, "Though Jesus may be the shortest or even the highest way to heaven, He isn't the only way."

People who adopt a theology of Universalism either have to say Peter was wrong or a liar when he spoke the words of Acts 4:12 to the Sanhedrin: "Salvation is found in no one else, for there is no other name under heaven given to men by which we must be saved." Worse yet, they call Jesus a liar. Thomas asked Jesus how to get to heaven. Jesus answered, "I am the way and the truth and the life. No one comes to the Father except through Me" (John 14:6). We certainly can't say Jesus was wrong, can we? We can't say it's a matter of interpretation, can we? Jesus makes it clear that it is only through Him that one gets to heaven. When He said the words, He was headed to the cross. Why? To earn a place in heaven for us through His death and resurrection.

We know "salvation is found in no one else" other than You, Lord Jesus. Thank You for showing and giving us the way. Amen.

ROGER R. SONNENBERG

Acts 16:31

It's the Truth!

They [Paul and Silas] replied, "Believe in the Lord Jesus, and you will be saved—you and your household." Acts 16:31

A good friend of mine in Mobile, Alabama, consistently tells me, "There's only one truth." What a great line! What he means is that the truth need not be embellished. He also means that the truth will eventually win out. Speak the truth; you have nothing to hide.

Paul and Silas, led by the Holy Spirit, were able to do just that. Though they had been imprisoned in what must have been squalor, they spoke the truth when the frightened jailer found they had remained behind in jail after the doors had been flung wide open by God. He recognized that they were motivated by a higher force than fear. They were—their motivation was love! Spiritually, the jailer was in prison; they were free. He was in search of the truth. They gave it to him in all its beauty and simplicity: "Believe in the Lord Jesus, and you will be saved—you and your household."

Often we are tempted to judge people's motivation for coming to a congregation or Christian day school. Whatever it is they want, we have the one thing they really *need*—the Good News of salvation through Jesus Christ. May we never be ashamed of the Gospel of Jesus Christ, but, rather, speaking the truth in love, tell them, yes, *show* them what they need to know: "Believe in the Lord Jesus, and you will be saved—you and your household."

As Christ's ambassadors we are equipped with everything we need to proclaim this truth by the indwelling of the Holy Spirit. Great challenge, great opportunities, great motivation, great news, great Spirit, great satisfaction!

Gracious God, give us opportunities to tell others of the one thing they need most—to believe in the Lord Jesus Christ and be saved. May we never be ashamed of the Gospel but speak it and live it. Amen.

JAMES W. FREESE

Acts 17:11

Search the Scriptures!

They received the message with great eagerness and examined the Scriptures every day to see if what Paul said was true. Acts 17:11

With the cable-TV industry growing, our airwaves are full of all types of stations and programs. Several networks run only Christian programs, as do some locally owned Christian stations. Including radio stations, most people have access to a variety of Christian programs.

With the wide variety of denominational, nondenominational, and independently owned programs, a Christian needs to use some discernment. There have been some well-publicized scandals concerning TV evangelists involved in dishonest financial dealings and sexual misconduct. Their shameful deeds have caused many to fall away from the faith.

The Bereans set a good example for us. Even with the apostle Paul, they "examined the Scriptures every day to see if what Paul said was true." The Bible is our source for judging whose teachings are true and faithful. It tells us of Christ, our Savior and Redeemer. It is on Him we rely for salvation.

When, as the Bereans, we read our Bible every day and seek the Holy Spirit's guidance to understand it, we can be more certain of discerning between false teachers and true ministers of God's Word. True ministers and the Bible will point us to our Savior, Jesus Christ.

How precious is the book divine,
By inspiration giv'n!
Bright as a lamp its teachings shine
To guide our souls to heav'n.
("How Precious Is the Book Divine," by John Fawcett)

Lord, keep us faithful to Your Word. Amen.

JIM WIEMERS

Romans 1:17

The Best Day of the Month

For in the gospel a righteousness from God is revealed, a righteousness that is by faith from first to last, just as it is written: "The righteous will live by faith." Romans 1:17

The best day of the month is when I get my bank statement. It is not that I enjoy taking the time to go through all the checks written during the previous month, balancing the checkbook against the bank records. What makes it the best day is that then I have the clear, written guarantee that the companies I sent checks for payment accepted that payment and declared the debt removed.

That is what the resurrection of Jesus is all about, God declaring that the payment Jesus made in His crucifixion is acceptable and our debt of sin is paid. In place of the debt caused by our sin, God declares the gift of righteousness. All of the righteousness of Christ is given to us, and we are right with God.

This rightness with God comes in faith, with the Holy Spirit gathering us to God as children, just as He gathered the Old Testament faithful. Only then, as children being right with their Father, can there be real life. Payment is made for the debt hanging over us, and the debt is cleared. In Jesus Christ we can truly live in hope and move with courage. Our oneness with God empowers us to love and forgive, to share and witness, to help and support others in the life we have received in Jesus.

Merciful God, we praise You for Your love in bringing us into unity with You by the gift of Jesus, our Savior. Amen.

PAUL J. ALBERS

Romans 3:28

Salvation Is God's Gift

For we maintain that a man is justified by faith apart from observing the law. Romans 3:28

One of the tenets that sets Christianity apart from other religions is that salvation and eternal life are not dependent on things we do or laws we keep. In many religions the individual is constantly on a quest to achieve a higher level of holiness or must be careful to follow all the rules and regulations of his or her faith.

Sometimes, even Christians become so concerned about what they should or shouldn't do and spend so much time dwelling on their anger or guilt that they forget that there is nothing of their own doing that can make them right with God.

Being declared right with God (justification) has nothing to do with our works or efforts. It is a gift God gives to us through Jesus' coming into the world, His dying on the cross for our sins, and His rising again. This forgiveness is distributed to us freely in Baptism.

Does this mean that the Law has no function in our life? No, as St. Paul continues in this chapter (v. 31), there is one very important law for us to remember—to love one another. "Love is the fulfillment of the law" (Romans 13:10).

Lord, keep us ever mindful that salvation comes from Jesus, not our works, and help us show His love for us by loving others. In Jesus' name we pray. Amen.

JIM WIEMERS

Romans 5:1–4

Access to the Throne of Grace

Therefore, since we have been justified through faith, we have peace with God through our Lord Jesus Christ, through whom we have gained access by faith into this grace in which we now stand. And we rejoice in the hope of the glory of God. Not only so, but we also rejoice in our sufferings, because we know that suffering produces perseverance; perseverance, character; and character, hope. Romans 5:1–4

Ask any up-and-coming salesperson what she needs the most to make her deals, and she'll reply, "That's simple—access!" To get ahead, you have to be able to get to the top, to access the decision-maker—the big cheese. If not, you'll get the runaround.

The process of the Christian life revolves around access. Christians have access, says Paul, to the very grace of God! We stand in the throne room of grace before our God. Consider that location—it is the Holy of Holies. And it is our home.

Now how did we get there? The door of access to the throne of grace is justification by faith. This is the doctrine Martin Luther called the "one solid rock." Justification, Luther stated, is this: "By faith alone in Christ, without works, are we declared just and saved." The action of Christ alone opens the door of access to the throne. All other doors are locked and shut! We stand in grace through faith because of Christ. There is no stronger position in heaven or on earth.

Because our God has made grace accessible, we can rejoice through every trial and difficulty because our hope in the glory of God is already sure. Life's difficulties can be faced squarely when we stand in God's accessible grace!

Dear Lord, thank You for the door of access to Your eternal grace. May I remain strong through trials because of the grace in which I stand. Amen.

DAVID H. BENKE

Romans 5:8

Love without Condition

But God demonstrates His own love for us in this: While we were still sinners, Christ died for us. Romans 5:8

New Testament writers used three Greek words for "love." *Philia* is the love of friends; *eros* is the love of intimacy. We applaud these expressions of love. True, they can be abused, and sexual harassment occurs. But friendship and intimacy are good experiences. The problem, however, is that both of these types of love are tentative because they depend on the lovableness of the one loved. "I just don't love her anymore" is the reason some have given for divorce. Something happened so that a spouse no longer seems to be lovable. The same is true with friends whose friendship dissolves.

The marvel of God's love is in Himself, not in the lovability of the people He loves. We are sinners! Unlovable! Not deserving of any favors—but loved with such a love that God gave His only Son to be our Savior. Not as soon as we get good enough! Not as soon as we do enough good works! But because God is love we are loved. This third kind of love is called *agape*. God had such *agape* for the world that He gave His one and only Son. God has such *agape* for you and me that we received faith and were brought into His family by the gift of the Spirit. God has such *agape* that He desires all to be saved and to come to the knowledge of the truth. This is truly love "while we were still sinners."

Keep us, O Lord, in Your love that we may ever be with You. Amen.

PAUL J. ALBERS

Romans 6:4

From Death to New Life

We were therefore buried with Him through baptism into death in order that, just as Christ was raised from the dead through the glory of the Father, we too may live a new life. Romans 6:4

Water has many uses. It can be used for cleansing, for refreshment, for helping things grow. Many of these images are reflected in Baptism. One image, though, is often overlooked: Water can kill. Baptism does kill. Paul reminds us of that when he says that "we were ... buried with [Christ] through baptism into death."

Baptism brings death, death to our old ways of thinking and acting. Baptism says that our problem is not that we need a few minor moral adjustments. It's not that we need improvement. Rather, Baptism says that we are so enslaved to sin that nothing less than daily death will do. That's what Martin Luther was getting at when he said that baptizing with water and the Word means "that the Old Adam in us should, by daily contrition and repentance, be drowned and die with all sins and evil lusts and, again, a new man daily come forth and arise, who shall live before God in righteousness and purity forever."

With the daily deaths to sin come the daily resurrections, where "just as Christ was raised from the dead through the glory of the Father, we too may live a new life." Since we daily die and rise in remembrance of our Baptism, in daily repentance, we need not fear death because we have been practicing for it each day.

> All who believe and are baptized
> Shall see the Lord's salvation;
> Baptized into the death of Christ,
> They are a new creation;
> Through Christ's redemption they will stand
> Among the glorious heav'nly band
> Of ev'ry tribe and nation. Amen.
>
> ("All Who Believe and Are Baptized," by Thomas H. Kingo)

HENRY GERIKE

Romans 6:23

Earned or Given?

For the wages of sin is death, but the gift of God is eternal life in Christ Jesus our Lord. Romans 6:23

Everyone always worries about their pay rate. Unions are formed to protect workers' pay and strikes are called to demand greater pay. Conflicts in the church arise over what a pastor or a teacher will be paid compared to what other people are paid. Call this selfishness or call it greed, but call it reality. We are all concerned about what we are going to be paid, and we believe we deserve every penny.

The only pay we are guaranteed, however, is the payment of death, for "the wages of sin is death." "All have sinned and fall short of the glory of God" (Romans 3:23), and "the soul who sins is the one who will die" (Ezekiel 18:4). You sin, and I sin. As sinners we deserve only death.

Only in knowing what we deserve (death) can we truly experience what we are given—eternal life in Christ Jesus, our Lord. Not earned, not gained by merit, not accomplished by decision or good works, but given, free and clear. How marvelous is the love of God that Jesus Christ was born, suffered, and died on the cross in our place. How much beyond our understanding that Jesus rose again on the third day to declare the final and ultimate victory over death. How much more gracious that we are given unity with Jesus by faith.

Lord, keep me in Your love that I may always receive Your gift. Amen.

PAUL J. ALBERS

Romans 8:1–2

Live Free

Therefore, there is now no condemnation for those who are in Christ Jesus, because through Christ Jesus the law of the Spirit of life set me free from the law of sin and death. Romans 8:1–2

In John 8:1–11 we read the story of a woman brought to Jesus because she was guilty of adultery. The religious leaders wanted her stoned according to the law. Jesus recognized that the woman was guilty, she had been caught in the act of sinning. But instead of stoning the woman, Jesus said that whichever religious leader was without sin should cast the first stone. One by one the leaders left. None of them could condemn her, for each was also guilty of some sin. Finally the woman was alone with Jesus. Jesus said to the woman, "Neither do I condemn you, go now and leave your life of sin" (John 8:11).

We find that same attitude when we come to God repenting and confessing our sins. There is no question that we are guilty. But rather than being condemned or rejected because we have failed again, we are forgiven. Jesus didn't come to condemn the world, but to save it (see John 3:17).

So why are we so quick to condemn one another? The minute a friend or acquaintance lets us down, makes wrong choices, or falls into sin, we point fingers. We spread gossip and lose respect for that person. Yet each one of us is guilty of our own sins. We need to be kind and gentle with one another and quick to forgive. We are all guilty but not condemned. We are loved.

Holy Spirit, bring to my mind sins I need to confess to receive forgiveness. Teach me to be forgiving and noncondemning toward others. Amen.

BOBBIE REED

Romans 8:16

Innocent Children of God

The Spirit Himself testifies with our spirit that we are God's children.
Romans 8:16

The age of innocence is over. Children are bombarded with sights and sounds that jade the soul from infancy. This overexposure of children to harsh evil images drives parents to distraction. It seems there is no safe haven. Unrest invades the family circle as well, and as the ancient Chinese proverb has it, "Nobody's family can hang out the sign, 'Nothing's the matter here.' "

Only the Spirit of God can bring the fresh breeze of restored innocence into souls staled and stolen by the cultural winds. And it is precisely the Spirit's function to breathe in us a simple sentence that changes everything: "We are God's children."

What a fresh start! In truth, there never was an age of innocence. We are "by nature sinful and unclean." We originate that way, so innocence had to be imported.

And it has been. Because of the Father's love, through His only-begotten Son, and by the power of the Holy Spirit in Baptism we are declared innocent. We are declared to be God's children. This heavenly family is forever. This family has a dear Father. This family has a brother named Jesus. And all of us in the family can hear the voice of the Spirit calling us as God's children.

Holy Spirit, breathe in me the innocence of Christ to make me a child of God. Keep me safe in the arms of my dear Father forever for the sake of Jesus. Amen.

DAVID H. BENKE

Romans 8:18

The Wrong Question

I consider that our present sufferings are not worth comparing with the glory that will be revealed in us. Romans 8:18

The disciples asked Jesus, "Rabbi, who sinned, this man or his parents, that he was born blind?" (John 9:2). In effect they asked, "Why did this happen to him?" *Why* is a question that always drives me back to myself—my pain, my sorrow. And the more I become wrapped up in myself, the more wretched I become.

"But this happened so that the work of God might be displayed in his life." Is this answer any better? Am I a pawn of God, a plaything He enjoys knocking around to see how I bounce? No, a thousand times no. The sacrifice of His only Son on the cross has paid for all our sins and has redeemed the world, which was condemned by our sin. That sacrifice demonstrated His love to us. He cannot negate that love by toying with our lives.

That is why Jesus' answer is liberating. He teaches us to ask, "To what end?" The answer to this question draws our attention away from ourselves to God's plans for our future. We are given a new direction, for we know that "in all things God works for the good of those who love Him, who have been called according to His purpose" (Romans 8:28). We are hopeful even in the worst situations because we know that we are headed for the best that a loving God can plan for us. We know that our present sufferings, no matter what they may be, lose their significance in light of the glory that will be revealed in us at the last day.

Holy God, You know Your thoughts toward us, thoughts of good and not of evil. Fix our eyes on Jesus so that we trust Your plans and await Your deliverance by the power of Your Holy Spirit. Amen.

DONALD W. SANDMANN

Romans 8:26

Lord, Teach Us to Pray

We do not know what we ought to pray for, but the Spirit Himself intercedes for us with groans that words cannot express. Romans 8:26

"Pastor, I made a big mistake in my prayer life," said the parishioner. "I asked God for something, and I *got* it!"

"I shouldn't have prayed that way," comments another parishioner. "I forgot to add, 'If it be *Your* will, O Lord.' I was concentrating on what *I* wanted!"

How often we misunderstand *how* to pray and what to pray *for.*

- We err when we fail to ask for the wisdom to pray properly. The problem is we often try to impose our will on God's will. But we need God's wisdom, not our own.
- We err when we ask God to bless our plans. (You want to make God laugh? Tell Him your plans.) Rather, we are to ask, "Lord, what would *You* have me do?"
- We err if we merely inform God about our trouble. He already knows what's going on. Instead, we are to seek to make *God's* will our own will.
- We are not to depend on prayer to solve our problems. We are to depend on *God.*

Only the Spirit of God can teach us how to pray. May you and I better learn from the Master Teacher in the best of times and in the worst of times to pray continually, to be thankful constantly, and to rejoice always (1 Thessalonians 5:16–17).

But, as in everything, when we fail in our prayer, may we turn to Jesus and ask for forgiveness, knowing that through His blood on the cross it has already been granted. Jesus is the ultimate answer to prayer! "Evening and morning and at noon I will pray, and cry aloud, and He shall hear my voice" (Psalm 55:17 NKJV).

"Lord, teach us to pray" (Luke 11:1); always in the powerful name of Jesus Christ and according to Your holy will. Amen.

DONALD L. DEFFNER

Romans 8:28

Faith—Share Now and Later

We know that in all things God works for the good of those who love Him, who have been called according to His purpose. Romans 8:28

Many years ago while in the waiting room of an attorney's office, I began browsing through a book. It contained listings of many items that had been included in wills. Since my purpose for seeing the attorney was to draw up a will to name legal guardians for our children if my husband and I should die, the contents of the book were most interesting to me.

One of the prototype wills stated that if the writer could give his heirs anything, it would be the salvation of Jesus Christ. However, since he could not do this, he bequeathed them his earthly goods.

Immediately, my thoughts turned to my young children. If I were to die while they were young, I wanted my will to speak God's words to them. It did not take long to choose Romans 8:28 to be included in the will. As the years passed, the children learned that this verse had been chosen for them and the reasons why. My husband and I wanted them to know that even if we had died while they were young the Lord would have taken care of them. They were to know that there may be times when they won't understand why something happens but that God knows best and that things will work out for their good in the end.

Although the children are long past any need for minor guardianship, they will always be in need of knowing that "in all things God works for the good of those who love Him, who have been called according to His purpose."

Today, my will affords me the opportunity to share my faith in Jesus with future generations and to share monetary gifts to help spread the Good News after I die.

Do you have a will? Does it reflect your faith in Jesus?

Dear Father, thank You for the comfort Your words give at all times in our lives. Amen.

IDA MALL

Romans 8:32

Questions and Answers

He who did not spare His own Son, but gave Him up for us all—how will He not also, along with Him, graciously give us all things? Romans 8:32

Few passages in Scripture summarize the assurance of a Christian better than Romans 8:31–39. There are four questions asked with four answers.

1. Q: "If God is for us, who can be against us?" (v. 31)
   A: "He who did not spare His own Son, but gave Him up for us all—how will He not also, along with Him, graciously give us all things?" (v. 32)
2. Q: "Who will bring any charge against those whom God has chosen?" (v. 33a)
   A: "It is God who justifies." (v. 33b)
3. Q: "Who is He that condemns?" (v. 34a)
   A: "Christ Jesus, who died—more than that, who was raised to life—is at the right hand of God and is also interceding for us." (v. 34b)
4. Q: "Who shall separate us from the love of Christ?" (v. 35a)
   A: "No, in all these things we are more than conquerors through Him who loved us." (v. 37)

Think of the assurance these verses give to the Christian journeying to the cemetery to bury her husband of 50 years. Or the Christian who lives alone, who never hears from anyone, including his own children. Or the woman who has just been told by her husband that he wants a divorce because he no longer "feels in love." No matter what the situation or the circumstance, God assures us that "He who did not spare His own Son, but gave Him up for us" will give us everything that we need. Everything! Forgiveness! His love! Whatever we need!

Everlasting Father, we rejoice that You are for us, and so, most assuredly, no one can be against us. We rejoice that no one can

bring any charge against us. No one can condemn us because of our many sins. You died for us. You won for us forgiveness. We rejoice that nothing or nobody can separate us from Your love. Thank You. Amen.

ROGER R. SONNENBERG

Romans 8:34–39

He Brings Us Back

For I am convinced that neither death nor life, neither angels nor demons, neither the present nor the future, nor any powers, neither height nor depth, nor anything else in all creation, will be able to separate us from the love of God that is in Christ Jesus our Lord. Romans 8:38–39

Many people act like individuals lost on a ship at sea. They're scuttling the boat, knocking down the bulkhead, toppling the mast. Their boat is sinking, and they are wailing in distress.

They remind me of Tennessee Williams' response when someone asked him: "What are you trying to say in your plays?"

He responded: "All I'm trying to say is: HELP! HELP!"

That's all some people do: cry for help.

At an apartment ministry worship service in Dallas, the pastor pushed his hand through the bills in the offering plate and found a simple, crumpled note. It read: "God, I hurt!"

But that's all some people do is hurt, and grope, and search. And they never admit to the need for help from *outside* themselves. They are like the college student whose friend asked him: "What're ya doin'?"

"Oh," said the student, sighing: "I'm searching for God."

"Oh!" replied his friend. "Is *He* lost again?"

That is the basic problem of our generation. We think that God is lost, and we all have to go and find Him. But *it's just the other way around!*

Yes, the Savior is looking for *us. We* are the ones who have often separated ourselves from our loving, caring Savior. But He has given His life to pay for our sins and to bring us back to Him.

Now I will not wander, Lord. Now I shall not be in want. Thanks be to God for His Son, the Good Shepherd, who has formed us and made us His own! Amen.

DONALD L. DEFFNER

Romans 9:1–5

A Remnant Will Be Saved

I have great sorrow and unceasing anguish in my heart. For I could wish that I myself were cursed and cut off from Christ for the sake of my brothers, those of my own race, the people of Israel. Theirs is the adoption as sons; theirs the divine glory, the covenants, the receiving of the law, the temple worship and the promises. Theirs are the patriarchs, and from them is traced the human ancestry of Christ, who is God over all, forever praised! Romans 9:1–5

What a heart-wrenching lamentation! Paul's words hark back to Exodus 32. Moses had gone to the mountain to meet with God. The Israelites' became impatient and commissioned Aaron to make a golden calf for them to worship. They had just been wondrously delivered from their Egyptian slavery, miraculously fed and given water in the desert, and supernaturally led through the wilderness. Yet they wanted a god of their own making to worship. Imagine how Moses felt when he returned from his summit conference with God to see them worshiping an idol.

Despite all the advantages listed by Paul in our text, which God had provided for the descendants of Abraham (and Paul was one of them), they had largely chosen to resist the action of God on their behalf. They were rejecting the work of the Son of God for them, which could have given them the abundant life that Christ promised. It's no wonder Paul is in anguish. Let us anguish, too, over those who are rejecting what God has to offer. But let us at the same time rejoice greatly that He has called us out of our darkness into His marvelous light!

Dear Father, thank You for calling us into Your family. Use us to make known Your love and salvation in Jesus Christ. Empower and equip us to be powerful witnesses as You provide opportunity, especially to those who are rejecting You and Your promises, through Christ, our Lord. Amen.

DANIEL SCHLENSKER

Romans 14:8

Living and Dying to the Lord

If we live, we live to the Lord; and if we die, we die to the Lord. So, whether we live or die, we belong to the Lord. Romans 14:8

To some, including myself, there are times that our lives seem to revolve around a sports team. It is even said that some people live and die with their favorite team.

For a former pastor, who was also a dear friend, life was good or bad depending on whether the Texas Longhorns football team won or lost. Since the two of us delighted in being on opposite sides on any given subject (especially sporting events), a football game on New Year's Day provided one of those opportunities. Upon the arrival at the pastor's home, I gleefully announced that my loyalty would be with the Texas Longhorns. With his head, but not his heart, Pastor rooted for the opposing team.

Within a few years, he accepted a call to another congregation in the special world of Texas. For several additional years, this pastor enjoyed life, living to the Lord. In God's time, and at a relatively young age, Pastor was called to his heavenly home, dying to the Lord. His earthly life and cheering for Texas were completed.

Like Paul, who had said, "If we live, we live to the Lord; and if we die, we die to the Lord," so in his life and in death Pastor's faith was shared with many people. It was very easy for him to converse with people of different life histories.

Knowing that Pastor had lived and died in the Lord and knowing that God is faithful to His promises, I am assured that he has life eternal. Therefore, like my pastor, we know that whether we live or die, the only thing that really matters is that we belong to the Lord.

Do our lives share our faith?

Dear Father, help us to always live to You so that our death will mean living with You forever. Amen.

IDA MALL

Romans 15:13

Joy—A Humming Sound

May the God of hope fill you with all joy and peace as you trust in Him, so that you may overflow with hope by the power of the Holy Spirit. Romans 15:13

What causes you to hum for no reason? Usually our unplanned or unexplained humming is an indication of a deep abiding peace or overflowing joy. Does it happen at the spectacular beauty of the majestic mountains, the sight of a small child peaceably asleep, the melodious sounds of chirping birds, the miracle of the birth of a child, the glorious color of a sunrise or sunset?

Small children seem to find great joy in filling a pitcher or glass with water to overflowing. The faster the water goes over the sides the brighter their eyes sparkle. The cascading water running over the glass edge produces an excitement and joy that cannot be contained. They will jump up and down and clap. It is their form of humming.

Adding God's power through the words "in the name of the Father and of the Son and of the Holy Spirit" to the very simple water enjoyed by the children gives us hope now and forever. The God of hope, who has done everything needed for our eternal life, is ready to fill to overflowing each one of us with this joy and peace as we trust in Him. Jesus says, "I have come that they may have life, and have it to the full" (John 10:10). He would have joy and peace brim over the edges of our lives to touch others. He makes our lives hum.

Do other people see the overflowing joy, peace, and hope in our daily Christian walk? Are you humming?

Dear Father, may our daily Christian lives of overflowing joy, peace, and hope touch those who do not know You. Amen.

IDA MALL

1 Corinthians 1:27

An Upside-down Deity—to Us

But God chose the foolish things of the world to shame the wise; God chose the weak things of the world to shame the strong. 1 Corinthians 1:27

Our God's stock in trade seems to be surprise. No, wait—maybe that's really not so. He is steady in His purpose and consistent in the way He works. We are the ones with twisted expectations, warped by our way of thinking. Isaiah punches a hole in the thinking of those who don't see this by quoting the Lord, "My thoughts are not your thoughts" (Isaiah 55:8).

A couple verses earlier in this chapter (1:25) Paul made that same point, saying, "The foolishness of God is wiser than man's wisdom, and the weakness of God is stronger than man's strength." There's our problem—we think we know the mind of God, or what it ought to be; but He doesn't work that way.

For the topsy-turvy way we think the Lord's mind works, look to the cross and the plan of salvation He established. It makes no human sense, but it gets us all home. And by what route? By faith in Christ Jesus. How odd of God, say some! How divine, say we!

Lord, help us see Your ways as best and trust in them. Amen.

CHARLES S. MUELLER

1 Corinthians 2:9

We Can Hardly Wait

However, as it is written: "No eye has seen, no ear has heard, no mind has conceived what God has prepared for those who love Him." 1 Corinthians 2:9

God has prepared an eternity of indescribable beauty for His children. We can get a hint of it by looking around.

We can see God's handiwork in creation. In his poem *Trees*, Joyce Kilmer identified the shadow of eternity in forests: "Poems are made by fools like me, / But only God can make a tree."

Sunsets give a hint, too, as do mountain ranges, miles of waving wheat, dancing porpoises, and rainbows. You can add to the list love in bloom, your child's smile, and the fun of growing older. Those are all wonders of the first order. But they don't capture the beauty of His readied home for us.

While we can't describe heaven, this we do know: It's more of and better than anything we've experienced here on earth. God's promise is that for all who trust in the work Christ has done on our behalf the best is yet to come.

Jesus, as You have made eternity possible for us, ready us also to find it through faith in You. Amen.

CHARLES S. MUELLER

1 Corinthians 3:16

A Living Temple

Don't you know that you yourselves are God's temple and that God's Spirit lives in you? 1 Corinthians 3:16

My father was a saintly man. I never heard foul language come from him. If anyone would curse within earshot of my older brother or myself, he would ask the person, "Do you eat with that mouth?" He got across his point.

At Baptism Christians become the dwelling place of the Holy Spirit. God Himself takes up residency, working mightily in us and through us, shaping us, working in us the mind of Christ. What sort of living conditions do we provide? Do we fill our lives with godly things, or do we defile ourselves by what we take in? What witness do we give of our house guest? Do we speak in a way that shows we are controlled by the Spirit, or do we pollute others by our language and conduct? A sign on my professor's office door succinctly stated, "A Christian should be an *alleluia* from head to foot." Such a tall order is only possible with the help of God.

Thanks be to God, we are forgiven through Jesus' blood and merit and assured of God's never-ending love. He never gives up on us, but daily cleanses and restores us, enabling us to continue to be His vessel throughout our earthly days.

Christ Jesus, Lord and Savior, come, open wide my heart, Your home. Amen.

JAMES W. FREESE

247

1 Corinthians 6:9–11

Face the Music!

Do you not know that the wicked will not inherit the kingdom of God?
... But you were washed, you were sanctified, you were justified in the
name of the Lord Jesus Christ and by the Spirit of our God.
1 Corinthians 6:9–11

Have you ever wondered where the phrase "face the music"
comes from? A Chinese legend tells the story of a corrupt man who
became part of the Emperor's orchestra, even though he could not
play an instrument. Every time the orchestra would perform, he
would raise a flute to his lips, but no sound was produced. He was
a fake! One day, the Emperor declared that each member of his
orchestra would have to play a solo.

The man became frantic! He hired the best flute teacher money
could buy, but still he could not play a note. He pretended to be
deathly ill, but the Emperor's physician examined him, finding him
fit. Finally, the day of his appointment for his solo came. He could
not "face the music," and so he killed himself.

God reminds us that one day each of us will have to "face the
music." We will all stand before the judgment seat of God. And
because of our sinfulness, we do not deserve to inherit the kingdom
of God. Yet, for those of us who believe in Jesus Christ, we have
Someone who faced the music for us. On the cross, Jesus took our
place. He suffered our punishment for our sins.

Our faith in Jesus Christ assures us that at our time of judgment
we will be declared, "Not guilty!" Even though we could not face
the music of our sinfulness, God declares us righteous through His
Son, Jesus. In Him we were washed, sanctified, and justified.
Because of Him, we can rest assured that we will inherit the
Kingdom. What a great God we have!

**Dear Jesus, thank You for facing the music for me and taking
away my sins. Amen.**

LUTHER C. BRUNETTE

1 Corinthians 6:19

Now, Wait a Minute Here!

Do you not know that your body is a temple of the Holy Spirit, who is in you, whom you have received from God? You are not your own. 1 Corinthians 6:19

The Bible is full of startling truths. Some explode with an insight that some people can hardly handle. This verse often has that effect. To the *me* generation (an it's-my-life-to-do-with-as-I-please people), Paul says, "You are not your own." You belong to God. Boom!

Belong to God? What an incredible thought! Does it mean that God wants me? Does it mean that God cares about me? Does it mean I have value to Him? Yes. Yes. And yes. You are so valuable that the Father sent His Son to the cross to gain you again for Himself. Yes, He wants you. But that's not the whole of it.

He also wants you to act like a divinely wanted person. Maximize life. Treat yourself like the person of value you are. And treat that body for which He died like it's His. It is. You are His. Twice over. He made you. He bought you back.

Father, empower me by the Spirit to treat myself like I'm Yours—for I am. Amen.

CHARLES S. MUELLER

1 Corinthians 10:13

Yes, You Can

No temptation has seized you except what is common to man. And God is faithful; He will not let you be tempted beyond what you can bear. But when you are tempted, He will also provide a way out so that you can stand up under it. 1 Corinthians 10:13

Folks who say, "It's more than I can bear," or "I can't stand it," need Paul's good news. For those facing difficulty, let's unpack this verse:

1. You are not the only one with your type of burden. Others have it, too. Look around and find comfort in a shared burden.
2. God is faithful. He's on the side of all who have problems. He never abandons the suffering. Never.
3. No, it's not more than you can bear. Your burden may be more than you *want* to bear, but it's not more than you *can* bear. You can make it.
4. Open your eyes. The road to relief can be found. Look for it. The God who brought Christ down from the cross to a victorious resurrection is full of amazing blessings. He can and will help you handle your burden.

Christ, on the cross, still called God *Father*. In His darkest moment, He cried out "My God …" In your darkest moments, you, too, can cry out to your Father—and He will hear you.

Jesus, let me find the way out—and up. Amen.

CHARLES S. MUELLER

1 Corinthians 13:5

Who's on First?

[Love] is not self-seeking. 1 Corinthians 13:5

It's just about the only thing that isn't. It's really difficult to find anything today, any action, any philosophy, any motive that isn't out to pad the account of number one.

Love, Christian love, is a tiger of a different stripe. The truth outlined in this verse is startling: "[Love] is not self-seeking." Imagine that in a world as grasping as ours. Christian love isn't outraged when life treats it unfairly, doesn't go into a blue funk when others prosper for efforts no better than our own. It doesn't send us on our way to look out for our so-called rights. (Whatever made them our rights, I'd like to know. We have to be careful when talking about rights. Careful consideration makes us shudder at the thought of what we rightfully have coming.) Christian love would have us ignore these so-called rights and eliminate altogether the personal element from our calculations.

The Bible often pulls us up short with its notions so contrary to our own. Having what is rightfully yours loses out to not being interested in what is yours at all, but in being interested in the other person instead. "Whoever wants to become great among you must be your servant" (Matthew 20:26). Happiness, satisfaction, and fulfillment consist simply and solely in being useful to somebody else.

"[Love] is not self-seeking." However, you can't just say it ought to be that way and bring it off. It takes something more than clenched fists and a yank at your bootstraps. It takes that mind in you that was also in Christ Jesus. That mind is Christ's gift to His people.

Teach me, dear Savior, to think and do as You, to come not to be served and sated, but to wait upon my fellow citizens, for in doing so will I fulfill what is the law of Christ. Amen.

ARNOLD KUNTZ

1 Corinthians 15:55

The Final Healing

Where, O death, is your victory? Where, O death, is your sting?
1 Corinthians 15:55

When I was a child, death held a fearful presence but no sting or victory. It was remote and only intruded into my world by the sudden fury of an accident or a one-in-a-million disease. But now I am older. Death is an almost daily event touching one friend here and another there. Death hurts. What do I do?

I have found the pain to be less oppressive when I get the order of events straight. When Paul speaks of death, he starts with *victory*. Then he turns to talk about *sting*.

When the matter of victory is considered first and understood as a triumph (in the balance of this chapter, especially verses 20–23, Paul explains Christ's conquest of death by His self-sacrifice on the cross), then the sting of separation loses its bite, leaving only a temporary loneliness in its wake.

Christ achieved the victory first. Death's sting was numbed second. Knowing and believing this I can even laugh in the face of this defanged adversary.

Dear Lord, Your death on the cross for us neutralized the feared appearance of death. May we be Spirit-led to claim Your work as ours and see this old enemy as nothing more than the door to eternity. Amen.

CHARLES S. MUELLER

1 Corinthians 15:58

Therefore ...

Therefore, my dear brothers, stand firm. Let nothing move you. Always give yourselves fully to the work of the Lord, because you know that your labor in the Lord is not in vain. 1 Corinthians 15:58

Therefore is a wonderful, transitional word. When a *therefore* shows up, you usually find that a long line of reasoning has been developing, leading to compelling implications.

This particular *therefore* reaches a long way back into 1 Corinthians. A good way to understand its place is to read everything from 1 Corinthians 10:1 through 15:57 as the preamble, building a case. Now, Paul is ready to draw a conclusion. He shows this with the word *therefore*.

And what is the conclusion? In the light of all he develops from 10:1 to 15:57, Paul urges both a change in any flawed lifestyle and a reinforced commitment to a positive one. In rapid-fire order he gives his *therefore* meaning by urging three life responses to six chapters of truth: stand firm (Yes!), immovable (Yes!), always giving yourself in the Lord's work (Yes! Yes!). And then he gives his reason for these actions: knowing that when you live that way you are engaged in purposeful and eternal activity (Yes! Yes! Yes!).

Lord, help me to hear important things You have done for me and ready me to respond affirmatively to Your *therefore* with a life of *yes*. Amen.

CHARLES S. MUELLER

2 Corinthians 1:20

Promise Keeper

For no matter how many promises God has made, they are "Yes" in Christ. And so through Him the "Amen" is spoken by us to the glory of God. 2 Corinthians 1:20

Promise keepers? Promises, it would seem, are made to be broken. Native American Chief Black Elk stated eloquently 100 years ago that the white man "made us many promises, and broke them all." Leonard Sweet lists the number one personally broken promise as "I'll start dieting/exercising tomorrow."

However, at the deepest level, the most-broken promises are always those made to our God. Before Him we stand without excuse and without power to change.

Therefore, it is up to God and God alone to be the promise keeper. All of God's promises must be kept for us to have hope. They include life, health, strength, blessings, peace, contentment, love, and many more listed in Scripture; enough promises to keep the scribes searching for decades. So God has made it easy on us. All His promises are made good in Christ. In Him every one is a "Yes," says Paul. Check the little list above—in Christ, are they all promises made good? *Yes!*

All that is left is to live your life as one loud *Amen.* Which, being translated, is "Yes, indeed!" That is you, and that is me—"yes, indeeds" to our promise-keeping God.

Dear God, help me to be an *amen* to the promise of Christ, who lives within me. Amen and Amen!

DAVID H. BENKE

2 Corinthians 4:16–18

Old, but New

For our light and momentary troubles are achieving for us an eternal glory that far outweighs them all. So we fix our eyes not on what is seen, but on what is unseen. For what is seen is temporary, but what is unseen is eternal. 2 Corinthians 4:17–18

My 98-year-old neighbor was finally overcome by her infirmities and entered our local Lutheran Home for the Aging. She would shriek as she passed any mirror, horrified by her aged, shriveled appearance. During my last visit with her she pleaded, "Please tell the nurses I used to be somebody!" I was moved by the remark. To me she *was* still somebody special despite her appearance.

Time-worn Christians, bodies ravaged by age and the hardships of life, are still viewed as children by our heavenly Father. Feeble and of fading worth in the world's eyes, they are quite the opposite to those who know of the miracle of faith the Holy Spirit has worked in their lives. Bound for eternity, nourished and steeped in the Word, firmly rooted in the knowledge that they have been redeemed by Christ on Calvary, they stand on the very precipice of eternity, gathering their remaining strength to journey across the Jordan with angelic escort.

In his hymn "I Walk in Danger All the Way," Hans Brorson sums this up well: "For all the world I would not stay." Old on the surface, but new daily in faith and hope, they—and we—are bound for eternity. The past life on earth will gladly be forgotten. A glorious crown of life awaits. When this earthly tent in which we live is destroyed, God will have a home for us in heaven—one not made with hands.

> Renew me, O eternal Light,
> And let my heart and soul be bright,
> Illumined with the light of grace,
> That issues from Your holy face. Amen.
>
> ("Renew Me, O Eternal Light," by Johann F. Ruopp)

JAMES W. FREESE

2 Corinthians 5:15

"All" Reads "Each" and "They" Reads "I"

He died for all. 2 Corinthians 5:15

God does not deal with people en masse. When He looks down upon the human condition, it is the man baffled and bewildered because life keeps treating him so unkindly yet making no complaint, who comes into specific focus. It is the woman worried about her health and wondering how long she can keep going and what will happen to her loved ones when she finally must give in whom He spies. Mothers and fathers who are worried about their children whose characters seem subtly changed; young people grappling with pressures about which they dare tell no one; others who despise themselves and wish to God for some solution to turn their shame to peace and victory—these are who God sees.

The Gospel story is that God cannot bear to see us so weighted down by sin; that He goes into action to help us. Christ couldn't bear to see the poor mother at Nain, crying as if her heart would break as she stumbled along in the procession going out to bury her son: "Young man, I say to you, get up!" (Luke 7:14). Christ couldn't bear to see a leper, struck down by a slow and painful death: "Be clean!" (Matt. 8:3). As He hung on the cross, Christ couldn't bear to see men and women and children, all of whom He calls by name, caught in sin and tormented by past mistakes: "Father, forgive them" (Luke 23:34).

Christ could not bear to hear the human story, retold billions of times, each time with a different name. So a decree went out from Caesar Augustus; a baby was born; a perfect life was lived; there was a dreadful death, followed by a miraculous resurrection. "The Word became flesh and made His dwelling among us" (John 1:14).

Christ couldn't bear to see our misery, so He lived and died for us so that we, each of us, may live and die in Him and with Him rise again to life.

Love Divine, as shepherds on a quiet night broke the silence to proclaim Your coming, so would I, now, sing Your praise that, in this world of men and women, You have seen and You have saved even me. Amen.

ARNOLD KUNTZ

2 Corinthians 5:17

God of the Brand-new

Therefore, if anyone is in Christ, he is a new creation; the old has gone, the new has come! 2 Corinthians 5:17

There's that word *therefore* again. It sets the stage for a great insight: Those who trust the Lord distinguish their commitment by laying aside the old and wrapping themselves into the Lord. Result? A brand-new person.

New! As a child I enjoyed receiving a hand-me-down jacket. It spiced up my life for a moment. But what thrilled me to the core was getting a brand-new coat.

Christians who have been brought to faith in Christ by the Holy Spirit know that same kind of feeling. In the Savior they receive more than just a better attitude, an enhanced faith, or a livelier hope. They get a new life at two levels.

First, things change right here and now. We change. In so many ways we are re-formed by the Spirit! Second, and, most important, we are readied for eternity and the new life there.

And to think: it all started—and ended—with the Lord.

Thank You, Lord, for the newness that is ours in the Savior. It's all we'll ever need. Amen.

CHARLES S. MUELLER

2 Corinthians 12:9

Boasting of Weakness

But He said to me, "My grace is sufficient for you, for My power is made perfect in weakness." Therefore I will boast all the more gladly about my weaknesses, so that Christ's power may rest on me. 2 Corinthians 12:9

Christ's power is "made perfect in weakness"? What's that again? Here is just one more example of how upside-down Christ's ideas seem to be when viewed through the eyes of the world, which certainly does not admire weakness. It may be okay for the meek to inherit the earth, but weakness? That's a trait to pity, to abhor, and it is certainly not an avenue for power, of any kind, to be made perfect.

Except to Christ and His followers. Paul had three times pleaded with the Lord to take away the thorn in his flesh. We don't know the nature of that thorn. But we know from Paul's writings that God in His wisdom chose to answer Paul's prayer in a different way. He would use Paul's affliction to highlight His own divine power. In so doing, Christ's power was made perfect, and His grace was plenty.

And we are now to believe that Paul will gladly boast about his weaknesses? For some of us, that's taking things a bit too far. We prefer to boast of our accomplishments, or those of our children and friends. Yet to boast of our weakness is to be completely humble, knowing that it is Christ's working in us that produces any good.

Upside-down? Yes. A stumbling block to some? Certainly. But Christ has set things in perfect order. We are weak and He is strong.

Dear Mighty God, thank You for Your grace and power in my life. May I trust that You work in my weakness. Amen.

LAINE ROSIN

2 Corinthians 12:10

My God Is So Great

That is why, for Christ's sake, I delight in weaknesses, in insults, in hardships, in persecutions, in difficulties. For when I am weak, then I am strong. 2 Corinthians 12:10

One song that children love to sing includes the refrain, "My God is so great, so strong and so mighty; there's nothing my God cannot do." Children love to sing this because they flex their arms to show off their muscles; in their faith they know this is the power of God.

Paul the Apostle might have been flat on his back in the weakness of the thorn in the flesh, bent over in the hardships of traveling from one city to another, receiving insults and persecutions at every turn. Yet he says that this is when he is the strongest, for then he receives the fullest power of God.

When we imagine ourselves to be strong in ourselves, that is when we have the greatest weakness, for it is only our strength. But in our human weakness or sickness, then in faith the fullest strength of God comes to help us and carry us on. Paul seems to say, "Bring on the problem, the sickness, the difficulty; when I know I am weak, then the all-encompassing power of God comes by grace in Jesus Christ." Oh, for such a faith; yea, such a strength; truly such a gift of the power of God overcoming our weakness.

O God, You are so great; come help me in my weakness. Amen.

PAUL J. ALBERS

2 Corinthians 13:14

The Great Blessing

May the grace of the Lord Jesus Christ, and the love of God, and the fellowship of the Holy Spirit be with you all. 2 Corinthians 13:14

Boy, this says it all, doesn't it! This is the way Paul ends his letter to the Corinthians. And often this is what the pastor says at the end of his sermon.

It is more than Paul's blessing to the Corinthians. And it is more than the pastor's blessing to his congregation. It is God's blessing upon us. For in this blessing, God tells us about Himself.

This blessing tells us about God's great love for us, a love so great that He would seek a way for us to become acceptable to Him. For we are by our fallen sinful nature unacceptable to God, who is righteous and abhors sin. Not only do we carry the sin of Adam within us, but we carry our own sin within us daily.

God, however, loves us so much that He sent Jesus Christ, His only Son, to live as a man. To be the only perfect human being. Jesus said, "I will die for their sins. They will then be righteous and perfect in Your sight." It is by grace through faith in Christ's atoning death and resurrection that we are acceptable to God.

But God is not done with us yet. He sends us His Holy Spirit. Through the Holy Spirit, we are in fellowship with God and with each other. We are encouraged, we are comforted, and we are sustained in faith by this person of God.

This is a marvelous blessing. When the pastor shares this blessing with you, it is not merely a signal that the sermon is done, but it is a gift from God, an expression of His great love.

Dear God, Your love is so apparent. I thank You for loving me and for sending Your Holy Spirit to strengthen me. Help me to love others and share the news of Your great love. In Your Son's name, I pray. Amen.

KEVIN PARVIZ

261

Galatians 1:8

Beware of Adding to the Gospel!

But even if we or an angel from heaven should preach a gospel other than the one we preached to you, let him be eternally condemned. Galatians 1:8

The apostle Paul was not one to avoid strong language if the situation called for it. Here, in Galatians, the stakes couldn't have been higher. Paul had preached the Gospel to the Galatians. Then others followed, and they asserted that what Paul had said about Jesus Christ was well and good, but that in addition to faith in Jesus Christ it was necessary to obey some of the precepts of Old Testament law, most notably circumcision.

This issue is not only of historical interest, for it goes to the essence of the Gospel itself. God forgives our sins and declares us righteous solely for the sake of Jesus Christ. Nothing we do can earn this forgiveness and, contrary to what some in Galatia were teaching, we do nothing in addition to what Jesus does for us. When Jesus said, "It is finished," that is precisely what He meant.

To add something to the Gospel, to make something necessary beyond what God has already done for us in Jesus Christ, is to make everything depend again on something we do—even if it is something otherwise good like keeping God's law. To add to the Gospel is to preach a different Gospel. To add to the Gospel is to destroy the Gospel.

Because St. Paul understood that so well, he reacted to the situation as vehemently as he did. We can be confident and at peace, because our forgiveness and life rests totally in God's hands and not at all in our own.

Merciful God, out of Your mercy everything that needed to be done for our salvation was done in Jesus Christ. Always draw our attention to that accomplished fact whenever we might look elsewhere for our consolation. Amen.

DAVID LUMPP

Galatians 2:20

It Is Not I

I have been crucified with Christ and I no longer live, but Christ lives in me. Galatians 2:20

St. Augustine (354–430 A.D.) was one of the greatest church fathers. But in his youth he was a noted profligate. It was only through the influence of his mother, Monica, that he was "converted"—turned around and headed on a path of Christian virtue and piety.

One day, later in his life, he was walking through a certain section of town he had frequently haunted during his "hell-raising days." A prostitute recognized him from her window and called down to him: "Augustine! It is *I!* It is *I!*"

Augustine just kept walking. Again the woman called out: "Augustine! It is *I!*"

But Augustine just continued straight ahead, his face turning neither to the right or the left, as he replied: "But it is not *I*."

He had a new *I* in Christ. The old *I* no longer existed.

Paul expressed this to the Romans: "For we know that our old self was crucified with Him [Christ] so that the body of sin might be done away with, that we should no longer be slaves to sin" (Romans 6:6).

He repeated it to the Colossians: "For you died, and your life is now hidden with Christ in God" (Colossians 3:3).

O Lord, may I ever affirm with the apostle Paul, "I have been crucified with Christ and I no longer live, but Christ lives in me" (Galatians 2:20). Amen.

DONALD L. DEFFNER

Galatians 3:26–27

Borrowed Finery

You are all sons of God through faith in Christ Jesus, for all of you who were baptized into Christ have clothed yourselves with Christ. Galatians 3:26–27

When we are baptized it's as if we wrap ourselves in a robe named Jesus Christ. So says St. Paul.

Ever wonder what we must look like decked out in such borrowed finery? Like a child wearing daddy's clothes: coat draped over the shoulder and dragging on the ground; his hat plopped on our head, sagging down around the ears; tiny tootsies disappearing into huge shoes? You think we look like that?

Oh, no. The robe fits. We are perfectly garbed. Haberdashers twist the truth a little when they say that clothes make the man. That's not really true. Clothes may mask reality for a moment, but truth will always finally be served. However, when we are wrapped up in Christ, through Baptism, we are transformed and end up looking like Him! We share in His accomplishments! We receive His honor! And better yet, when the Father looks at us, standing before Him dressed in the Savior's righteousness, He doesn't see us. He sees a forgiven daughter or son, styled for eternity.

Lord, we thank You for all that has come to us through Baptism. We praise You for making us into that which we could never become on our own. Amen.

CHARLES S. MUELLER

Ephesians 2:5–6

The Greatest Blessing

[God] made us alive with Christ even when we were dead in transgressions—it is by grace you have been saved. Ephesians 2:5

What is the greatest blessing you could experience in this life: wealth, health, power, a happy family life, peace? The list of possibilities is almost endless. While the Christian enjoys countless blessings from God, there is one above every other. It is the forgiveness of sins.

The psalmist reminds us that none of us could ever come into God's presence if God would keep a record of our sins (Psalm 130:3). Our sins have separated us from God. We have done what we should not have done and not done what God has commanded us to do. We sin in thoughts, desires, words, and deeds. In fact, according to Paul's letter to the Ephesians, without Christ we are spiritually dead.

We justly deserved to be punished. How can it be that we are not and never will be punished for our sins? It is because the Father punished His Son on the cross for our sins. Through Christ we were made spiritually alive. Our sins are now fully forgiven, even forgotten (Hebrews 8:12). The wall of separation between God and humankind has been destroyed. "God was reconciling the world to Himself in Christ, not counting men's sins against them" (2 Corinthians 5:19).

Thanks be to God who gives us the victory through our Lord and Savior, Jesus Christ. There is no greater blessing than God's gift of forgiveness, which He freely gives us by grace for Christ's sake.

Lord, thank You for forgiving my sins for Jesus' sake. Amen.

ANDREW SIMCAK JR.

Ephesians 2:8–9

Christ Is the Only Way

For it is by grace you have been saved, through faith—and this not from yourselves, it is the gift of God—not by works, so that no one can boast. Ephesians 2:8–9

In *A Study of Generations*, Lutheran sociologist Merton Strommen found that of 5,000 Lutherans interviewed, 40 percent agreed with the following statements:

- Salvation depends on being sincere in whatever you believe.
- The main emphasis of the Gospel is on God's rules for right living.
- God is satisfied if a person lives the best life he or she can.
- If I say I believe in God and act right, I will get to heaven.
- Although there are many religions in the world, most of them lead to the same God.

The one thread leading through these five fallacious statements is a belief in salvation through our own good works, not through faith in Christ alone.

Scripture says, "For it is by grace you have been saved, through faith—and this not from yourselves, it is the gift of God—not by works, so that no one can boast" (Ephesians 2:8–9). God's Word refutes each of the five statements:

- Sincerity in what you believe does *not* get you to heaven. Only trust in Christ does. "By this gospel you are saved … otherwise, you have believed in vain" (1 Corinthians 15:2). You may be sincere in thinking your bus is headed for Chicago, but if San Diego is its true destination, that's where you will go.
- We *can't* keep God's commandments. We fail utterly. Only Christ *in us* can keep the Law perfectly—we are unable to. (See Colossians 1:27 and Philippians 2:13.)
- Trying hard isn't enough to please God. The best we can

do isn't good enough for God—"All our righteous acts are like filthy rags" (Isaiah 64:6). We plead for His mercy. Christ in us is our only hope.

- I can't "act right." On my own I am a walking disaster area. "There is a way that seems right to a man, but in the end it leads to death" (Proverbs 14:12). Throwing myself on Christ's indwelling power I have hope. In New Testament terms that means the *certainty* of heaven.

- *Christ* is the only *way* back to the Father. He *alone* saves me. "Salvation is found in no one else" (Acts 4:12).

I believe in Christ, my *only* Savior. It is by *grace* I have been saved! All praise and thanks be to You, dear Lord. Amen.

DONALD L. DEFFNER

Ephesians 4:15

Speaking the Truth in Love

Speaking the truth in love, we will in all things grow up into Him who is the Head, that is, Christ. Ephesians 4:15

St. Paul knew how the church was built up both externally and internally. He knew that the one key ingredient to the growth of Christ's church was that the Gospel of Jesus Christ be central to all its teaching and activity.

The readers of Paul's letter are to be "speaking the truth in love," and this rich phrase tells them both what they are to say and how they are to say it. Their message is the truth, and there is no greater truth for anyone to hear than the Gospel of Jesus, who described Himself as the way, the truth, and the life. The message of His death and resurrection for us is God's promise to us that we have forgiveness of sins, life, and salvation.

We speak that truth to each other "in love." Finally, there is no more loving thing we can do than to remind one another of the truth that our sins have been forgiven. Our life with God is now secure because in Baptism we have been joined with Him who died and was raised from the dead.

When the Gospel is spoken to us and when we speak the Gospel to others, extraordinary things happen. We are joined to Jesus Christ and become part of His body. We grow up into Him who is our head, and He now directs our activities. Above all, as part of His body, we draw our life from Him and serve Him as His willing instruments.

Merciful Lord, keep us always mindful of the truth from which everything else in our lives is derived, the message of Jesus Christ for the forgiveness of all of our sins. Amen.

DEBB ANDRUS

Ephesians 6:10–20

Ready for Action

Finally, be strong in the Lord and in His mighty power. Put on the full armor of God so that you can take your stand against the devil's schemes. Ephesians 6:10–11

In Ephesians 6:10–20, Paul warns believers to be prepared to fight against Satan. The Lord is not sending us out as spiritual cannon fodder; He just wants us to be fully outfitted for the fight.

If Paul were speaking today he'd say something like this: "God has all power and has won the war, but our enemy, Satan, still surrounds us in many evil guises, taking sniper shots at us. So grab that ammo belt of truth. Don't forget your flak jacket of righteousness! Or the combat boots, the gospel of peace! Strap on the bulletproof helmet of salvation, pick up your M-1 rifle of God's Word—and then let's fight, praying for everyone on our side all the way!"

If this sounds like the story line of a war movie, it is because Christians are, in fact, at war. We dare not relax or fall asleep at our post. We are called to courageous conduct knowing that our "weapons" from God are capable of both protecting us and stopping that old evil foe in his tracks.

Lord Jesus, as You fought the fight of faith and gained the victory for us, embolden us to be Your Christian soldiers. Amen.

CHARLES S. MUELLER

Ephesians 6:13

Fight Satan

Put on the full armor of God, so that when the day of evil comes, you may be able to stand your ground. Ephesians 6:13

How does a Christian wage war in his or her daily life against an antagonist who is invisible, powerful, the avowed adversary of God and dedicated enemy of humankind, whose sole purpose is to destroy a personal relationship with God? It is not easy.

The devil, the ringleader of all the fallen spirits cast out of heaven, is determined to do all he can to wean us away from our Savior. His focus is not on those who do not believe in Jesus as their Savior. He's after you and me. The Bible pictures him as a roaring lion prowling around looking for victims (1 Peter 5:8). Even as he tempted Christ, he tempts us. His temptations are subtle, sinister, sneaky, and sugar coated.

We are told to "resist the devil, and he will flee from you" (James 4:7). Christians on their own cannot fight successfully against Satan. They can't subdue Satan one-on-one. Only with Christ and through what He did for us on the cross can we resist the devil and defeat him. Jesus has overcome Satan for us. With Him at our side the victory is always ours.

Put on the full armor of God (Ephesians 6:13) so that you can be more than conquerors through Him who loved us (Romans 8:37).

Lord, stand with me and help me overcome the wiles of Satan. For Your sake, I pray. Amen.

ANDREW SIMCAK JR.

Philippians 1:3–6

Christian Friends

I thank my God every time I remember you. In all my prayers for all of you, I always pray with joy because of your partnership in the gospel from the first day until now, being confident of this, that He who began a good work in you will carry it on to completion until the day of Christ Jesus. Philippians 1:3–6

Remember. Friends. Prayer. Partnership. Gospel.

As I sit in my chair and ponder on these five words, my mind drifts in so many different directions. Sooner or later, my traveling mind will remember friends who prayed, cried, and laughed with me. Our partnership in the Gospel truly united us.

Have you ever had to make a decision where there was no right or wrong answer? Recently I had to make such a choice between going with my husband on a business trip to Europe or attending the wedding of a young man who is like family to me.

As a child, this son of a dear friend had helped me to better understand the meaning of *friends, partnership,* and *Gospel* with the words, "Miss Ida, what are you doing?" His question was prompted by my attempt to steal a few packets of artificial sweetener.

It was the last night of our joint two-family vacation. We were on our traditional Friday-night-out meal at a restaurant. Knowing that we would have no artificial sweetener for our last meal's coffee away from home on Saturday morning, I decided to take a couple packets. And that was when the searing question was asked. This young friend reminded me that as a Christian, I am a witness at all times and in every situation. That simple question reminded me of the sweet life that Jesus chose to give up to come to earth to die for my sins.

And now I faced a choice: Europe or wedding? Although either choice is all right, I chose to attend the wedding. While traveling and attending the many activities associated with the wedding, I remembered the many years that we lived as backdoor neighbors. Over the years, our friendship grew as we forgave, prayed, laughed, and cried together. Our memories and friendship are truly meshed by our partnership in the Gospel.

Has a child ever asked you a question that helped you grow in your faith?

Dear Father, thanks for the partnership of friends to remember, pray with, and share Your Gospel. Amen.

IDA MALL

Philippians 2:6–11

The Word Became Flesh

Christ Jesus: Who, being in very nature God, did not consider equality with God something to be grasped, but made Himself nothing, taking the very nature of a servant, being made in human likeness. ... He humbled Himself and became obedient to death—even death on a cross! Philippians 2:5–8

We like to say, "I'm as good as my word." Unfortunately, we know that we often fail to keep our word. We also have a rather low view of words and what they can do. We would rather see deeds than words. But words do have power in that they can hurt others or isolate.

God knows the power of His word. "The world was created by the word of God" (Hebrews 11:3 RSV). "In the past God spoke to our forefathers through the prophets at many times and in various ways" (Hebrews 1:1). And God's word did what it said it would do: create, condemn, heal, forgive.

"But in these last days He has spoken to us by His Son" (Hebrews 1:2). John reminds us that "the Word became flesh and made His dwelling among us" (John 1:14). The Word made flesh is Christ Jesus, "who, being in very nature God, did not consider equality with God something to be grasped, but made Himself nothing, taking the very nature of a servant, being made in human likeness. ... He humbled Himself and became obedient to death—even death on a cross!" (Philippians 2:5–8).

The Word made flesh, Jesus the Christ, did not return to God empty but accomplished God's purpose of forgiveness of sins and new life for us.

> **Thy strong word did cleave the darkness;**
> **At Thy speaking it was done.**
> **For created light we thank Thee,**
> **While Thine ordered seasons run. Alleluia!**
> **Amen.**
>
> ("Thy Strong Word," by Martin Franzmann, © 1969 CPH)

HENRY GERIKE

Philippians 2:14–15

The Perfect Model

Do everything without complaining or arguing, so that you may become blameless and pure, children of God without fault in a crooked and depraved generation, in which you shine like stars in the universe. Philippians 2:14–15

"Mom loves him best." "Teacher's pet." "She always gets the best job." "I've done my share, now it is time for someone else to do it." Most of us have probably uttered one or more of these statements at one time or another. It is difficult to take second place to others. Imagine what our lives would be like if Jesus had chosen to have the best or had waited for someone else to die on the cross.

Throughout Philippians 2, we see the perfect picture of humility, the example of Christ. He "made Himself nothing, taking the very nature of a servant, ... And being found in appearance as a man, He humbled Himself and became obedient to death" (vv. 7–8). Paul encourages the Philippians and us to model our lives after Christ.

The model or road map for Christian living is indicated by first being united with Christ and having fellowship with the Spirit. Our journey will also take us into His Word for strength and guidance. This will produce joy, peace, and like-mindedness in spirit and purpose. As we travel the road, we will put the interests of others first. With this God-pleasing relationship with Christ and others in place, we can do things without complaining and arguing so that others may see us as shining stars for Jesus' sake.

Even though Jesus was God, He humbled Himself to follow the road to Calvary. It completed His perfect model of humility for us. This allowed us to become the children of God.

Is it difficult to serve without complaining? What can we do to lessen or eliminate the arguing and complaining?

Dear Father, help us to live our lives without arguing and complaining so that we can shine like stars for You. Amen.

IDA MALL

274

Philippians 3:20–21

Citizens or Aliens?

But our citizenship is in heaven. And we eagerly await a Savior from there, the Lord Jesus Christ, who, by the power that enables Him to bring everything under His control, will transform our lowly bodies so that they will be like His glorious body. Philippians 3:20–21

We might laugh about aliens from outer space, but we are very concerned about illegal aliens from other countries. Many U.S. citizens do not want people entering the country without the proper permits and visas. Often it is because we do not want other people to benefit from government welfare programs unless they are legally entitled to them.

The apostle Paul calls us aliens on earth, trespassing on God's turf in our selfishness and sin. It is in God's power to deport us. Instead, God redeems us, gives us a citizenship that we cannot earn and we do not deserve, a citizenship in heaven by faith in Jesus Christ.

The benefit of that citizenship is a transformation that we cannot possibly imagine, the transformation of our physical body into the likeness of His glorious being. We cannot vote about it, enact a law to accomplish it, call a legislative session into being to discuss it. God gives this citizenship in the gift of faith by the power of the Holy Spirit. We have this citizenship in heaven by the loving grace of God that gives us the Savior, the Lord Jesus Christ.

O Lord, You have made us Your own, Your holy nation, citizens of Your heavenly home. We thank You and praise You. Amen.

PAUL J. ALBERS

Philippians 4:4–8

Always Reason for Thanks

Rejoice in the Lord always. I will say it again: Rejoice! ... Do not be anxious about anything, but in everything, by prayer and petition, with thanksgiving, present your requests to God. Philippians 4:4, 6

The Thanksgiving table was set. The turkey was a golden brown. Mashed potatoes and gravy, cranberries, and creamed corn surrounded the main entree. Before the residents of this small boarding house ate, they held hands and gave thanks.

"I thank You for each friend who shares this house with me," spoke one woman.

Another said, "I thank You for all Your blessings, dear Lord, especially salvation through Jesus Christ."

Each shared his or her thanksgiving, and finally at the very end, one of the more elderly ladies gave her thanks: "I thank You, Lord, for two perfectly good teeth, one in my upper jaw and another in my lower jaw, that match so I can chew that delicious turkey in front of me. Amen."

St. Paul was in prison when he spoke the words of Philippians 4:4–9, and yet he gave thanks. He reminds us that we, too, have reason to give thanks, no matter what our circumstance or situation. In fact, he says, "Rejoice in the Lord always."

St. Paul tells us to "rejoice" as well! Rejoice because through faith in Jesus Christ we're friends with God! Through Jesus' life, death, and resurrection the wall of sin that once separated us has been broken down. We have a mediator—Jesus Christ. We can talk to God about anything and everything, with thanksgiving, knowing that He's working all things out for our good because we are family.

Lord God, we rejoice in knowing that we can bring "everything, by prayer and petition, with thanksgiving" before You. May Your peace be ours. Amen.

ROGER R. SONNENBERG

Philippians 4:11

Godliness with Contentment

I am not saying this because I am in need, for I have learned to be content whatever the circumstances. Philippians 4:11

Joyce was a middle-aged woman suffering from an advanced stage of multiple sclerosis. She was confined to a wheelchair and resided in a nursing home. The only family she had were some distant cousins. Members of her church felt a need to visit her but were reluctant because Joyce also had a problem speaking clearly.

When the church members finally decided to visit Joyce, they wondered what they could talk about and how they might be able to cheer her up. They needn't have worried. As soon as they arrived, Joyce smiled broadly and immediately asked them how they were and what their families were doing. Her cheerfulness and interest in her visitors made the time go by quickly. She lifted the spirits of those who had come to try to lift hers.

Joyce had learned to be "content whatever the circumstances." She knew Jesus loved her and had saved her, and because Jesus loved her, she wanted to share that love with others. One way she could do that was by showing an interest in others and building up those who came to see her. Her display of Christian love encouraged her friends and motivated them to come more often to visit with her.

"Godliness with contentment is great gain" (1 Timothy 6:6).

Lord Jesus, teach me to be content with my circumstances and help me learn how to be a blessing to others. Amen.

JIM WIEMERS

Philippians 4:13

Power to Do Everything

I can do everything through Him who gives me strength. Philippians 4:13

Everything takes in a lot of territory. To begin a sentence "I can do everything" seems a childish boast. For such a boast to emanate from behind bars makes it more ludicrous. Yet it was Paul the prisoner who penned these words. What could he do from a jail cell? In retrospect, we know that all Paul managed to do while imprisoned was to oversee and direct the entire gracefully growing mission enterprise called the Christian church!

How does a boast become as expansively inclusive as *everything?* Only "through Him who gives me strength," says Paul.

Ralph Waldo Emerson wrote, "a great man stands on God." Paul was a great man who knew he was a nobody—the "chief of sinners." His ability to "do everything" derived completely from the dynamic power of Christ within him. Christ was his strength, pure and simple.

Christ was and is and will be the power of life available for us. Each of us journeys through our customized territory called "everything." Paul's encouraging challenge is that the entire territory belongs to Christ and can therefore be accomplished in Christ! He is everything in you for everything you do!

Dear Lord, may everything I am and do be dedicated to You. You are my strength and shield! Amen.

DAVID H. BENKE

Colossians 1:11–12

Develop Endurance

Being strengthened with all power according to His glorious might so that you may have great endurance and patience, and joyfully giving thanks to the Father, who has qualified you to share in the inheritance of the saints in the kingdom of light. Colossians 1:11–12

Wilma decided to become physically fit and so bought a home-exercise machine. She was not used to exercising. The first time Wilma used the machine she lasted two minutes before her heart pounded, her breath came in short gasps, and her muscles ached unbearably. She had to stop. It was several days before she tried again. She had the same results. Wilma never used the machine consistently and never developed endurance.

Wilma's daughter, Sami, runs six miles a day and exercises 40 minutes every other day. Over the years she has developed her ability to work out. Sami tried Wilma's machine and stayed with the exercise for 40 minutes her very first time. Sami had developed endurance.

Tough times in life are opportunities to exercise our faith and to develop endurance and patience. When we have shocks and losses in life, we can come to God in prayer. We can ask for what we need: strength, courage, patience, and/or faith. Each time we survive a crisis (great or small) we have strengthened our faith "muscles." It is a little easier to have faith when the next crisis comes. We can endure longer, suffer less, and forget to worry. We know that God created the world, worked the miracles in the Bible, and proved to be faithful in the past. We believe that God will get us through whatever comes our way.

Access to God's power and provision is one of the things we inherit as children of an awesome God.

God, grant me endurance for the life course I must master and patience for the process of becoming what You want me to be. Amen.

BOBBIE REED

Colossians 1:18

The Supremacy of Christ

And He is the head of the body, the church; He is the beginning and the firstborn from among the dead, so that in everything He might have the supremacy. Colossians 1:18

This verse from Paul's letter to the Colossians is one of his greatest texts affirming who Jesus is and what He has done for us.

When Jesus Christ came into this fallen world, everything changed. The Son of God, who with the Father and the Holy Spirit created the universe and everything in it, came to our rescue in the person of Jesus. In His life He did what we had failed to do, and in His death He suffered our well-deserved death. But this was only the beginning. In Jesus' resurrection the Father has accepted the sacrifice of His Son. Paul assures us in this text that Jesus is "the firstborn from among the dead"; that is, because He has risen, we, too, will be raised at Jesus' final return.

In Baptism, we share in Jesus' death and resurrection. In the Lord's Supper we receive the very body and blood that was sacrificed for us. We worship Him who now sits at the right hand of the Father. As Paul declares at the end of this verse, Jesus Christ is now first in everything.

He is also the head of His body, the church. The church is not just a place for like-minded people to get together. The church is the present agency for declaring what Jesus has done for us and for the entire world through His death and resurrection for the forgiveness of sins.

The mission of the church is given by the risen Jesus Himself. In this mission it is not left to do its job on its own. Jesus promises to be with the church through the Gospel and sacraments to empower and sustain it—until He returns to take us all to Himself.

Gracious God, keep us ever mindful of the gifts and blessings You have given us, and continue to strengthen us through Him who is our head, Jesus Christ. Amen.

DAVID LUMPP

Colossians 2:9

True God and True Man

For in Christ all the fullness of the Deity lives in bodily form. Colossians 2:9

"If Jesus Christ is not true God, how could He help us? If He is not true man, how could He help us?" So wrote Dietrich Bonhoeffer. So are posed the great questions concerning the nature of the God-man, Jesus the Christ.

We need help. The problems we face through life and into eternity are pervasive and terrifying. We seek higher purpose and live lower purpose. We know that we fall short of the glory of God. The primary relationship in life is our relationship with God—but we have blown it. Strip away all the defenses and that is what you get. Help to restore this relationship must come from the outside. Our salvation depends on Christ being true God. He must inhabit the fullness of the Deity. And His resurrection tells us that He does!

He must also be a true mediator, an authentic go-between, a real human being. If not, His help would be above and beyond us, at another level. And so He is true man, flesh and bone like you and me. He takes on the burden of humanity. His crucifixion unto death tells us that He does so.

We need help—and help has come in the person of Christ!

Heavenly Father, for the precious gift of Your Son, true God and true man, I give You thanks. Amen.

DAVID H. BENKE

Colossians 2:11–12

Baptized into Christ's Name

In Him you were also circumcised, in the putting off of the sinful nature, not with a circumcision done by the hands of men, but with the circumcision done by Christ, having been buried with Him in baptism and raised with Him through your faith in the power of God, who raised Him from the dead. Colossians 2:11–12

Old ways of doing things are hard to give up. That's how many Colossian Christians felt. They thought that by going back to the ancient rites and regulations they could find release from the complexities and responsibilities of Christian freedom. That freedom can be challenging because it asks us to make decisions.

To be sure, God had given circumcision as a sign of His gracious covenant that He would be the God of the Israelites and that He would bless them. It may be somewhat understandable that there would be those who would want to return to this old way of life. Yet these people were forgetting that when God came in the flesh in His Son, none of His ancient blessings were lost. Jesus the Christ gathers all blessings to Himself and gives them to us.

As circumcision set aside a people for God, so Baptism in Christ sets us aside to be God's people. In Baptism the old way of regulation, the old way of sin and death, have been cast off and buried. In Baptism we are united with Christ who died for our sins and was raised by God for our justification. In Baptism we are made children of the heavenly Father. We live as His children, knowing that because of Christ we have been forgiven.

> My loving Father, here you take me
> Henceforth to be your child and heir;
> My faithful Savior, here you make me
> The fruit of all your sorrows share;
> O Holy Ghost, you comfort me
> Though threat'ning clouds around I see. Amen.

("Baptized into Your Name Most Holy," by Johann J. Rambach)

HENRY GERIKE

Colossians 3:12–14

The Best Dressed

Bear with each other and forgive whatever grievances you may have against one another. Forgive as the Lord forgave you. And over all these virtues put on love, which binds them together in perfect unity. Colossians 3:12–14

"Father, forgive them, for they do not know what they are doing" (Luke 23:34). "Forgive as the Lord forgave you" (Colossians 3:13). "Forgive us our debts, as we also have forgiven our debtors" (Matthew 6:12). These sentences can sear one's heart. Have you ever encountered a situation where you thought you could not forgive another person? If you pick up any newspaper, listen to talk radio, or watch television news, you can readily see and hear examples of sin. In so many cases, the sin is against children and our heart hurts.

On Calvary's cross, the Father saw His child. His child hurt and bled. When Christ spoke the words, "Father, forgive them, for they do not know what they are doing," He was the world's prime example of one clothed in compassion, kindness, humility, gentleness, and patience. His love for us poured from the nail prints in His hands and feet and from His pierced side.

God's chosen Son has made us God's chosen children by the love He showed on that cross. We are invited to use the power given to us through the forgiveness exhibited on the cross to forgive others. On our own, we could never forgive someone for wronging us. Only with the power of the Holy Spirit are we able to forgive others.

With God's forgiveness in our hearts and knowing that we are His chosen, holy, and dearly loved people, is there any other way to live than to be on the best-dressed list by wearing compassion, kindness, humility, gentleness, patience, and love?

Dear Father, help us to be properly dressed. Amen.

IDA MALL

1 Thessalonians 4:11–12

A Christian Lifestyle

Make it your ambition to lead a quiet life, to mind your own business and to work with your hands, just as we told you, so that your daily life may win the respect of outsiders and so that you will not be dependent on anybody. 1 Thessalonians 4:11--12

We live in a world that gets increasingly fast-paced each year. People are in a hurry to get where they're going; their lives are crowded with a demanding job, parental responsibilities, and organizational obligations. Even though we often feel overstressed, we think we need to keep up a hectic schedule to get ahead in the world.

In stark contrast the apostle Paul tells the Thessalonians to "make it your ambition to lead a quiet life, to mind your own business and to work with your hands." An "ambition to lead a quiet life" almost seems like a contradiction of terms, but actually it is a worthy goal for finding contentment. Quietly going about your business, not gossiping, and doing an honest day's work can, as the apostle says, "win the respect of outsiders."

More important than winning people's respect, our life is a testimony to our faith in God. Jesus said, "Let your light shine before men, that they may see your good deeds and praise your Father in heaven" (Matthew 5:16). No matter what our job or station in life is, a godly lifestyle will give glory to the Gospel as we witness to others about the Savior, who loves and redeemed them.

Lord, let me find contentment in my labor and may my life be a witness to Your love. In Jesus' name I pray. Amen.

JIM WIEMERS

1 Thessalonians 5:16–18

The Secret to Happiness

Be joyful always; pray continually; give thanks in all circumstances, for this is God's will for you in Christ Jesus. 1 Thessalonians 5:16–18

People are always looking for the secret to happiness. Some think it will come when they win a large lottery prize or become successful in their occupation. Others are looking for the inner joy they think will come from Eastern meditation or positive thinking. Even Christians sometimes feel their lives are not happy and lack inner joy.

True happiness is not found in external possessions or in one's self. It is not even found in the love of other people. True peace and joy come from the knowledge and assurance that our heavenly Father sent His Son, Jesus Christ, into the world to redeem us. Our salvation is accomplished. No matter what we may face in this world, God loves us and has prepared a life of eternal joy in heaven for all who believe in Him.

Today's reading also gives us some guidelines for coping with our daily earthly problems. "Pray continually; give thanks in all circumstances." A close and constant communication with our Lord will help us keep the proper perspective on our daily activities and give us that happiness and joy we truly want.

> **In You is gladness**
> **Amid all sadness,**
> **Jesus, sunshine of my heart. Alleluia! Amen.**
> ("In You Is Gladness," by Johann Lindemann)

JIM WIEMERS

2 Thessalonians 1:5

Your Kingdom Come—to Me

You will be counted worthy of the kingdom of God. 2 Thessalonians 1:5

In the Second Petition of the Lord's Prayer we pray that the kingdom of our heavenly Father will come to us. How does that kingdom come to us?

The child of God needs to pray constantly that God's kingdom of grace (undeserved love) will come to him or her. We cannot come into the presence of the holy and almighty King, except by grace. "If You, O LORD, kept a record of sins, O LORD, who could stand?" (Psalm 130:3). None of us can ever do enough to become a member of God's kingdom, for the King insists that we be perfect. It is only by God's undeserved love that we "are counted worthy" and numbered among the members of His kingdom of grace. "By grace you have been saved, through faith—and this not from yourselves, it is the gift of God—not by works, so that no one can boast" (Ephesians 2:8–9).

Incredible! A King humbling Himself, leaving heaven, suffering and dying on a cross! We didn't choose Him; He chose us. It is only in Him that we are counted worthy of the kingdom of God.

By faith in Jesus as our Savior we have the assurance that all our sins are forgiven. May our lives lived in tribute to His name show our thanks to Him, the King of kings.

Heavenly King, increase my faith in You as my Savior and keep me a faithful member of Your kingdom. Amen.

ANDREW SIMCAK JR.

1 Timothy 4:8

For Now and Forever

For physical training is of some value, but godliness has value for all things, holding promise for both the present life and the life to come. 1 Timothy 4:8

Riding a stationary bicycle has tremendous benefit. Using a stepper or a ski simulator machine provides exceptional benefit. The key is in the "riding" and the "using," for there are many such pieces of exercise equipment that stand idle. Many people who use such machines talk about their feeling of self-worth increasing because they are losing weight and getting into better physical condition. That is wonderful and every encouragement for exercise needs to be given since we are described more and more as a nation of "couch potatoes."

All that exercise and fitness is beneficial for right now. There is more to life than physical fitness, though; there is spiritual fitness. St. Paul repeatedly speaks of this with Timothy as "godliness." He speaks of a deep reverence for God that is expressed in a good and holy life. No spiritual corners are cut, no great determination at self-justification for weakness or unfaithfulness. Rather Paul exhorts us to such a relationship with God that we demonstrate that faith in what we do and say, and the attitudes we express. That godliness is only possible through the Holy Spirit bringing us ever closer with Jesus Christ in His death and resurrection.

Help me, O Lord, to exercise daily—my body and my faith. Amen.

PAUL J. ALBERS

2 Timothy 1:7

Power, Love, and Self-Discipline

For God did not give us a spirit of timidity, but a spirit of power, of love and of self-discipline. 2 Timothy 1:7

What an interesting combination of attributes! Power, love, and self-discipline. They don't seem to go together well, do they?

When we think of power, we think of power over someone or something. In business, to be timid is to fail. We want to be in a "position of power." In hockey, the "power play" is desired because the team with the power has the advantage.

So what does power have to do with love? Love is a wonderful feeling, but it hardly seems powerful. To be in love is to sacrifice our needs for another's. To be in love is to consider someone else more important than ourself. To be in love is, in a way, to put someone else in a position of power over us.

But wait, there is a third spirit that God gives us—the spirit of self-discipline. Self-discipline is what tempers our desire for power. Self-discipline is what helps us in love. Self-discipline in the Spirit helps us balance the power that we have with the love that we have.

In faith in the death and resurrection of Jesus, God gives us the spirit of power. It is not power over others, but power over ourself. It is power over our sinful desires, power over Satan within us, power over our death. And it is with this power that we can love.

The spirit of love leads us to sacrifice our needs for the needs of others. Love gives us humility and helps us serve others. This is Christ's love for us, that we can confidently, with no trace of timidity, share with others. What power there is in love!

Dear Lord, I thank and praise You for the many gifts You have given me. May I boldly love others as You have loved me and powerfully share Your good news. Amen.

KEVIN PARVIZ

2 Timothy 3:16–17

Staying in Bed

All Scripture is God-breathed and is useful for teaching, rebuking, correcting and training in righteousness, so that the man of God may be thoroughly equipped for every good work. 2 Timothy 3:16–17

One night a boy fell out of his bed. The next morning when he told his mother, she asked him how it happened. He answered, "I don't really know, but I expect I stayed too close to where I got in."

There are many people who also stay too close to where they originally got in when it comes to their faith. They join the church but never grow in their faith. They go to church on Sunday but never open their Bibles during the week. They never attend Bible studies. Thus, they never move deeper in their walk with the Lord. When a Christian stops growing in his or her faith, he or she runs the danger of falling out of the bed of faith!

Growth in faith comes through the Word, the Bible. The Bible is, after all, "God-breathed"—God's inspired Word to us. It not only makes us "wise for salvation through faith in Christ Jesus" (2 Timothy 3:15), but is "useful for teaching, rebuking, correcting and training in righteousness, so that the man [and woman] of God may be thoroughly equipped for every good work."

Each of us must ask whether we're growing in our faith. If not, we must do something about it. "Therefore let us leave the elementary teachings about Christ and go on to maturity" (Hebrews 6:1).

Lord God, through Your Word You have made us "wise for salvation through faith in Christ Jesus." Through the study of Your Word, continue to instruct us, teach, rebuke, correct, and train us in righteousness, so we might be thoroughly equipped for every good work. Amen.

ROGER R. SONNENBERG

2 Timothy 4:7

Finish the Race

I have fought the good fight, I have finished the race, I have kept the faith. 2 Timothy 4:7

A brother and sister trained for the Olympics as speed skaters. Both were excellent. It appeared they would both make the United States Olympic Team. However, a year before the Calgary Olympics the sister developed leukemia and had to drop out. The brother worked to hone his skills so he could win the gold medal and dedicate it to his sister. He had always been an excellent skater, but now he became outstanding and was selected for the team. He was consumed by thoughts of being the best skater, of winning the gold, and of being a hero for his sister.

The day of the race he was so determined to win, he made a false start. He returned to the starting line embarrassed. The officials signaled the start of the race and the boy took off. Seconds later he lost control, kicked one skate into the other and fell. He was out of the race.

We are not called to be spectacular or to finish first. We are expected to run the Christian race with patience and to finish the course God has outlined for us. When we focus on winning honors, we may lose control and fall. But when we focus on running with a steady pace, we can keep the faith and finish the race. For those who are faithful, who finish the race, there is a crown of righteousness waiting (see 2 Timothy 4:8).

Will you finish the race and receive the crown? Or will you lose control and drop out?

God, grant me the stamina to keep on keeping on despite the challenges life may bring. Help me keep the faith and finish the race. Amen.

BOBBIE REED

Titus 2:3–4

Relationship Mentoring

Teach the older women to be reverent in the way they live, not to be slanderers or addicted to much wine, but to teach what is good. Then they can train the younger women to love their husbands and children. Titus 2:3–4

Have you ever made a cake? assembled a bicycle? quilted a quilt? learned to drive a car? To do any of these the first time, you probably had to follow a cookbook or manual that supplied explicit details or have an individual by your side to assist you with the task.

Many of us learn new skills easiest by watching others perform them. My grandmother was my teacher and mentor. She taught me how to milk a cow, make a pie crust, hoe the garden, use kind words, be patient, and go the "extra mile."

This woman was God's living example for me and others to be "reverent in the way they live, not to be slanderers or addicted to much wine, but to teach what is good." Still to this day I can hear her say, "If you don't have something good to say about a person, don't say anything." Moreover, she encouraged me not even to think hurtful thoughts.

As each of us ages, we are given the opportunity to live lives that provide "cookbooks" or "manuals" for younger people to follow. It is to be done so that others may see the Word of God in action in our daily walk. What an awesome opportunity and responsibility!

Have you helped or mentored a younger woman or man in fulfilling her or his special niche for the Lord?

Dear Father, help each of us to be a mentor to others. Amen.

IDA MALL

Titus 3:3–8

He Saved Us

He saved us through the washing of rebirth and renewal by the Holy Spirit, whom He poured out on us generously through Jesus Christ our Savior. Titus 3:5–6

Who gets the credit? That is a major concern in our lives. Copyrights are established so no one else can use the work of another without permission—"I did it, I want the credit." Copyrights are necessary and commonplace today. Even in church worship folders we give credit acknowledging the authors of the hymns.

God, too, deserves credit for what He has done. Too often we want credit for giving ourselves to God, for inviting God to come into our lives, for being willing to be called a child of God. We act as if we are doing God a favor by accepting Jesus as our Savior.

Yet, God's Word makes it clear: "He saved us"; we didn't save ourselves. The fullness of the mercy and love of God is that He gathered us in Baptism; He gave the Holy Spirit to bring us into unity with Jesus Christ. The work and the credit belong to God. It is a good thing, too, because in our sinful nature we would have stayed away from God.

God comes to us in mercy; God gathers us in love; God gives us new birth in His family. We receive the blessing, the faith, the eternal promise. It is a sure thing because it all depends on God. God holds the copyright on our souls. Only He deserves the credit.

O Lord, I praise You for You have called me Your own. Amen.

PAUL J. ALBERS

Hebrews 5:11–6:1

Grow Up in the Lord

Solid food is for the mature, who by constant use have trained themselves to distinguish good from evil. Hebrews 5:14

Age is not entirely a matter of calendar years. Much depends on how we guard our health. A dissolute actor who died at age 50 was said to have had the worn-out body of a 90-year-old man. Conversely, some people at age 80 are in better shape than those half their age. When Moses died at the age of 120, "his eyes were not weak nor his strength gone" (Deuteronomy 34:7).

How old are you? It could well be that you are younger than you think. You are young in *body* if you keep fit through daily exercise. You are young in *mind* if you keep on learning, maintain an interest in life around you, can adjust to changing conditions, and stay hopeful about the future.

Above all, we need to measure our age in the spiritual realm—in our Christian faith. Here the emphasis is on growth. We don't want to remain what St. Paul calls "mere infants in Christ" (1 Corinthians 3:1) when we have the opportunity to be mature men and women. God has given us the means for spiritual development: His Word and sacraments. He desires that we, in the words of St. Peter, may "grow up" in our salvation. To discover every day how wonderful is the love of God, who sent His Son to give us life and peace and pardon, is to stay spiritually young—in the psalmist's words, to renew our youth "like the eagles" (Psalm 103:5). At the close of his second letter St. Peter urges us: "Grow in the grace and knowledge of our Lord and Savior Jesus Christ" (2 Peter 3:18).

Let us look for specific opportunities this week to let Christ's light of the Gospel shine in and through our lives.

Dear Lord, may Your Holy Spirit keep my faith alive and fresh by drawing me ever closer to Jesus, my Savior. Help me today to put my faith into action and demonstrate Your love to those I meet. Amen.

RUDOLPH F. NORDEN

Hebrews 10:25

The Value of Church

Let us not give up meeting together, as some are in the habit of doing, but let us encourage one another—and all the more as you see the Day approaching. Hebrews 10:25

A common expression heard today is, "I don't have to go to church to be saved." Sometimes great figures in history like Abraham Lincoln are held up as examples of men of faith who did not hold membership in a church. How many people, however, know that Lincoln was prepared to join the New York Presbyterian Church in Washington D.C. in 1865?

The death of his son, Willie, in 1864 and the continuing tragedy of the Civil War caused Lincoln to more actively seek the advice and counsel of clergymen to help him learn more about the Savior. Lincoln was set to join the church on Easter Sunday, 1865; he was assassinated on Good Friday, two days earlier.

Can we be saved without holding church membership? Yes. The apostle Paul told the jailer in Philippi, "Believe in the Lord Jesus, and you will be saved" (Acts 16:31). It's that simple. Jesus paid the price for our salvation.

But believers, as Abraham Lincoln discovered, need to continue in the Word and be encouraged by other believers, lest they drift away from their faith and fall into despair. God has many blessings He wishes to bestow upon us through other believers and through His church.

> **Lord, keep us steadfast in Your Word … .**
> **Defend Your holy Church that we**
> **May sing Your praise triumphantly. Amen.**
> ("Lord, Keep Us Steadfast in Your Word," by Martin Luther)

JIM WIEMERS

Hebrews 12:1–13

Focused!

Let us fix our eyes on Jesus, the author and perfecter of our faith, who for the joy set before Him endured the cross, scorning its shame, and sat down at the right hand of the throne of God. Hebrews 12:2

A new addition to professional athletics is the sports psychologist. This person's task is to help the athlete to concentrate. You hear of this person in tennis, golf, and all team sports. Easily distracted athletes especially need this special assistance.

This text was written to Hebrew Christians who were being distracted from their faith. They had the great stress of persecution and had temptations to turn away coming from so many directions that they needed something extra. The writer reminded them of that extra power for running with perseverance the race marked out for them. That power is in focusing only upon Jesus, the author and perfecter of our faith. He is the one who went to Calvary; He is the one who rose again on the third day and assured the victory. Now Christians need only to continue running toward the goal.

In this Christian faith it is not winning that is the goal. Jesus has already won the race. The goal is finishing the race, running in faith with Jesus all the way to the victory of life in His very presence. Concentrate! This is the advice to an athlete. Look to Jesus alone! This is the exhortation in faith.

Lord, help me look only to You for only in You is victory. Amen.

PAUL J. ALBERS

Hebrews 13:5

A Big Heart

Keep your lives free from the love of money and be content with what you have, because God has said, "Never will I leave you; never will I forsake you." Hebrews 13:5

He was a large man. He wore size 52 bib overalls. His heart was even bigger than his body. Although he had not been blessed with exceeding earthly riches, the Lord had blessed him with an overflowing love for others. Day after day, people came to his house to borrow any and every kind of item from water to machinery.

On many occasions, this big-hearted man either loaned money directly or co-signed bank notes for people in need. If you didn't know him, you would say his lending of money was foolhardy. However, it is fact that of all the money lent, only one $50 loan was not repaid.

At his funeral, the small country church where he had been a member overflowed with people, many of whom shared that their lives had been blessed by this man who loved people more than he loved money.

Throughout his life, he acknowledged that the Lord had given him what he had. In life and in death, the Lord was glorified by this big man's willingness to share whatever monetary gifts he had with those less fortunate.

As the Lord blesses each one of us with much or with little, may we be content with what we have knowing that God says, "Never will I leave you; never will I forsake you."

Dear Father, thank You for our material blessings. Help us to be thankful and keep our lives free from the love of money. Amen.

IDA MALL

Hebrews 13:8

Something We Can Depend On

Jesus Christ is the same yesterday and today and forever. Hebrews 13:8

Things and places change. Maybe you recall having to walk to school a mile or even two miles—there was no school bus. Perhaps you can recall Christmas programs in public school where the name *Jesus* was mentioned. Do you remember starting the school day with the Pledge of Allegiance? Maybe you can remember when ice cream was homemade. There was a time when families ate dinner together. Today, less than 10 percent of the families in America eat one meal a day together. Most ice cream is store-bought!

Just as things and places change, so do people. They think differently. Their attitudes change. Their appearance alters with time.

Thank God there is one who never changes—Jesus Christ. The God who loved Abraham, Isaac, and Jacob enough to die for their sins is the God who keeps loving us. He doesn't turn His love off and on as we do. It's constant. He "is the same yesterday and today and forever." He is the same omnipotent, omniscient, eternal, kind God that He has always been! He is the one who daily forgives and strengthens. He is the one who never leaves us. Someone wisely said, "The same Christ who was with them is with you and will be with those who come after us, even to the end of the age. Yesterday He was with the fathers; today He is with you; and He will be with your posterity for evermore."

Lord Jesus, thank You that though things, places, and people change, You never change, for we know You are the "same yesterday and today and forever." Amen.

ROGER R. SONNENBERG

James 1:14

The Problem of Sin

Each one is tempted when, by his own evil desire, he is dragged away and enticed. James 1:14

There is definitely not a shortage of problems in the world. Hatred, murder, famine, poverty, disease, natural disasters—these are some of the many serious problems confronting humankind. There is one overriding problem, however, that confronts everyone—sin. James gets to the heart of our problem when he says each person is dragged away by his *own* evil desire. The author of the hymn "Rock of Ages" once claimed that every youth of 20 has committed 630 million sins. At the age of 50, so Augustus Toplady figured, a man is guilty of 1,500,000,000 sins.

We do not know how accurate these calculations are. We do know that sin separates God and humankind (Isaiah 59:2). There is nothing worse in this world than to be separated from God because of sin. Nor can any of us remove the barrier that separates us from Him. Only God Himself can do that. "God was reconciling the world to Himself in Christ, not counting men's sins against them" (2 Corinthians 5:19). God has given us the greatest blessing a person can possess—the forgiveness of our sins.

How grateful we should be that the Father laid our sins upon His Son on the cross. Our Savior was forsaken by His father on the cross (Matthew 27:46) so that we might hear Him say, "Take heart, ... your sins are forgiven" (Matthew 9:2).

Savior, I look to You, my only Savior from sin, and find my comfort there. Amen.

ANDREW SIMCAK JR.

James 1:17

Fix Your Eyes on Jesus, the Perfect Gift

Every good and perfect gift is from above, coming down from the Father of the heavenly lights, who does not change like shifting shadows. James 1:17

People of all ages like to give and to receive gifts. When we give a gift to someone, we try to find something that will be particularly meaningful or useful to that person. Ideally, we would like it to be something "special," something that the recipient will always associate with the giver.

But our gifts often wear out. They have to be replaced. At best, the gifts we cherish most from others point beyond themselves to the relationship from which such an exchange of gifts arises. When in this life even the best of relationships end with one person's death, the gift is an occasion both for joy and sadness.

Gifts are intended to point to the person who gives them to us. James reminds us that God's gifts are good and perfect, as He is. To an extent even greater than a loving parent, God knows what is best for us. He knows what we need most. He even knew that before we would recognize and trust Him as our Father He would have to redeem and restore us as His children, and He did so through the death and resurrection of Jesus Christ. God gives us the righteousness of His Son, and in doing that He gives us an eternal life with Him.

The gift of eternal life is truly a good and perfect gift; it is abiding and unchanging, like Him who gives it to us.

Merciful God, keep our eyes and hearts focused not so much on the gifts we receive but on You as the giver of all that is good, most especially the gift of life in Jesus Christ. Amen.

DAVID LUMPP

James 4:10

Comparing Ourselves

Humble yourselves before the Lord, and He will lift you up. James 4:10

It is part and parcel of our sinful nature to compare ourselves with other people. Such comparison often makes us look good. We see ourselves as better than the other person.

In the parable Jesus told about the Pharisee and the tax collector, the Pharisee bragged to God how good he was in comparison to the tax collector. He gave himself high marks alongside what he perceived to be the failures of someone else.

The tax collector, on the other hand, offers us a wonderful example. He assumed his total lack of worth before God, did not even look to heaven. He beat upon his chest, an outward sign of inward sorrow over his sins. Those sins were forgiven because he turned to the Lord and asked God for mercy. He did not place his trust in what he did or did not do, in what he was or was not. He placed his trust in the mercy and grace of God, asking God to forgive him.

James exhorts us to "humble yourselves before the Lord." If we are going to compare ourselves with others, make the comparison with Jesus. It's a humbling experience. When you stand alongside Him, you won't be apt to call attention to your acts and attitudes. You'll find a great deal more comfort in the acts and attitudes of Christ by which you have been forgiven and adopted into the family of God.

Lord, help me glory only in the cross of Christ, my Savior. Amen.

ANDREW SIMCAK JR.

James 5:13–16

Come to Me

Is any one of you in trouble? He should pray. ... Is any one of you sick? ... The prayer offered in faith will make the sick person well; the Lord will raise him up. If he has sinned, he will be forgiven. Therefore confess your sins to each other and pray for each other. James 5:13–16

Many times during Jesus' public ministry, people of all ages gathered around Him, people with problems. As Jesus looked over the crowd, He may have pointed to one over here and one over there, extended His arms toward them, and invited them to approach Him with their burdens and anxieties.

This same invitation is extended by the same Savior to you and me. Jesus knows we are "weak and heavy-laden, cumbered with a load of care." He knows our trials, troubles, and tribulations, our pains and problems. And Jesus extends His arms to us and invites us to come to Him in prayer. He promises to hear and answer us. He forgives every sin, even those that are especially burdensome. He offers comfort to the lonely, if loneliness is what is making one's life miserable. He heals. He cheers. He makes the weak strong, the lame to walk, and the deaf to hear.

"Come," He says. "Come to Me, all you who are weary and burdened, and I will give you rest" (Matthew 11:28). Gladly and willingly accept our Savior's invitation to come and receive from Him the rest and relief that He is prepared to give.

> What a friend we have in Jesus,
> All our sins and griefs to bear!
> What a privilege to carry
> Everything to God in prayer!
> ("What a Friend We Have in Jesus," by Joseph Scriven)

Jesus, help me, heal me, give me rest, according to Your will. Amen.

ANDREW SIMCAK JR.

1 Peter 1:3

Hope against All Hope

Praise be to the God and Father of our Lord Jesus Christ! In His great mercy He has given us new birth into a living hope through the resurrection of Jesus Christ from the dead. 1 Peter 1:3

My mother was the most hopeful person I ever knew. Though severely debilitated with crippling arthritis and in constant pain, she never lost hope. She often remarked that tomorrow things would get better. When the lights of her life flickered out and she was laid to rest, her hope saw fulfillment—things *did* get better.

As Christians, purchased and won by the blood of Jesus Christ, baptized into His name most holy, we are given a new birth and a living hope—a hope for what is yet to come. As we travel and travail through life to eternity, we are buoyed by the sure promise of Jesus, "Because I live, you also will live" (John 14:19). Such a promise helps us put our difficulties into perspective. St. Paul writes, "For our light and momentary troubles are achieving for us an eternal glory that far outweighs them all" (2 Corinthians 4:17). Our life, then, becomes a journey, not a destination; a place to labor as we await our rest in heaven; and a place to hope in surety as we await the fulfillment of our hope—the coming of our Lord Jesus Christ. The writer to the Hebrews gives such sweet encouragement, "Let us hold unswervingly to the hope we profess, for He who promised is faithful" (10:23).

Loving Father, give us a sure and certain and living hope in You and Your promises to us that we may always trust in You. Amen.

JAMES W. FREESE

1 Peter 1:6–7

Proof of God's Love

For a little while you may have had to suffer grief in all kinds of trials. These have come so that your faith—of greater worth than gold, which perishes even though refined by fire—may be proved genuine and may result in praise, glory and honor when Jesus Christ is revealed. 1 Peter 1:6–7

How often do we in the weakness of our faith question God's love, power, and presence in our daily lives? When disappointments, troubles, and trials come, how often do we feel that God doesn't love or care for us—that He's not there for us?

The Christians undergoing persecution at Peter's time certainly may have felt like that at times. Peter reassures them, however, by pointing to Jesus. He tells them the trials of faith are valuable because they prove faith's genuineness and will result in glory and honor when Jesus is revealed. He reminds them that they were redeemed not with perishable items but with the precious blood of Christ, a lamb without blemish, and he exhorts them to continue putting their faith and hope in God (vv. 18–21).

In the midst of our trials of faith, how often do we look for evidence—proof—of God's love? God, Himself, has given us all the proof that we will ever need. Again we are pointed to Jesus. "For God so loved the world that He gave His one and only Son, that whoever believes in Him shall not perish but have eternal life" (John 3:16). The Christ of Calvary's cross is proof positive that God loves us. He purchased us "not with gold or silver, but with His holy, precious blood and with His innocent suffering and death."

Through all the circumstances of life, we place our confidence and trust in Jesus, our Savior.

Dear Jesus, through all the trials of my life, remind me that Your love for me is so great that You died for me to make me Your own. Strengthen my weak faith and help me keep my eyes focused on You. For Your sake, I pray. Amen.

ANDREW SIMCAK JR.

1 Peter 1:17–21

Just Passing Through

Live your lives as strangers here in reverent fear. 1 Peter 1:17

At the end of our vacation this summer, I asked our children if they would like to continue staying in the hotel. Their response was immediate: "No! We had fun, but we want to go back home."

Placed here on this earth, the only existence we've ever known, we as Christians have a difficult time realizing that we are only here temporarily. In 2 Corinthians 5:6, St. Paul says, "As long as we are at home in the body we are away from the Lord," that is, from our eternal home in heaven. Our mansion has already been prepared. Our guarantee is the price our Savior paid for our redemption—His very life!

Aware of that tremendous sacrifice, we live life from another point of view—that of a guest and a stranger here, just as Christ Himself was a guest and stranger. Our lives are lived in thankfulness to God for His unfathomable love. To be sure, we live here fully enjoying the life and material blessings God has granted us, but we do so in anticipation of that even greater life to come in heaven. Our confession of faith in the Nicene Creed, then, takes on heightened meaning when we say, "I look for the resurrection of the dead and the life of the world to come."

O almighty God, keep me ever mindful of the fact that heaven is my home. Guide me safely through this life to You. Amen.

JAMES W. FREESE

1 Peter 2:9–10

Declare His Praises

You are a chosen people, a royal priesthood, a holy nation, a people belonging to God, that you may declare the praises of Him who called you out of darkness into His wonderful light. 1 Peter 2:9

In this passage Peter underscores that all who believe in Jesus have the wonderful task of sharing about our great God and His mercy with others. God, who has called us out of the darkness of our sin to be His own people and given us eternal life, gifts us in different ways for work in His kingdom and wants us to declare His praises—to tell others about Him.

We are to spread the good news of the Gospel of Christ to all the world, to every person in it. What is the good news, the glad tidings for which we praise our God? It is that "God so loved the world that He gave His one and only Son, that whoever believes in Him shall not perish but have eternal life" (John 3:16). Our Lord wants all people to become members of His kingdom of grace, the holy, Christian church. Jesus died for all, to save everyone for time and for eternity. Through faith in Jesus we have become subjects of the King. Now the King commands us, "go and make disciples of all nations" (Matthew 28:19).

There are only two eternal kingdoms: the kingdom of Satan and the kingdom of our heavenly Father. The kingdom of the Father is the kingdom to which those who accept the free forgiveness of sins belong. May we as loyal subjects thank God that His kingdom of grace includes us and through us reaches out into all the world. May we for Christ's sake seek ways to communicate His love to those around us in their language and culture, even when it is different from our own, so that they will come to know the Savior.

Gracious Lord, "here I am, send me, send me." Amen.

ANDREW SIMCAK JR.

1 Peter 3:15

Witness for Christ

Always be prepared to give an answer to everyone who asks you to give the reason for the hope that you have. 1 Peter 3:15

A church building was destroyed by fire. The fireman saved only a statue of Jesus. He placed it on the sidewalk in front of the burning church. Some of the neighbors joined a few of the members who were watching the fire. Noticing the statue of Jesus, one of the neighbors remarked to a church member: "This is the first time you have taken Christ out of your church."

It is true, unfortunately, that some Christians do not share Christ with their friends or their neighbors or their relatives. We become engrossed taking care of our own souls but neglect the desperate need of others who do not know that Jesus is their Savior or believe that He has come to bring them forgiveness, life, and salvation.

Determine to "take Christ out of your church" by sharing the good news about what He did for us on the cross and at the open tomb with those with whom you come into contact in your daily life.

Lord Jesus, lay someone upon my heart who does not know You and help me to share the good news about You with that person. In Your name, I pray. Amen.

ANDREW SIMCAK JR.

1 Peter 5:7

Take It to the Lord in Prayer

Cast all your anxiety on Him because He cares for you. 1 Peter 5:7

A television commercial for V-8 vegetable juice once showed a woman who became frustrated in trying to find just the right drink that would meet her particular craving. After rejecting several choices, she finally hit her palm against her forehead as she came to the realization, "Wow, I could have had a V-8!"

How many times in our lives do we find ourselves fighting a vexing problem that leads to frustration? We can't make up our mind what to do or whom to consult. No matter which way we turn we seem to come to a dead end. When it seems we have nowhere else to turn, suddenly we remember, "Wow, I could have turned to God!" As a last resort we come to our heavenly Father in prayer.

Our Scripture reading says, "Cast all your anxiety on Him." There is no burden too large or too small for His concern. The God who loved us so much that He gave His Son to suffer and die for us is ready and eager to hear our cries of distress. In His Sermon on the Mount Christ said, "Your Father in heaven [will] give good gifts to those who ask Him!" (Matthew 7:11).

We can save ourselves many hours of anxious thought if we establish a regular prayer life and come to God first with our cares.

Lord, thank You for caring about all my concerns, both great and small. Help me to seek You first in times of need. I ask this for Jesus' sake. Amen.

JIM WIEMERS

2 Peter 1:20–21

The Scriptures Testify to Christ

No prophecy of Scripture came about by the prophet's own interpretation. For prophecy never had its origin in the will of man, but men spoke from God as they were carried along by the Holy Spirit. 2 Peter 1:20–21

Sadly, there are many theologians and churches today that do not believe in the inerrancy and inspiration of the Bible. They do not believe that certain events as recorded in Scripture actually occurred, and they debate whether Jesus actually said many of the things recorded in the gospels.

To maintain a strong Christian faith we must believe that what the Bible tells us is true. "Faith comes from hearing the message, and the message is heard through the word of Christ" (Romans 10:17).

When we read the accounts of Christ's crucifixion and resurrection, the testimony recorded adds details to the same events. There are no contradictions. Scripture interprets Scripture. Verses that appear unclear can be clarified when compared to other verses that discuss the same topic.

The Bible, itself, addresses the issue of whether we should doubt some of the writers. "For prophecy never had its origin in the will of man, but men spoke from God as they were carried along by the Holy Spirit" (2 Peter 1:20–21). There may be variations in writing style, but the contents all come from God.

Our Bible is true and inspired; and its message is clear: Christ came into the world to save us.

Lord, keep us faithful to Your holy and inspired Word, for in it we find the words of eternal life. In Jesus' name we pray. Amen.

JIM WIEMERS

1 John 1:9

Go and Sin Some More!

If we confess our sins, He is faithful and just and will forgive us our sins and purify us from all unrighteousness. 1 John 1:9

"What do we have to do to get forgiveness from God?" asked the teacher. There was no response from the class. Exasperated, the teacher repeated the question, and then said: "Boys and girls, you know the answer I want!" Finally, one boy brightly replied: "Sin!"

This incident illustrates how we can misunderstand the serious nature of sin, God's judgment and His mercy, and what we call "Law and Gospel." For one thing, we do not just sin more that grace may increase (Romans 6:1). Also, God doesn't just forgive us *because* we repent.

Law and Gospel are confused when we lead a person to assume that contrition (being sorry for sin) is the cause for forgiveness. Rather, God has acted already in the face of and despite our sin. God forgave us before we were born—even before the world was created, when He determined that the Lamb (Jesus) should be slain for us (Revelation 13:8). "This is love: not that we loved God, but that He loved us and sent His Son as an atoning sacrifice for our sins" (1 John 4:10).

So we are called to genuine repentance. Jesus didn't say, "Go and sin some more," but "go and sin *no* more" (John 8:11 NKJV).

Therefore we daily affirm with St. John: "If we confess our sins, He is faithful and just and will forgive us our sins and purify us from all unrighteousness."

Lord, may I honestly repent of my sin and put on my baptismal garment each morning, knowing that I am buried with Christ through my Baptism and now live a new life. Amen.

DONALD L. DEFFNER

1 John 3:1

Never Left Alone

How great is the love the Father has lavished on us, that we should be called children of God! And that is what we are! 1 John 3:1

The news carried a report about a man who was washing his car in a self-service car wash when he heard what sounded like a cry from the next bay. Immediately he went to investigate and found an abandoned baby. When we hear accounts such as this, we are always touched and saddened. How could a mother feel so helpless to care for her child that she would feel compelled to such action?

We have not been abandoned by God, but we have run away from Him. Fortunately for us, God came after us, again and again, to gather us close to Himself and love us.

What a description St. John uses: "How great is the love the Father has lavished on us." Don't you love that word *lavished?* It pictures God giving and giving and giving—not material things, but love, the love that gathers the runaways and the abandoned to Himself as children. God's children! It is exciting to have parents that love us and to be parents that love our children. But it is infinitely more exciting to be children of God, members of God's own family, the ones upon whom love is *lavished.* The great price of such a love is the sacrifice of God's only Son, Jesus. The great benefit is our being God's own for all eternity.

Yours, only Yours, O Lord; make me only Yours. Amen.

PAUL J. ALBERS

1 John 3:16–23

Behaving in Love

This is how we know what love is: Jesus Christ laid down His life for us. And we ought to lay down our lives for our brothers. ... And this is His command: to believe in the name of His Son, Jesus Christ, and to love one another as He commanded us. 1 John 3:16–23

There is a fictional story told of the pope standing on the balcony in St. Peter's Square. Thousands of people stood below awaiting his blessing of peace. Instead, the pope came out and said, "I have some bad news for you, my children. The doctors tell me I need a heart transplant. Which of you would be willing to give me your heart so that I can continue to serve God and my people?"

Thousands waved their arms in the air, shouting, "Me, Papa; Me, Papa."

The pope found it almost unbelievable that so many people would be willing to give up their lives to save his. There were so many people that he had to choose which one would have the privilege, and so he said, "Dearly beloved, I will throw out a feather and the person it lands on, that person will have the great privilege of giving me his or her heart."

The pope threw the feather from the balcony. The feather floated downward; however, it seemed to hover in the air forever. It never seemed to land.

The pope went to the ground floor to see what was wrong. He discovered that whenever the feather got close to a group of people, they all blew with great gusto! It became apparent to the pope that what the people said and what they were willing to do were two different things.

John makes it clear that love isn't just some fancy word that you use to describe how you might be feeling about someone, but it is something very concrete. It is active. It is more than "being in love," it is "behaving in love." It is loving another as God in Christ loves us.

St. Paul also describes what love is: "Love is patient, love is kind.

It does not envy, it does not boast, it is not proud. It is not rude, it is not self-seeking, it is not easily angered, it keeps no record of wrongs. Love does not delight in evil but rejoices with the truth. It always protects, always trusts, always hopes, always perseveres. Love never fails" (1 Corinthians 13:4–8). In this passage Paul points out that love is more than talk. It is walking the talk. It is kindness in more than words—it is kindness in deeds! It is protecting, trusting, hoping, persevering. It never fails!

This is God's love toward us. It never fails, even when we were His "enemies, we were reconciled to Him through the death of His Son" (Romans 5:10). "This is how we know what love is: Jesus Christ laid down His life for us."

Heavenly Father, teach us to love even as You love us. Amen.

ROGER R. SONNENBERG

1 John 4:8

God's Universal Love

Whoever does not love does not know God, because God is love. 1 John 4:8

Dios es amor. Gott ist Liebe. Dieu est Amour. Boh je laska. These three words, "God is love," so simple and yet so profound, have been translated into hundreds of languages worldwide.

The message is universal. It's the Christmas message. Although not as familiar as the Luke 2 account, 1 John 4 tells us God, "sent His one and only Son into the world that we might live through Him" (v. 9). The next verse is the message of the Easter season: "He loved us and sent His Son as an atoning sacrifice for our sins" (v. 10). Indeed, the messages of Christmas and Easter are one and the same: God's love for us is so great He sent His Son to be born in a humble manger; suffer and bear our sins in His body; die and then rise triumphant to conquer death for us.

What is our response to such great love? Verse 11 says, "since God so loved us, we also ought to love one another." We share God's great gift to us with the whole world.

Lord, thank You for Your great love in sending Your Son for our redemption. May others see this love in us. Amen.

JIM WIEMERS

1 John 5:4–5

Look to Jesus

This is the victory that has overcome the world, even our faith. Who is it that overcomes the world? Only he who believes that Jesus is the Son of God. 1 John 5:4–5

When problems seem to overwhelm us, we suppose that we can solve them by our own efforts. While God wants us to employ the strength and wisdom He has given us, only Jesus offers real help and deliverance.

The biblical account of God's people in the desert offers insights for our situation. For a time while the Israelites were in the wilderness, venomous snakes brought about the death of many. They could not save themselves. God told Moses to construct a bronze snake and place it on a pole. Anyone who was bitten by one of the poisonous snakes slithering around would live if he or she looked up to the bronze snake on the pole (Numbers 21:6–9).

What gives us victory over the problems and difficult situations we encounter in this world is not looking inward to our own strength and ability but upward to the cross of Christ and all that it represents. God sent His Son to die on a cross and to offer to all the forgiveness of sins. The answer to our problems is to look to the cross and to Jesus who endured the cross for us.

Our look to Jesus on the cross is a look of faith and trust and hope. It is a look of faith—we lay hold of the good news of forgiveness and salvation. It is a look of trust—we lay ourselves and our future into the arms of God, holding to His promises. It is a look of hope—"We have this hope as an anchor" (Hebrews 6:19).

My Savior, help me always look to You for my help and salvation. Amen.

ANDREW SIMCAK JR.

Revelation 2:10

Faithful, Faithful, Faithful

Be faithful, even to the point of death, and I will give you the crown of life. Revelation 2:10

Every realtor will insist there are three things to consider in the purchase of a house: location, location, location. When we speak about our relationship with God, *faithful* is that description repeated over and over again. This word describes the relationship of God to His children and is used by Jesus to identify those who do not reject the gift of salvation (see Matthew 25:21).

Now John, in the book of Revelation adds that our faith is to extend "even to the point of death." In our day, especially in the free world, we will not likely face the kinds of persecutions the Christians of John's day faced—but we do experience temptations, both open and subtle. One time it will be to minimize the importance of faith. Another time the temptation will be to ignore our relationship to God. Over against these temptations we are called to faithfulness.

How? With what power can we remain faithful? Only through the power of "the one who calls you [who] is faithful" (1 Thessalonians 5:12). This is Jesus Christ, given for the forgiveness of sins to gather us into unity with His cross and resurrection. Only by this power in our lives can we experience "faithfulness" in our Christian living, in the expression of our unity with God in Jesus Christ. The result is clear, a crown that lives forever.

Keep me, O Lord, faithful in You. Amen.

PAUL J. ALBERS

Revelation 21:4

Thy Kingdom Come—Heaven

I saw a new heaven and a new earth .... Now the dwelling of God is with men, and He will live with them. ... He will wipe every tear from their eyes. There will be no more death or mourning or crying or pain, for the old order of things has passed away. Revelation 21:1–4

The Second Petition of the Lord's Prayer, "Thy kingdom come," is a prayer asking that God's undeserved love continue to come to us. We also pray in this petition that our King would empower and energize us to proclaim to a sin-sick world that Jesus Christ is our only hope, the only Savior from sin and hell. But there is more in these words of our Lord. When we pray, "Thy kingdom come," we are also asking our Father to take us to Himself in heaven. All Christians, because of God's undeserved love, become members of God's kingdom of grace and will some day by God's grace transfer their membership to His kingdom in glory, heaven.

Jesus has returned to heaven to prepare a place for us (John 14:2). Because of His death and rising again we look forward with certainty to being with Him in heaven. In God's good time He will call us out of this vale of tears to Himself in heaven to live and reign with Him forever. In heaven "there will be no more death or mourning or crying or pain, for the old order of things [will have] passed away."

With Paul we look forward to being with Jesus in His kingdom of glory. "Thanks be to God! He gives us the victory through our Lord Jesus Christ" (1 Corinthians 15:57).

Come, Lord Jesus, and in Your good time, take me to Your heavenly, eternal kingdom. Amen.

ANDREW SIMCAK JR.

Revelation 22:12–16

Come Back Soon!

Behold, I am coming soon! Revelation 22:12

During the nine years when I frequently traveled alone, one phrase sounded consistently from my family members, "Come back soon!" The prayer spoken at the end of many of my meetings, part of which says, "Make our ways safe and our homecomings joyful," never failed to put a lump in my throat as I visualized those anxious faces staring out the front window, their eyes brightening as I arrived back home.

Christians have a similar, indescribable longing for Christ's return. When that occurs, time will change to eternity, and a lifetime of hearing about and yearning to see Jesus will blissfully change to an eternity of seeing and being with Him. The apostle Paul further explains, "After that [the resurrection of the dead], we who are still alive and are left will be caught up together with them in the clouds to meet the Lord in the air. And so we will be with the Lord forever" (1 Thessalonians 4:17).

We, then, will be the ones whose eyes will widen as we see His loving gaze and *see* the salvation prepared for us. The angels' promise to the disciples at Jesus' ascension will then be fulfilled, "This same Jesus, who has been taken from you into heaven will come back in the same way you have seen Him go into heaven" (Acts 1:11). "Amen. Come, Lord Jesus" (Revelation 22:20).

Come, Lord Jesus! Come back soon! Amen.

JAMES W. FREESE